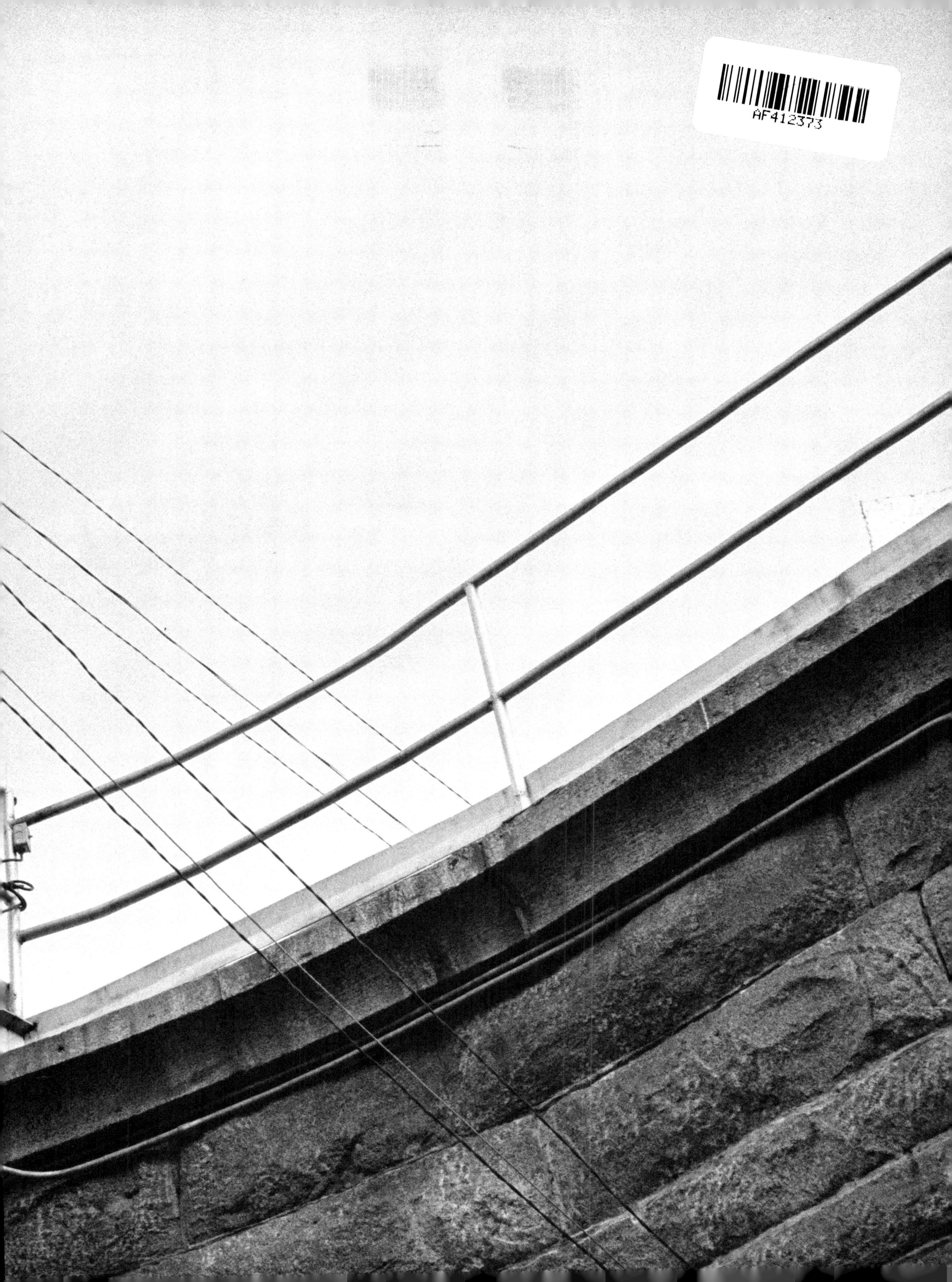

AF412373

JOHNNY CASH AT FOLSOM & SAN QUENTIN

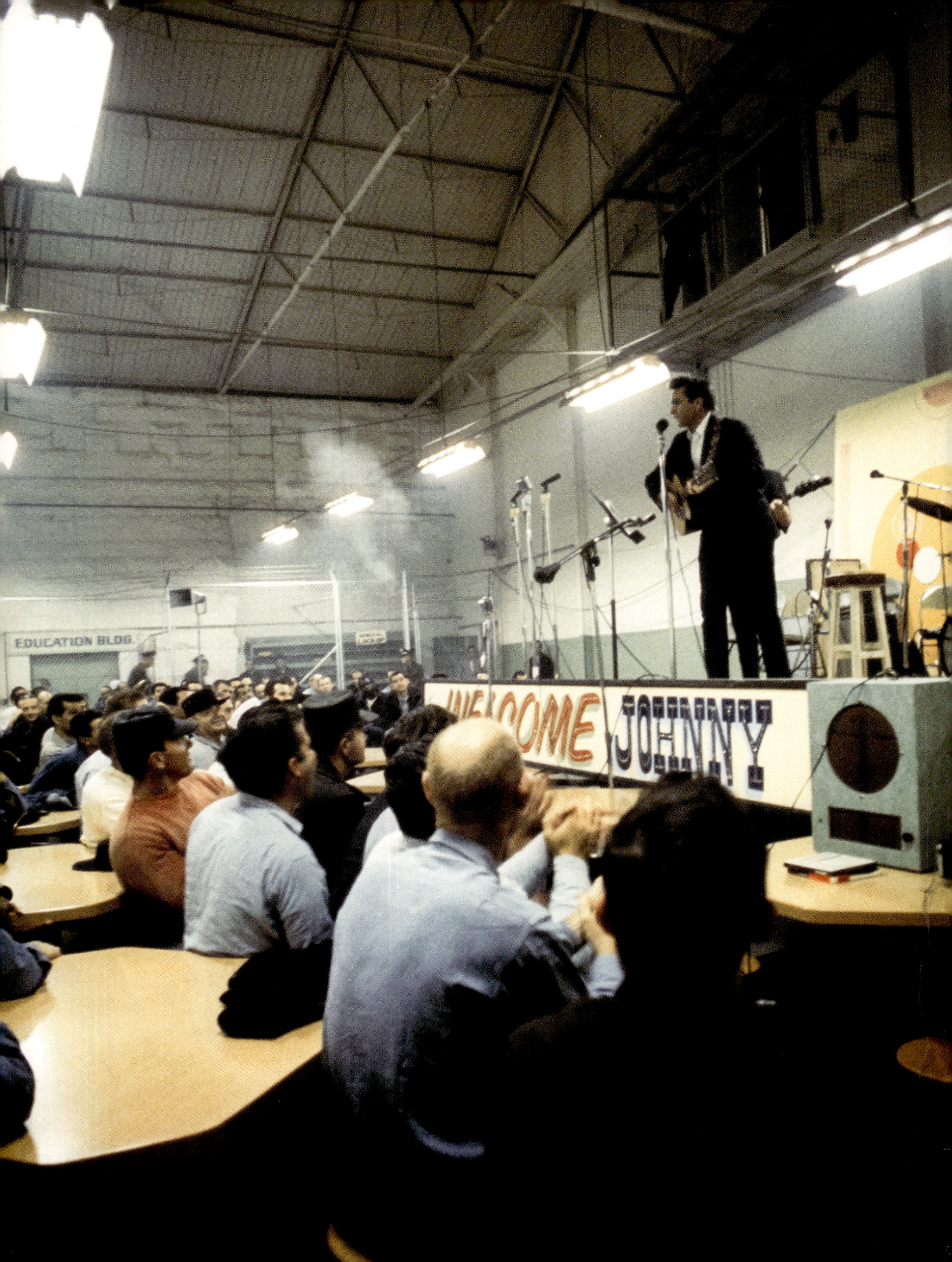
EDUCATION BLDG.
WELCOME JOHNNY

JOHNNY CASH AT FOLSOM & SAN QUENTIN

PHOTOGRAPHS BY
JIM MARSHALL

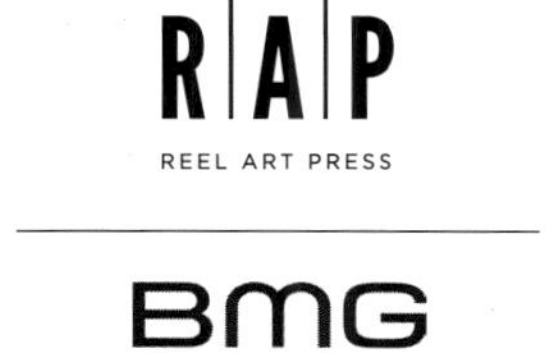

REEL ART PRESS

BMG

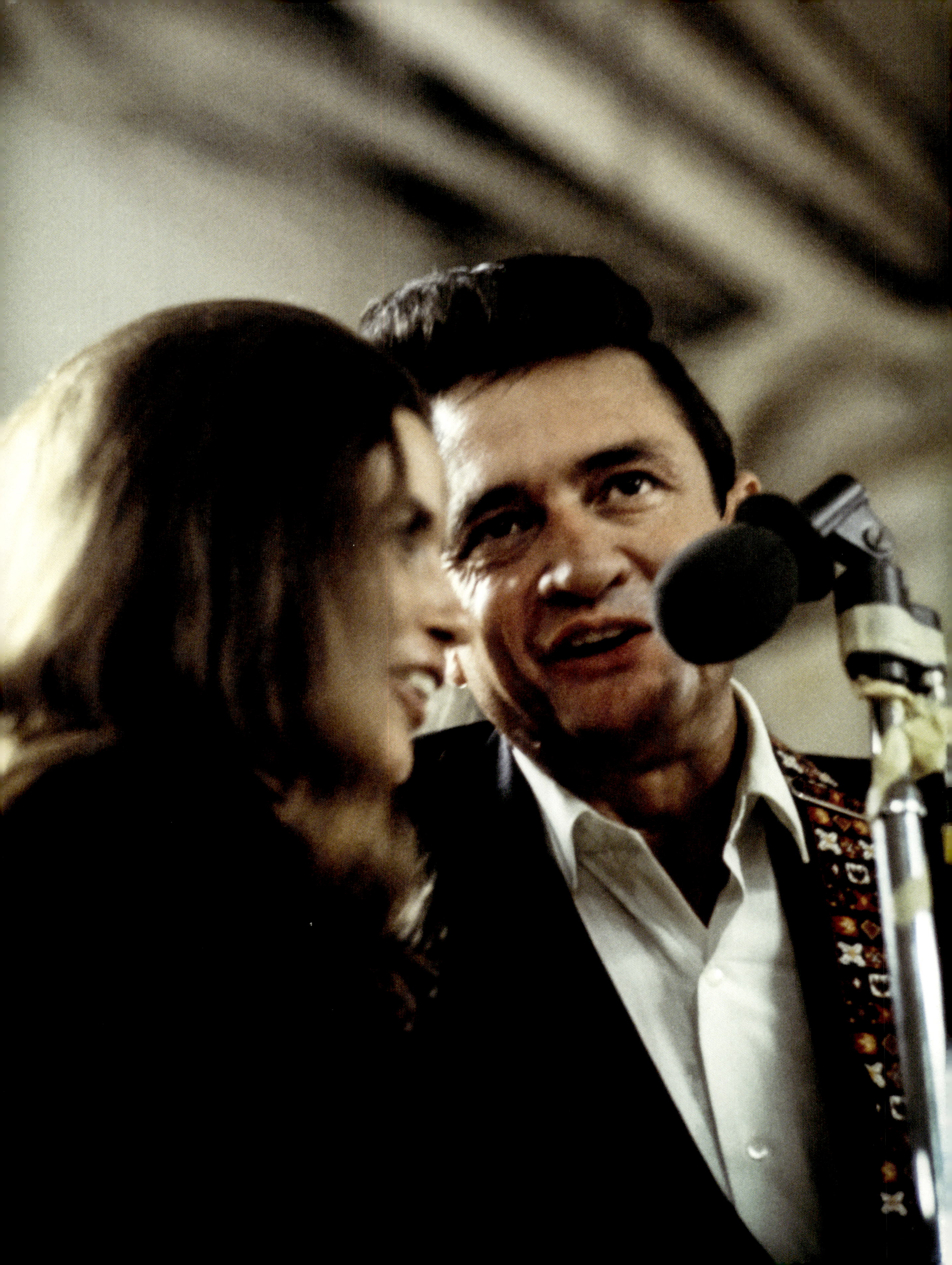

PHOTOGRAPHS BY

JIM MARSHALL

INTRODUCTION BY

MARTY STUART

EDITED BY

AMELIA DAVIS

TEXT BY

SCOTT B. BOMAR

ART DIRECTION AND DESIGN BY

JOAKIM OLSSON

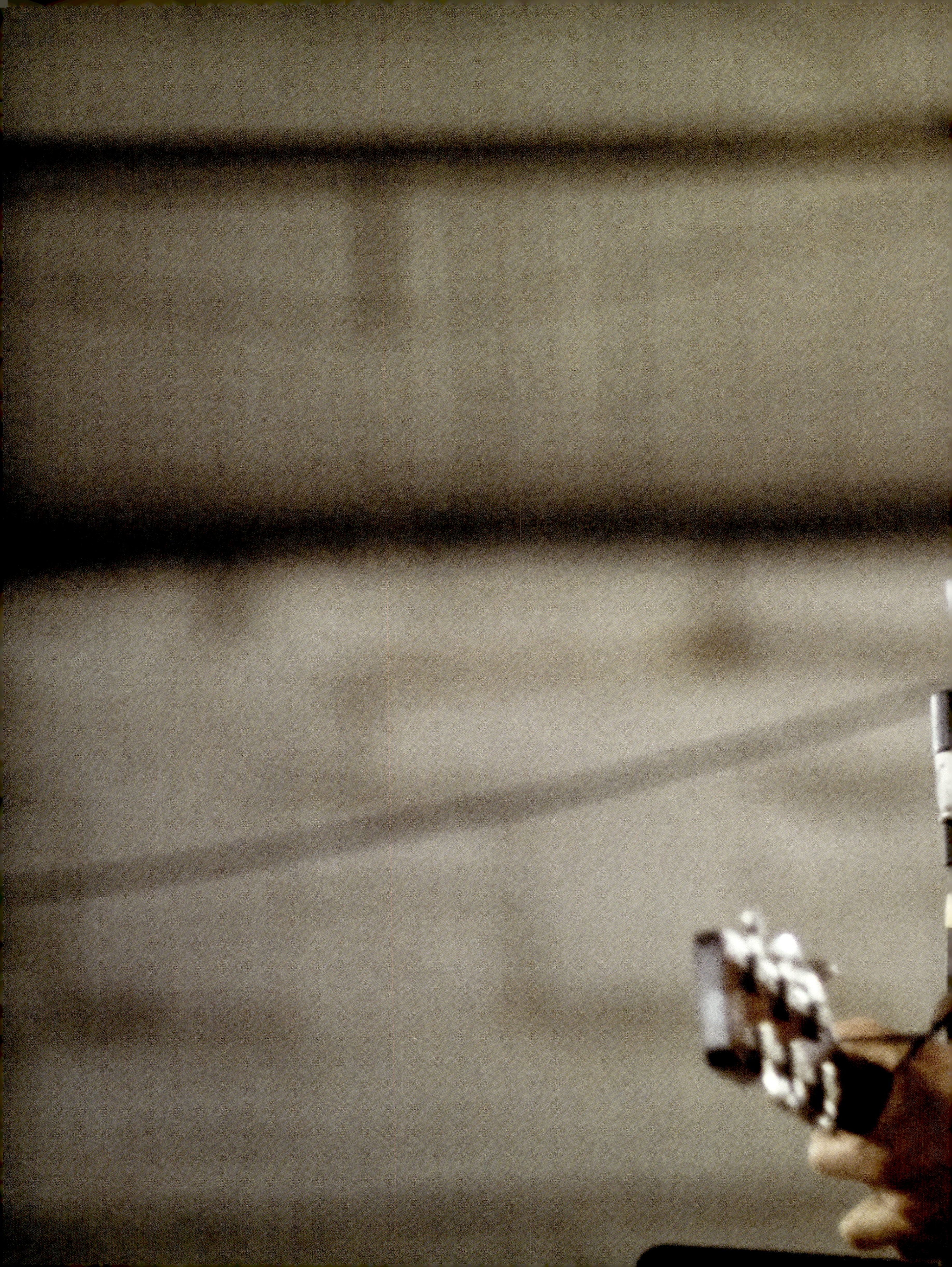

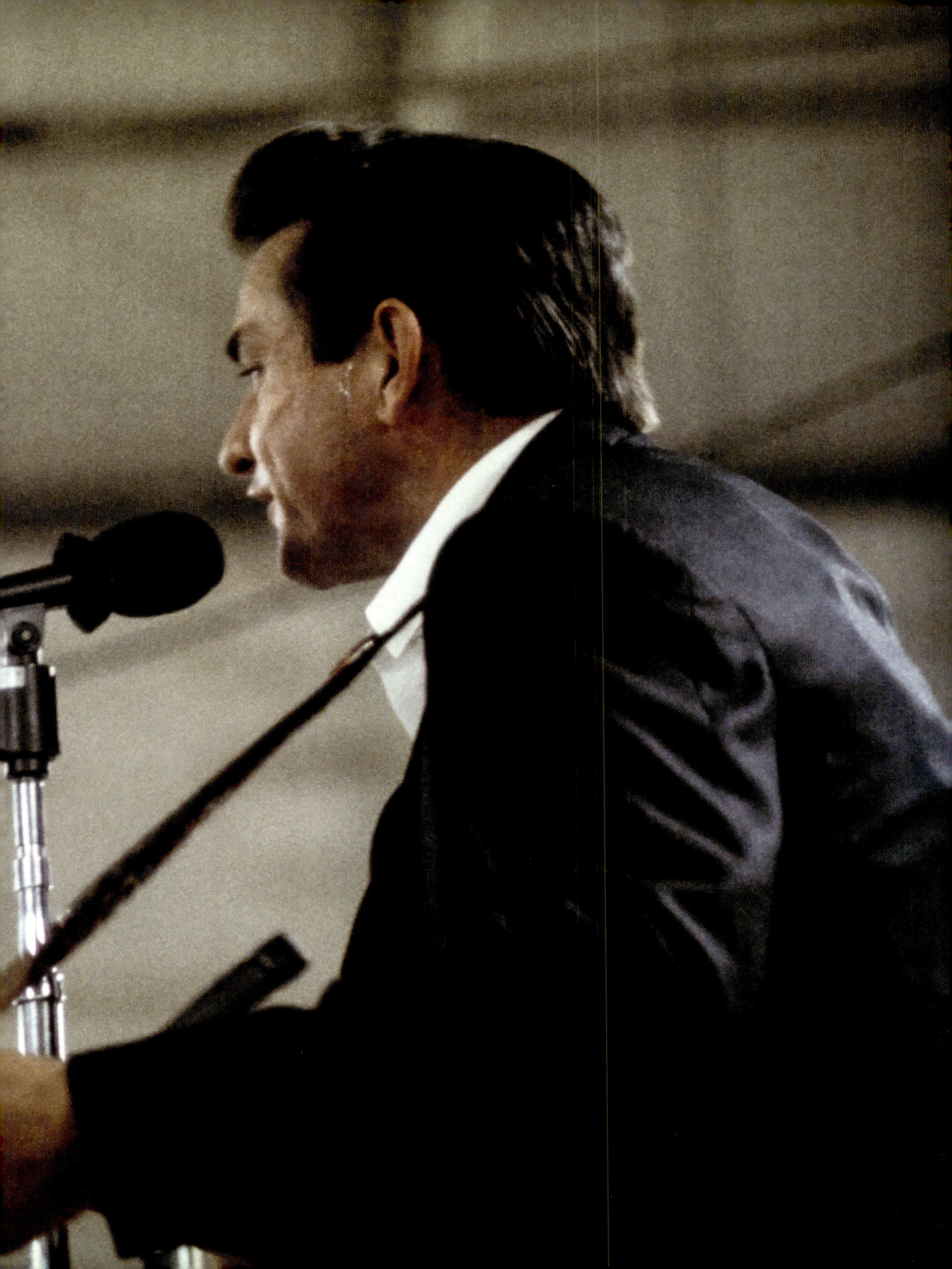

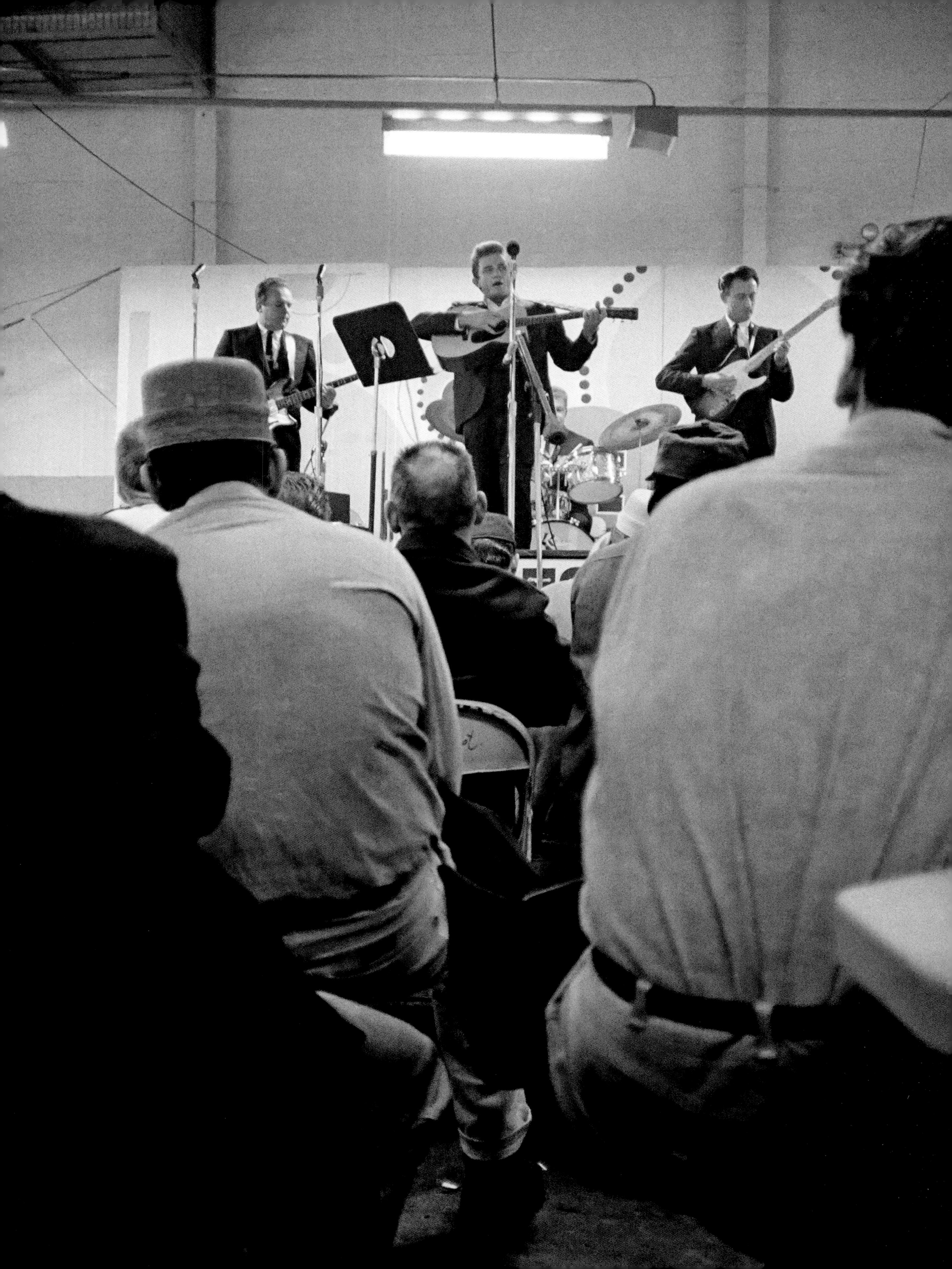

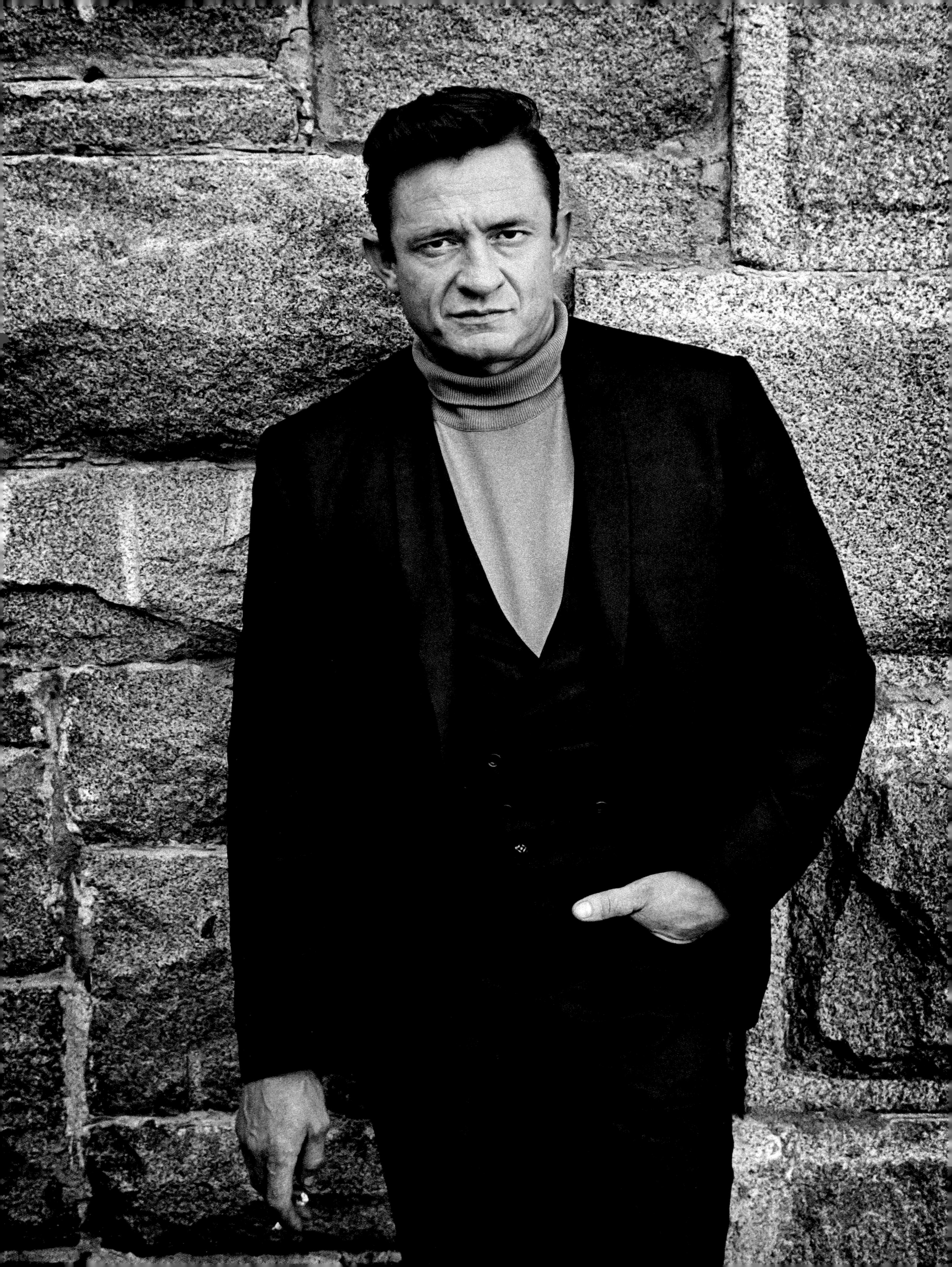

A FLOWER OF LIGHT IN A FIELD OF DARKNESS

"Behind all the rising and setting external forces of religion in the world, there has been a broad, fully developed stream of knowledge, always the same and always having the same object, namely the inner quickening and inner growth and evolution of a man to a higher level of himself."
Dr. Maurice Nicoll, *The New Man*

The first two records that I could call my own were *The Fabulous Johnny Cash* and *Lester Flatt and Earl Scruggs' Greatest Hits*. I was five years old when these recordings were given to me in 1963. Soon after came *The Sound of Johnny Cash*. After that, I lost sight of Cash for a time. Until one afternoon in the summer of 1968, as I was walking through the living room of my Aunt Waldine's house, I heard, "Hello, I'm Johnny Cash" coming out of the speaker of her radio. Then I heard people hollering as Luther Perkins played his famous intro and the music began. I did not know what I was listening to. I only knew that I couldn't move and there were goosebumps all over my body. I felt as if I were plugged into an electrical outlet in the wall.

In retrospect, I regard that moment as a divine appointment. I had no idea that I was listening to someone who would become my mentor, my lifelong chief, my band leader, my father-in-law for a time, my next-door neighbor, and one of the best friends I've ever had. My mother bought me the *At Folsom Prison* album. That record inspired me to start my first band. During that summer of 1968 the airwaves were filled with the music of The Beatles, The Rolling Stones, Jimi Hendrix, The Who and most of the other stars of the British invasion. Rock and roll ruled in my hometown of Philadelphia, Mississippi, but Johnny Cash and the Tennessee Three were my heroes. They were my Beatles, and I considered it my civic duty to fly the flag in my community for the kind of country music that Johnny Cash and his friend Merle Haggard played. My little neighborhood band had a set list of hard country songs—our showstoppers being "Mama Tried" and "Folsom Prison Blues."

On January 13, 1968, at Folsom State Prison in Folsom, California —and then again on February 24, 1969, at San Quentin Prison just outside San Francisco—Johnny Cash walked through the gates of an infamous jailhouse, empowered as if by divine authority with songs and dialogue that transported those congregations of prisoners to a sparkling world where they could freely breathe, far beyond the grim daily existence of being locked away behind stone walls and steel bars.

The "inner quickening and inner growth and evolution of a man to a higher level of himself" that Maurice Nicoll described seems to have applied to Ray and Carrie Cash's son as he traveled to his appointment at Folsom Prison on that January day. There was his life as he had known it before he made that record, and then his

life thereafter. John R. Cash served as a rogue minister at both the Folsom and San Quentin events. His sermons were three chord songs that spoke of railroads, horses, land, judgment day, family, hard times, whiskey, dope, courtship, marriage, adultery, separation, murder, prison, war, rambling, damnation, home, salvation, death, pride, humor, piety, rebellion, patriotism, larceny, determination, tragedy, rowdiness, heartbreak, work, love, mother, and God. He once referred to these subjects as "his musical values."

Cash sang his songs with heartfelt conviction, and he knew that the prisoners knew exactly what he was singing about. He delivered them from the depth of his being, conveying the kind of wisdom that can only be earned by living—or at the very least fully comprehending —the weight of each and every word. The absolute beauty of those prison concerts is the sheer empathy, understanding, love and kinship that John R. Cash offered to every man in his audience.

I've always believed J.R., as I called him, to be at his best when he had something to prove. As 1968 dawned, he was coming up out of the ashes of hell, to say the least. At 36 years old, he had already experienced more fame than most people could ever conceive. For the better part of a decade, however, he had squandered that fame as he walked a razor-thin line between life and death. By his own admission he had become a slave to amphetamines and had an ongoing relationship with all the demons that come along with that brand of addiction. His broader popular fan base had dwindled, and even the country music industry had all but dismissed him for his unpredictability. Cash was looked upon by most insiders as a pill-popping, hard-living, show-missing, adulterous rebel who was the next star candidate for a Hank Williams body bag. His marriage and family were slipping away; he had been arrested in El Paso for smuggling pills; arrested in Starkville, Mississippi for being drunk and picking flowers out of some nice lady's flower bed late at night; and arrested in Georgia for similar craziness. His greatest hit of the era (in terms of criminal activity) might have been the burning of five hundred acres of the Los Padres National Park, which resulted in a lawsuit from the State of California.

In his autobiography, *Man In Black*, Cash revealed that somewhere around that point in his life, he was so sick of himself that he crawled into a cave in south Tennessee to die, only to find that neither God nor the devil was ready for him. Somehow, in the depth of all that despair, John R. Cash found enough light to keep going. As he

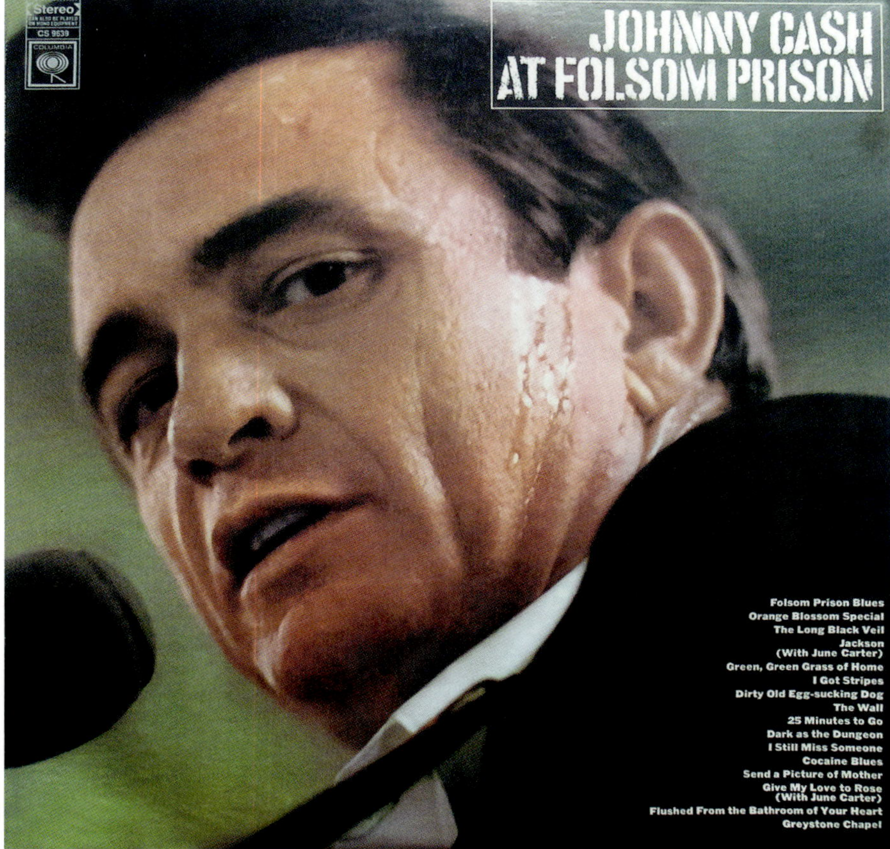

crawled out of that cave he had a newborn mission—to prove to himself that he wanted to live.

Miraculously, his band (Luther Perkins, W.S. "Fluke" Holland and Marshall Grant), his tour mates (Carl Perkins, The Statler Brothers and June, Helen, Anita and Mother Maybelle Carter), his manager Saul Holiff, and his record label stuck by Cash during his lowest times. So did his creative muse. Regardless of how it was fueled, John R. Cash's creativity seemed to be the one thing that he could count on in himself. He was absolutely fearless. If he had an idea or a song that he believed in, he stood by it regardless of what anyone else thought. He stayed true to what lived in his heart. Cash's recorded works from 1960-1969 are compelling, adventurous projects that in every way live up to the words Saul Holiff had printed on his stationary from that period: "Nobody, but nobody is more original than Johnny Cash."

Sprinkled in amongst his commercial efforts throughout the 1960s, J.R. created a counter melody of bold concept records. There was *Johnny Cash Sings the Ballads of the True West*; *Bitter Tears*, his stark portrait of Native American life; the *Mean as Hell* cowboy songs collection; a story songs narrative entitled *Ride This Train*, and even a journey into the corridors of warped humor entitled *Everybody Loves a Nut*. These projects undoubtedly meant more to him than they did to anyone at Columbia Records. To their credit, they let him roll. The loveliest misfit of all his conceptual recordings is the obscure, now highly collectible but nearly unlistenable *A Day in the Grand Canyon with Johnny Cash*. J.R. imagined that a full phonograph record of him walking around the Grand Canyon with his tape recorder and talking about things he saw would be an interesting listen. I wish I could have been there when he turned the project in to the A&R department at Columbia. The label passed. The Doral Cigarette Company signed on to sponsor the release, which was a commercial disaster but a monumental artistic triumph to the man who conceived it. He was extremely proud of it. He saw beauty within its grooves.

All of J.R.'s concept pieces have their individual merits, but the common thread that runs through each project is a man whose soul is on fire, burning with artistic integrity. Not your ordinary country or rock star, but a folk hero in the making. J.R. was an Old Testament style of man in search of excellence, peace and the ultimate higher evolution of himself. He threw himself into his concept projects by way of deep research and association with the authentic lifestyle pertaining to the subject matter—even creating and costuming characters for himself to portray on the album covers. In retrospect, these projects stand as timeless documents. They are to be regarded as the recordings that paved the way for *At Folsom*, *Live at San Quentin* and *The Holy Land*, which was undoubtedly the closest to his heart.

Cash's television appearances from the latter part of 1967 show a man on the move toward the better side of himself. The major networks didn't seem to be calling, but he and the Tennessee Three—sometimes along with Carl Perkins, the Carters and the Statlers—made the rounds of the syndicated Nashville country music shows performing medleys of the old hits. It's obvious that he'd gone and bought himself a couple of new black suits, tuxedo shirts and a black bow tie. The Cuban-heeled Beatle-style boots he wore only added to his visual appeal. Johnny Cash's cool factor never wavered in the midst of all of his struggles, but those television appearances suggest that his dignity and his glow were beginning to reappear. If you look between the lines of those 1967 performances, you witness a man warming up for bigger things to come—sketch padding, quietly finding his way back, rebuilding his life and career from the backroads out. As J.R. used to say when times got thin; "There ain't a thing wrong with us that a big hit wouldn't cure."

Cash found a kindred spirit to help him find that hit with Columbia staff producer Bob Johnston. Johnston was a bohemian of the highest order. A musical gypsy. His name appeared as producer on Bob Dylan's Nashville recordings, including *Blonde on Blonde* and *Nashville Skyline*. He had worked with Leonard Cohen as well as Simon & Garfunkel. The project he was working on when he and Cash began their talks was a suicide mission of an album featuring Lester Flatt, Earl Scruggs and The Foggy Mountain Boys recording songs written by Dylan, Shel Silverstein, Donovan and the like. Bob Johnston was always game for an out-of-the-box idea that reached beyond the standard Nashville fare.

Cash had already been taking his act to prisons for the better part of a decade and had experienced the sheer thunder of those audiences enough times to know that the setting of a prison as a theatre—combined with the combustible energy unleashed by the inmates—would light up the microphones and serve as the perfect canvas for a live recording. When J.R. presented him with the idea, Bob Johnston jumped at the chance and welcomed the opportunity to, as he once said to me, "go out to the rock and roll edge of the limb so far that we could hear it crack, baby." Bob's boss, Columbia executive Clive Davis, reluctantly greenlit the project. He gave the boys enough rope to hang themselves, believing all the while that a live recording made at a prison would ultimately damage—if not destroy—Johnny Cash's career. The legend goes that when the word came down to the Nashville office from New York that preparations could be made for a road trip to a prison, Johnston picked up the phone and called the wardens at both Folsom and San Quentin. Bob later said the Folsom project happened first because the warden of Folsom was the first one to pick up the phone.

In Michael Streissguth's impeccably written *Johnny Cash at Folsom Prison: The Making of a Masterpiece*, he writes,

Cash showed up at the prison in 1968 with crates of recording equipment and the hard hunger of a struggling salesman. ... But Cash lurched awake when the album he recorded there hit the record bins and began moving like the 20th Century Limited. ... The album signaled a resurgence that defined his place in musical history. Henceforth, in the eyes of everybody, he would once and for all be the poet for the little man (which he'd always been, anyway) and all would regard him a leviathan figure in popular music. The album opened vast commercial fields to Cash and escorted country music—his home base—to new heights."

When the record had finished its course, the world had a new superstar statesman. The year 1968 grew very loud for Johnny Cash. He had a mega hit on his hands; he married June Carter; he returned to prominence in the eyes of the general public; he was looked upon as an outlaw king; politicians sought his endorsement; and the country music establishment offered him their praise and handed him their most coveted awards. He was claimed by country folks, hippies, Christians, prisoners, rockabillies, folkies and academics as one of their own. The ABC Network signed him as the host of a weekly variety show that bore his name, and he embarked upon a journey to the Holy Land to look into the eyes of spiritual history—all the while searching for a deeper, renewed relationship with God.

John R. Cash became a bright light in a year that saw the assassinations of Dr. Martin Luther King in Memphis and Robert Kennedy in Los Angeles. All of this heartache was underscored by a nation that continued to witness an ongoing parade of flag-draped coffins coming home to America from a war in Vietnam that made no sense. The funeral that undoubtedly hit closest to home for John R. Cash in 1968, though, was that of guitarist Luther Perkins, who had succumbed to smoke inhalation after a fire at his home. In losing Luther, J.R. lost a brother, his musical soulmate and the cornerstone component of his sound. Even though the songs for *The Holy Land* album, which would be Luther's final sessions with Cash, were recorded post-Folsom, the Tennessee Three could not have planned a greater moment to call their swan song performance than that of their hit Folsom Prison concert.

When Johnny Cash and the boys stood on stage in the cafeteria at Folsom on that January morning they had been in business together for nearly thirteen years. From the unlikely beginnings of Cash—the unsuccessful vacuum salesman—and Marshall Grant and Luther Perkins—the two automobile mechanics—gathering in the living room of Grant's Memphis home for coffee and musical fellowship, they organized and began playing their clackity southern music. Johnny Cash and the Tennessee Two spent the latter part of the 1950s traveling around the world as Sun Records stars, thrilling audiences with hit songs such as "I Walk the Line," "Folsom Prison Blues," "Get Rhythm," and "Give My Love to Rose," to name a few. In the early 1960s drummer W.S. Holland came over from the Carl Perkins' band, thus transforming the Tennessee Two into the Tennessee Three.

The Tennessee Three were a power trio of oddball savants who at times hardly tuned their instruments and could barely change chords together. Even on their shakiest day, however, Johnny Cash and his band were never less than a mesmerizing collection of characters. The authorities charged with keeping an eye on the convicts at Folsom probably didn't have a clue as to the level of delinquency on that stage. They were looking at master architects of bad-boy band behavior—the undisputed kings of mayhem. One might not think—looking at Fluke, Marshall and Luther up there playing music so straight and respectable in their black church deacon suits— that they would smuggle a crate of baby chicks onto an airplane, then turn them loose at 32,000 feet. At the recording session for *At Folsom* that morning, the members of the Tennessee Three were probably packing enough black powder in their instrument cases to have blown the gates off the place. On the other hand, they were the kind of guys who adopted a stray dog who was loitering in front of their hotel in Des Moines, Iowa, named him James Louis Henry, bought him a suite, gave him a bath, set him up in bed, and ordered five-star room service meals for him for the duration of their stay. Many hotels around the country would not allow bands to stay at their properties due to the antics staged by Johnny Cash and the Tennessee Three during the course of their visit.

Any band is but a subtotal of the life experiences of all its members. The good, bad and ugly of everyone's existence somehow finds its way onto the bandstand and into the microphones. The two morning concerts at Folsom Prison sound like the culmination of everything Johnny Cash and the Tennessee Three had lived through together. They had played the majority of the songs on that set list countless times, but that morning was special. It was a masterful recital and, thanks to Bob Johnston—along with Columbia engineers Bill Britain and Bob Breault—the moment was brilliantly captured and lives on as one of the most significant recordings of all time.

Amongst the black coat society of Johnny Cash-ologists, there has been ongoing debate down through the years as to which of the prison recordings is best, *Folsom* versus *San Quentin*. Some archivists have differing opinions regarding the choices of performances that were selected between the two morning shows at Folsom that made their way onto the final record. The answer is that all three shows were great. But I personally choose *At Folsom*. I view it as a near-perfect work of art. I sense the danger of the unknown and J.R.'s instincts for a project that knew more about him than he knew of it. Everyone involved seemed to be hanging on for dear life, and that made for excellent theater and powerful music.

Concerning *Live at San Quentin* one need look no further than "The Wreck of the Old '97," "Wanted Man," the first take of "San Quentin," or the later-released outtake of "I Don't Know Where I'm Bound" to hear pure brilliance. The main difference in *At Folsom* versus *Live at San Quentin* is that the unknown now seems known. The troupe seems more at ease and the routines sometimes border on the familiar. But the project was an instant hit, helped along no doubt by the success of *At Folsom*. The real ringer inside the *Live at San Quentin* record that absolutely set the woods on fire was a talking blues piece written by Shel Silverstein entitled, "A Boy Named Sue." An off-the-cuff performance of Silverstein's song midway through the set had the magic that it took to propel all-things-Johnny-Cash into the stratosphere.

Michael Streissguth pointed out that the combined success of *At Folsom* and *Live at San Quentin* did for Johnny Cash what the '68 comeback special did for Elvis Presley. In the short amount of time between the Folsom and San Quentin shows, pictures and footage of Cash show an evolved man. Gone was most every trace of the Memphis greaser in the black sharkskin suit who performed at Folsom. The new version of Cash was the precursor to his Man in Black character. He now sported custom-tailored, nineteenth century style coats with Edwardian overtones. His crown was a softly teased pompadour. He looked iconic, primed as he was ushered onto the world stage. And, for a moment, J.R. held the world in the palm of his hand. He became a global commodity. From the vantage point of the top of the world, the newly-blessed man who looked down on that not-so-long-ago scene from Nickajack Cave—and the shell of a man who crawled out of it—must have seen a terrifying sight. But John R. Cash had proved to himself—and anyone who cared to watch—that he had, indeed, lived. "By merciful grace," he later said, "I was spared." In terms of his new-found life, the grace that had been gifted to him resulted in a deeper compassion for his fellow man. And he walked that out for the rest of this life.

The all-knowing, all-seeing eye from which the truth cannot hide is the camera. However, the camera is only as poetic as the artist looking through its lens. Jim Marshall was absolutely the right man to document the visual story of the making of *At Folsom* and *Live at San Quentin*. Coming from the worlds of jazz and rock, Marshall shot with an eloquent edge that few, if any, of his peers could have matched in these unique situations. Jim Marshall would have probably been the first to tell you that Johnny Cash was one of the most photogenic human beings to ever walk the earth. Whether he was peeling an apple, working in a recording studio, walking into a prison or performing on stage, the camera absolutely loved him.

From the first stanzas of the rehearsal the night before the Folsom show, all throughout the day of the concert, and again at San Quentin, Jim Marshall shot his heart out. He was beyond brilliant. In the early 1990s Jim invited me to his place in San Francisco. After we'd shot some pictures I asked him if he had his Folsom and San Quentin contact sheets. He left the room and came back with a handful of folders. When he spread them out they resembled a classical music score. Jim handed me his loop and I began looking at the pages. Frame after frame, there they were; the unseen treasures. At that time, I had not yet seen the images that he had taken at the rehearsal, or the shots of everyone mingling backstage, or the beautiful moment of J.R. shaking inmate Glen Sherley's hand after performing Glen's song "Greystone Chapel." There was the now-iconic shot of J.R. flipping the bird, but the image that has stuck in my mind since that day is the shot of John sitting on a stool, singing at Folsom with the soles of his boots sticking out over the edge of the stage. That may be one of the greatest performance shots ever taken of a musician at work.

Jim Marshall totally captured the significance, weight and mood of the prison shows. More importantly, his pictures are a perfect reflection of the music. It's almost as if he were a member of the band. Time has proven that Johnny Cash and Jim Marshall were a powerful duo. They were locked. J.R. must have fully trusted Marshall because, especially at Folsom, he let all his walls down and gave Jim total access to himself and every molecule of space around him. The bottom line of their story is this: Jim Marshall and Johnny Cash had a lot to do with enhancing the other's legend. The hands of time seem to fully support those legends, as they continually evolve into the realm of higher truth—or the place where perfect art goes to dwell for the ages.

Again, as if by divine appointment, tonight—January 10, 2018, three days shy of the fiftieth anniversary of the recording of *At Folsom Prison*—my band, The Fabulous Superlatives, and I played a concert at the Harris Center for the Performing Arts in the city of Folsom, California. To date, I've been through Folsom Prison twice. I've stood in the cafeteria where the record was made. I've seen the old hanging gallows. I've played music with the Folsom Prison country band. I have touched the walls of Greystone Chapel, and I've heard the ambient sounds that are so much a part of the record. Different voices, same sounds. They echo in my mind.

I did not feel the need for another tour inside Folsom today, but I did have someone drive me out to the prison so I could walk around, do some daydreaming, and think about how much I loved the people who came here half a century ago and made a record filled with songs that lit a fire in my heart and set me on my life's journey. Tonight, at the Harris Center, The Superlatives and I played Glen Sherley's "Greystone Chapel." The audience understood. It was a good feeling to bring the song back home. Nothing much has changed for me since my little neighborhood group first started playing those great country songs when I was a kid. I still consider it my self-appointed duty to fly the flag for the kind of music my heroes made. It's a worthy mission.

Back in the early 1980s, J.R. and I had a ritual for several years running. Usually around Christmas time, he'd call and say, "Let's go see Luther." We would meet up and ride together to Hendersonville Memory Gardens on East Main Street (now known as The Johnny Cash Parkway) in Hendersonville, Tennessee. We would take presents to Luther, or L.M. as J.R. called him. I'd always bring flowers, guitar picks or other guitar-related items. J.R. once brought him a newspaper and a road map (because Luther enjoyed driving). One year he took Luther a cup of coffee and a pill. That wonderfully warped sense of humor the two of them shared always surfaced during these visits. If the earth wasn't too wet, J.R. would lay down on the ground, light a cigarette and tell Luther how much better he felt since he'd quit smoking. That was a running gag they had between them. He would rag Luther for laying down there resting while the rest of us were busting our asses to make a living. These visits were all done in love and remembrance. We never left without J.R. saying, "Love you buddy, love you L.M, love you Luther. I miss you." As we were leaving the cemetery one afternoon after one of those visits, I asked J.R., "Was it ever the same after Luther was gone?" He didn't hesitate in answering, "No sir, it was never the same, and it hurts because he didn't get to enjoy the big stuff." Then he repeated, "Naw, it was never the same."

In the mid-1960s J.R. purchased a substantial amount of ground as a family plot at those Memory Gardens. At the time the land and its surroundings were very rural with fifty miles of elbow room on either side to spare, as the old Carter Family song says. Now here in the 21st century, thousands of cars pass by each day. There are housing developments that back up to the property, a Shell service station and a Bank of America on the nearby corners, and a Lowe's home improvement store behind an Exxon station directly across the street. Luther is now joined in that earth by J.R., June, Helen, Anita, Mother Maybelle, and J.R.'s mother and father, along with other close relatives, friends and loved ones of the Cash-Carter clan. Sometimes when I go there to pay my respects I'm taken with all the noise and busyness that surrounds what was once such a peaceful place. But I doubt J.R. would have a problem with that. After all, he was a forward-thinking man who was always on the move, always restless. He couldn't sit still for 30 seconds. There's not a day goes by that I don't miss him. I miss talking to him and playing music with him. I miss his wisdom, his counsel, and I especially miss his sense of humor.

A while back, J.R. made an appearance in one of my dreams. I was standing in some pretty country setting by a pond and he came walking up. He looked beautiful. He was tanned, peaceful and rested. His hair was black again and he glowed the way he did back in the early 1970s. I said, "Look at you, J.R., you look great." He said, "I feel great and I haven't wanted a cigarette since I've been here." I said, "That's wonderful." Then he laughed and said, "Do you know what else I've learned to do since I've been here? I can sing just like Merle Haggard." He showed me, and we laughed and we laughed. The visit was so happy. I called Merle the next day and told him what I had dreamed. He got a kick out of it and asked, "Was the dream in color?" I said, "Yes it was."

Thinking back to Hendersonville Memory Gardens and all the noise surrounding the place, I am reminded of the rogue minister, who in the midst of all the commotion at San Quentin that night, stilled the room when he sang ...

There will be peace in the valley for me
There will be peace in the valley for me, oh Lord I pray
Then ... the angelic voice of Anita Carter can be heard singing along with her mother and sisters ...
There'll be no sadness, no sorrow, no trouble I see
J.R. finished the last line of the song alone as he sang ...
There will be peace in the valley for me ... SOMEDAY.
I have no doubt he made it home.

MARTY STUART

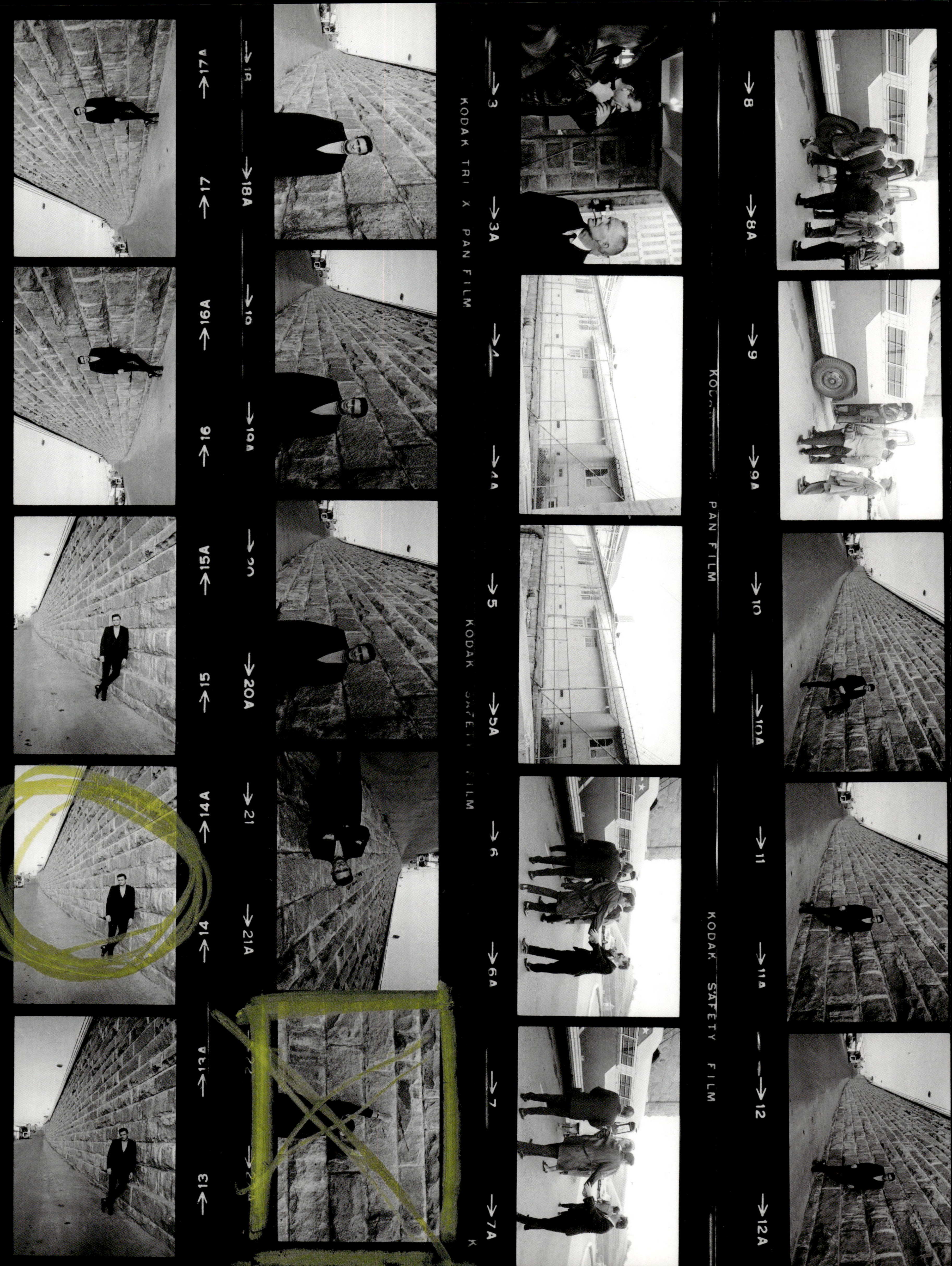

AT FOLSOM PRISON

SATURDAY, JANUARY 13, 1968

"There was no restriction. There was no asshole telling me you can't do this, you can't do that, you can't go here, you can't do that. That was it. I was there taking pictures. No one said you can't do this. That's the magic."
Jim Marshall

In 1955 John Cash, guitarist Luther Perkins and bassist Marshall Grant auditioned for Sam Phillips, who ran Sun Records in Memphis. The producer was drawn to "Hey Porter," a song Cash had written himself. Phillips encouraged the group to return to his studio when they had come up with additional original material. Cash went home and wrote the song that would become the group's first single, "Cry Cry Cry." Paired with "Hey Porter" and released in June under the newly-named Johnny Cash and the Tennessee Two, the single reached the Top 15 on Billboard's national country chart.

That December Sun released the group's follow-up single, featuring two more original compositions, "So Doggone Lonesome" and "Folsom Prison Blues." Both were Top 5 hits, but it was "Folsom" that became one of Cash's signature songs and an American standard. "'Hey Porter' / 'Cry Cry Cry' got our foot in the door," recalled Marshall Grant in a 2008 interview with author Michael Streissguth. "'Folsom Prison Blues,' when it came out, we didn't need to have our foot in the door. We just kicked the damn door down!"

"Folsom Prison Blues" was partially inspired by a 1951 Crane Wilbur B-movie called *Inside the Walls of Folsom Prison*. Cash saw the film in 1953 while he was stationed in Germany with the Air Force. It was one of his early songwriting efforts and, to complete it, John borrowed liberally from the melody and lyrics of "Crescent City Blues," a Gordon Jenkins composition that was also released in 1953. Originally performed as a slow blues, Phillips convinced Cash to rearrange "Folsom Prison Blues" into the up-tempo version that became the definitive recording.

Not surprisingly, the song was a favorite among prison inmates who heard it on the radio. Cash and the Tennessee Two received their most enthusiastic response to the song when they played it for the first time at the annual prison rodeo at the Texas State Penitentiary in Huntsville. Various conflicting dates have been reported—sometimes by Cash himself—as the first year they performed at Huntsville. The collection of original rodeo programs housed in the Texas State Library and Archives, however, confirms it was 1957. Despite performing outdoors in a thunderstorm that knocked out the electrical power, the inmates couldn't get enough. "They walked down in the rain to get close enough to hear me sing without the amplifier," Cash told Larry King many years later. "And I sang that song and they demanded that I sing it again and again and again. We all got soaking wet, but we had a great time." Cash was moved. "For reasons he didn't try to figure out," biographer Robert

Hilburn wrote, "he could identify with these men's lust for freedom and redemption."

In the wake of "Folsom Prison Blues" Cash scored a dozen Top 10 country hits with Sun, including a handful of #1 singles that also crossed over to the Top 20 on the pop charts: "I Walk the Line," "Ballad of a Teenage Queen" and "Guess Things Happen That Way." He signed with the larger Columbia Records in 1958 and moved to the Los Angeles suburb of Encino, California. The hits continued at Columbia with "Don't Take Your Guns to Town," "I Got Stripes," "Ring of Fire," "The Matador," and "Orange Blossom Special."

As his fame grew, "Folsom Prison Blues" remained a crowd favorite in Cash's live shows. He received letters from prisoners asking him to perform at the facilities where they were incarcerated. He returned to the Huntsville Prison Rodeo and soon began booking shows at other penitentiaries, including San Quentin in Marin County, California. One of the San Quentin inmates who saw Cash perform was Merle Haggard. It was a turning point for a man who would go on to become nearly as iconic as Cash in the pantheon of country music luminaries. "He'd lost his voice the night before over in Frisco and wasn't able to sing very good," Haggard recalled to *Rolling Stone* magazine many years later. "I thought he'd had it, but he won over the prisoners. He had the right attitude: He chewed gum, looked arrogant and flipped the bird to the guards—he did everything the prisoners wanted to do. He was a mean mother from the South who was there because he loved us. When he walked away, everyone in that place had become a Johnny Cash fan." Haggard pointed to that moment as the catalyst he needed to get serious about his own music and his resolve to change his life.

As prison performances became a semi-regular part of Cash's annual touring schedule over the years, he was increasingly compelled to do more than simply play a show and leave. "I guess I wanted to record in a prison ever since I played Huntsville," he confessed to biographer Christopher Wren. Nobody at Columbia Records was particularly excited by the concept, but producer Don Law reluctantly agreed to capture an already-scheduled July 6, 1965 show at the Kansas State Reformatory for a possible album release. The plan was derailed on June 27 when, in an amphetamine-fueled haze, Cash accidentally started a fire that burned more than 500 acres of California's Los Padres National Forest. With his drug addiction raging out of control, and in serious trouble with the authorities, Cash missed the date and Columbia canceled the planned prison album. He would have to wait until 1968 to finally realize his vision.

There's a narrative that says Johnny Cash's career was in grave danger at the time he made the Folsom album. That he was washed up and badly in need of a hit. As with many parts of the Johnny Cash myth, the reality was more complex. Though Cash wasn't the consistent hit maker he'd once been, half of the eight singles he released in the previous two years were Top 10 country hits. One of them was "Jackson," a song written by Billy Edd Wheeler and performed as a duet with June Carter, which earned Cash his first Grammy award. Columbia released two albums in 1967—*Johnny Cash's Greatest Hits, Volume 1* and *Carryin' On With Johnny Cash & June Carter*—that went to #1 and #5, respectively, on the country albums chart. When he stepped through the gates of Folsom Prison on January 13, "Rosanna's Going Wild" was on its way to peaking at #2 on Billboard's country singles chart.

While Johnny Cash was certainly not a has-been in the country field, his reputation in the country *industry* was reeling by the time he appeared at Folsom. Crippling addiction, arrests for drug possession and trespassing, a crumbling marriage, financial problems and a growing reputation for missing shows didn't endear him to the Nashville community. And while many country fans still loved him, Cash's wider appeal had certainly waned by the late 1960s. He hadn't cracked the Top 40 on the pop album charts since 1963, and he hadn't broken into the Top 20 on the pop singles chart since "Ring of Fire" that same year.

Perhaps most significantly, much of the material Cash had been recording in that era fell short of his own artistic standards. He was most energized by concept albums, which began with *Ride This Train* in 1960. He then released *Blood, Sweat and Tears* in 1963; *Bitter Tears: Ballads of the American Indian* in 1964; and *Sings the Ballads of the True West* in 1965. It was these projects of which Cash was most proud. He longed for another album that was infused with passion, but as his personal life unraveled it was difficult to focus.

As Johnny's marriage disintegrated he was embroiled in a tumultuous on-again-off-again affair with June Carter, who had joined his stage show in 1962. His failings as a husband and father ignited a burning shame that drove him deeper into drug addiction. The drugs, in turn, fueled his self-loathing, which pushed him toward further self-medication. The vicious cycle of misery affected his live performances and nearly cost him the woman he loved.

In late 1967 June was fed up with his substance abuse and left Johnny for what he feared was the final time. Jolted into reevaluating his behavior, Cash sought help for his drug habit from psychologist Nat Winston and resolved to turn the corner on his out-of-control personal life.

During that same era Bob Johnston was appointed to head Columbia Records' office in Nashville, where Johnny had moved in 1965 after separating from his first wife, Vivian. "He came into the office one day," Johnston recalled in a PRX radio interview, "and said 'I've always wanted to go to a prison to record and no one would ever let me in seven or eight years.' And he said, 'I don't suppose you will either; nobody will ever let me.' And I said 'really?' And I picked up the phone and called Quentin and called Folsom, got through to the warden at Folsom and said to the warden, 'I got Johnny Cash here and he's gonna come and do a concert for you.' And he said, 'My god, hand the phone to him.' So I handed Johnny the phone and left."

"I finally found the man who would listen at Columbia Records," Cash wrote in the liner notes for the *Folsom* album. "Bob Johnston believed me when I told him that a prison would be *the* place to record an album live."

The date was set for January 13, 1968, but it wouldn't be the first time Johnny Cash had performed at Folsom Prison. Always interested in the spiritual side of life, Cash had joined Reverend Floyd Gressett's Avenue Community Church in Ventura, California in 1963 when he was still living on the West Coast. The two became close friends. Johnny was inspired by Gressett's ministry to prison inmates, including those at Folsom. Gressett helped arrange Cash's first show at the prison in November of 1966, so Johnny was excited to record his long-awaited prison album in somewhat familiar territory.

Cash's divorce from Vivian was finalized a few days before Christmas, 1967. He was serious about getting his drug use under control, and June was back by his side. With his prison album just a few weeks away, Johnny was ready to start 1968 with a clean slate. It would be the personal and professional rebirth he needed, though it's unlikely even he could have predicted just how pivotal that moment would be.

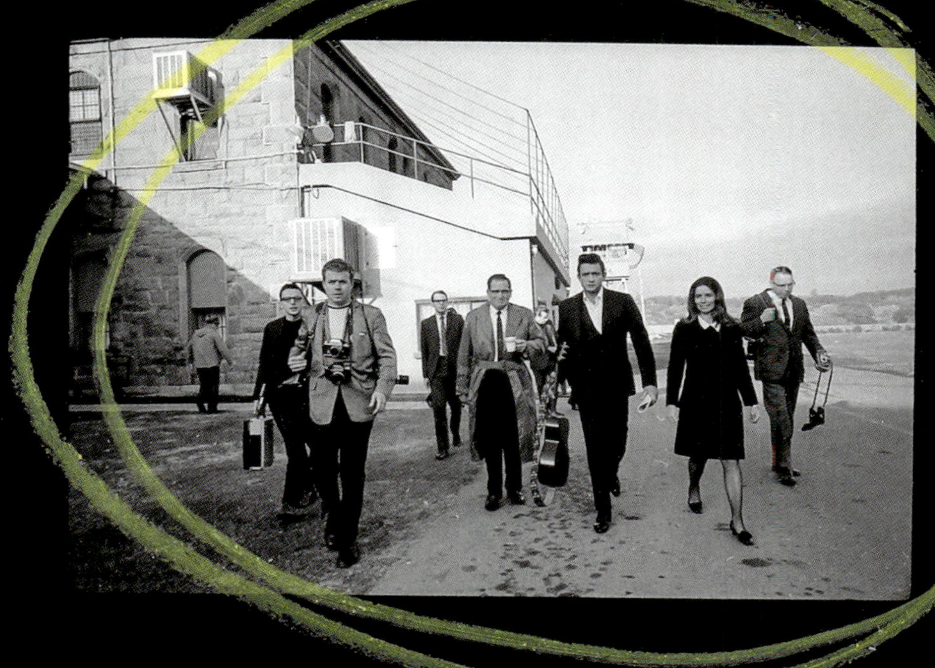
KODAK TRI X PAN FILM

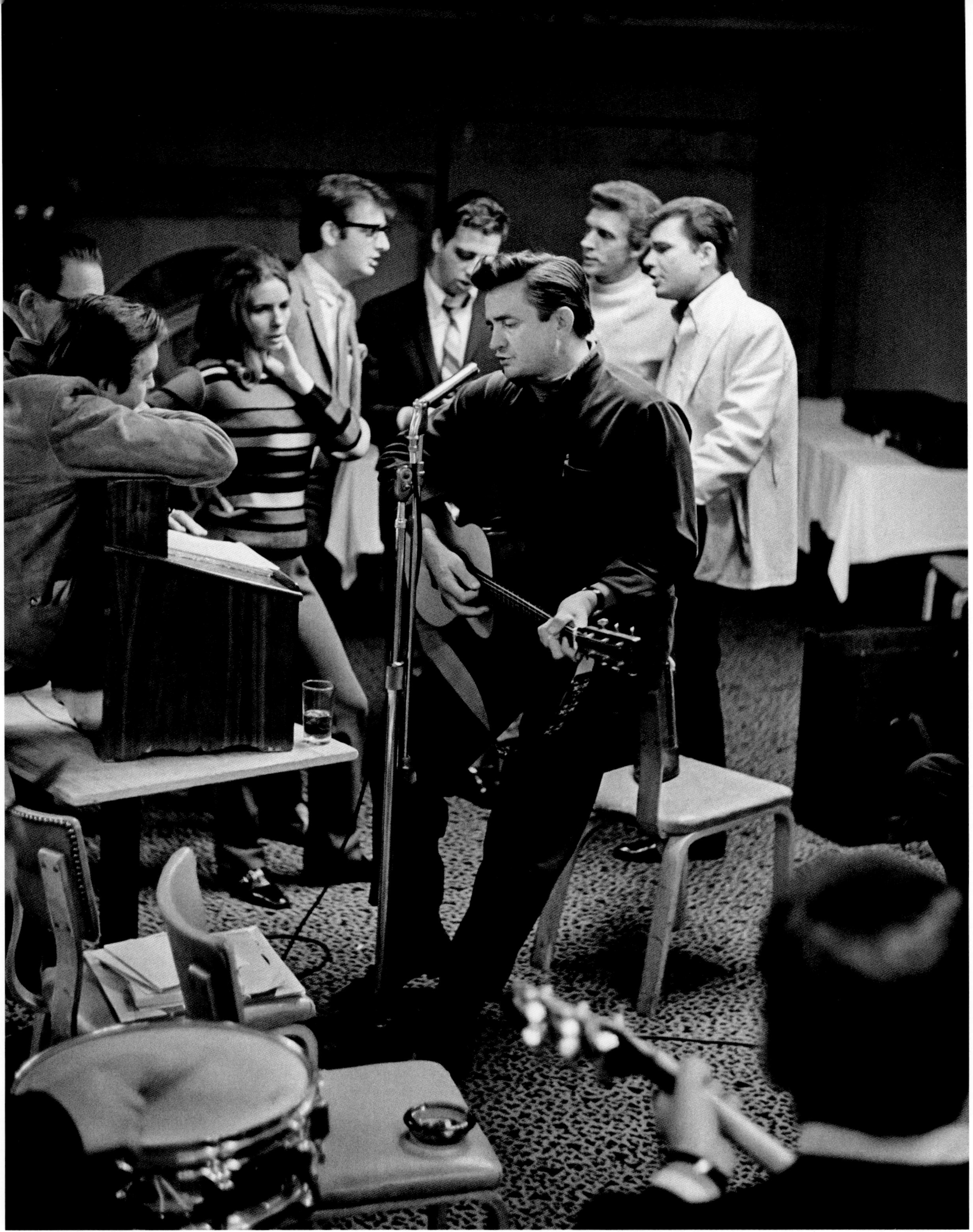

The day before the Folsom show Johnny and June flew from Los Angeles to Sacramento with Reverend Floyd Gressett, who was Cash's initial connection to Folsom. Gressett brought along reporter Gene Beley and photographer Dan Poush from Ventura's *Star-Free Press* to cover the story. They checked into the El Rancho Hotel and waited for the rest of his touring roadshow—The Tennessee Three, Carl Perkins, The Statler Brothers—and producer Bob Johnston to arrive from Nashville. When everyone had convened, the entourage huddled in one of the hotel's banquet rooms rehearsing and finalizing the plan for the following day. Johnston and Cash agreed to record two shows so they could use the best takes from each. Johnny generally had little patience for rehearsals, but he wanted to get this one right and kept everyone there late into the evening.

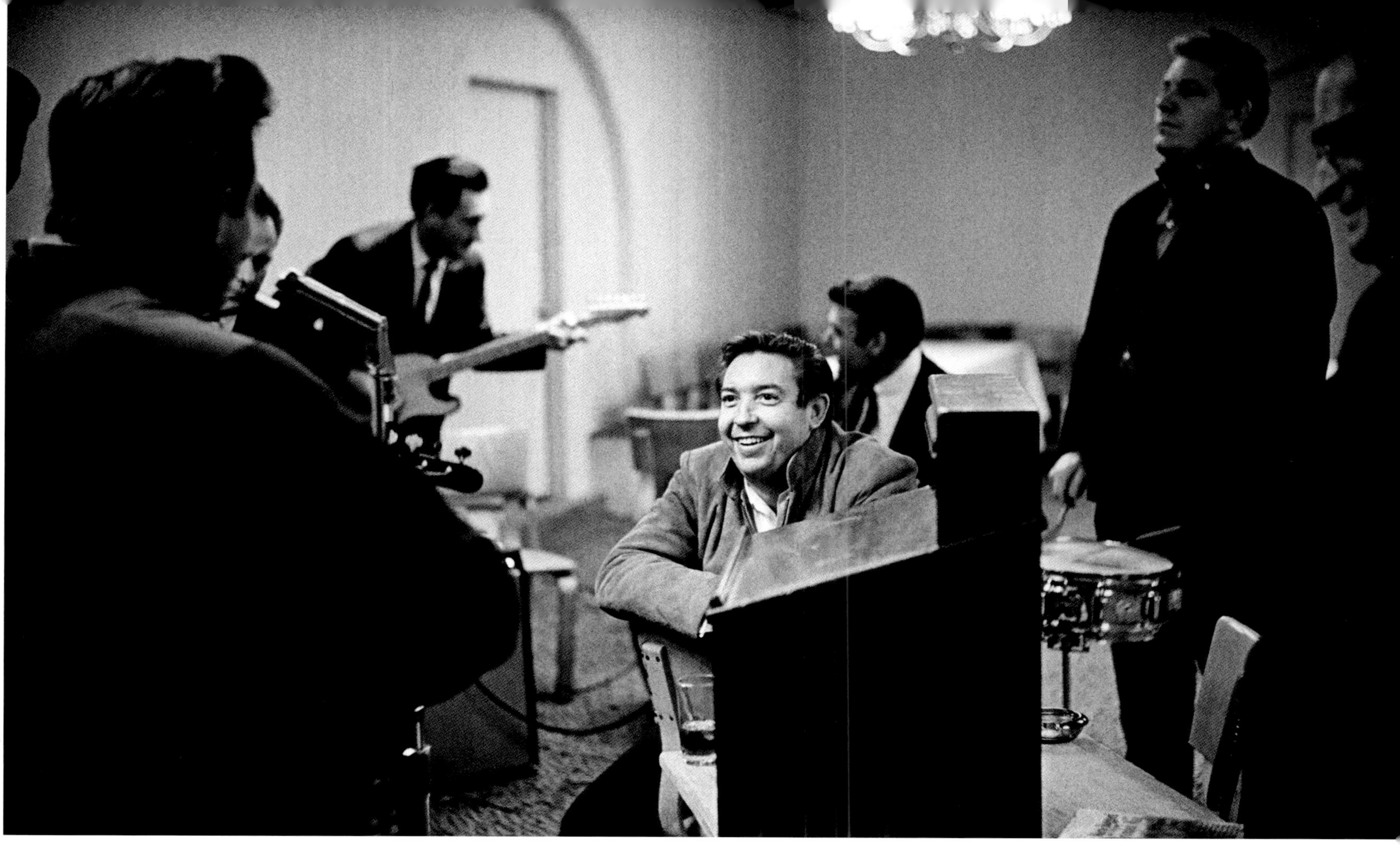

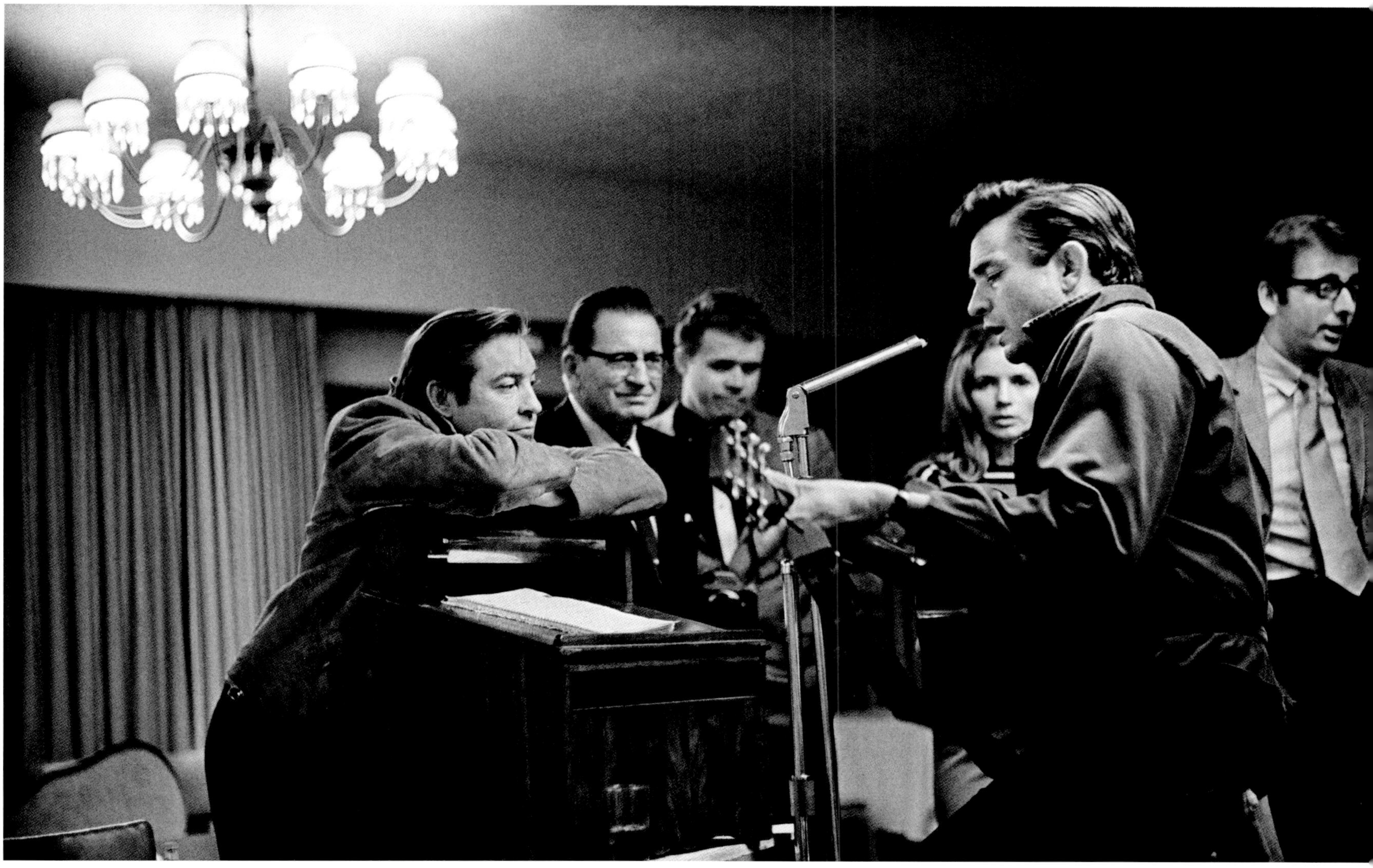

Opposite page: Cash flanked by (L-R) producer Bob Johnston, Rev. Floyd Gressett, journalist Gene Beley, June Carter, and The Statler Brothers—Don Reid, Harold Reid, Philip Balsley, and Lew DeWitt.

Top: (L-R) Cash, bassist Marshall Grant, guitarist Luther Perkins, producer Bob Johnston, guitarist Carl Perkins, drummer WS "Fluke" Holland, and Rev. Floyd Gressett.

Bottom: (L-R) Johnston, Gressett, photographer Dan Poush, June Carter, Johnny, and Statler Brother Don Reid.

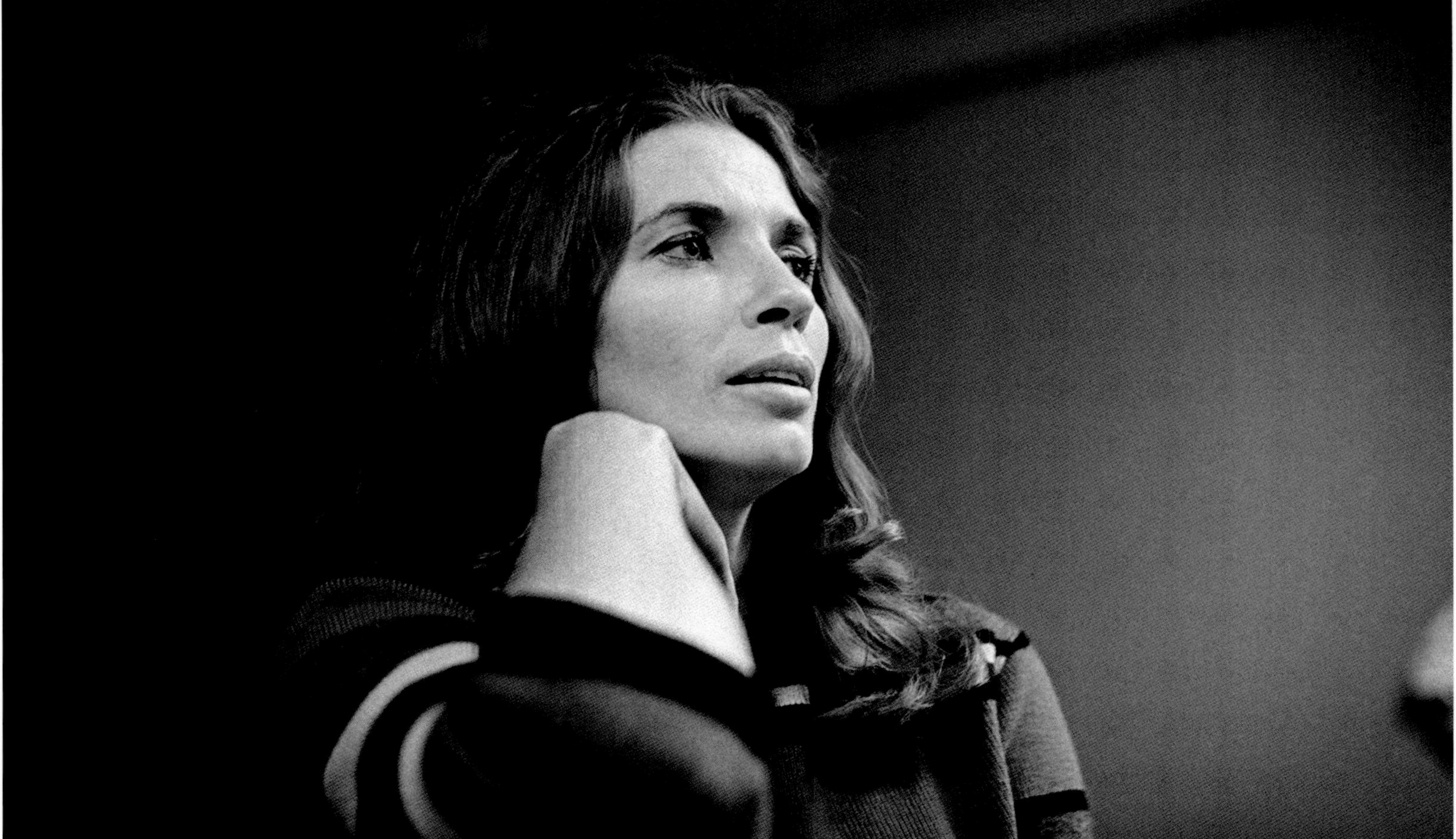

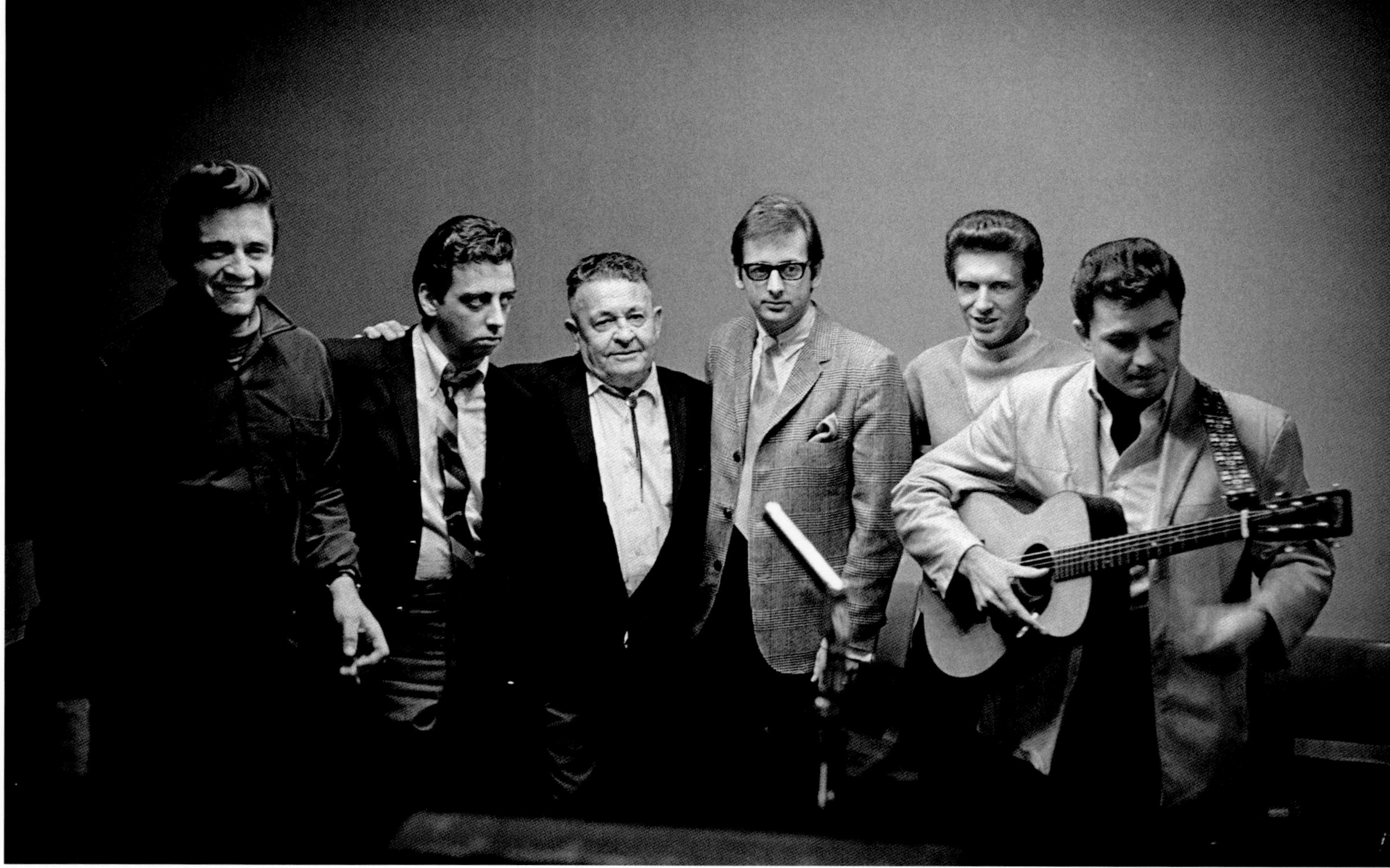

Jim Marshall had driven up from San Francisco and was the only official photographer present to capture images for the album. Cash loved Marshall's work and had personally requested his participation. The other notable person at the hotel was Johnny's father, Ray Cash. Though he was already a star, the younger Cash was never confident of his father's approval. He could sense that this was an important moment and wanted to make sure his dad was there to see it. California's then-Governor Ronald Reagan was hosting a fundraising dinner in another banquet room at the hotel and stopped in to greet Cash, who was pleased to introduce his father to the most powerful politician in the state.

***Opposite:** Johnny's father, Ray Cash, looks on as his son prepares for the following day's performances.*
***Above:** Johnny and Ray Cash (third from left) posing with The Statler Brothers' Harold Reid, Don Reid, Philip Balsley, and Lew DeWitt.*

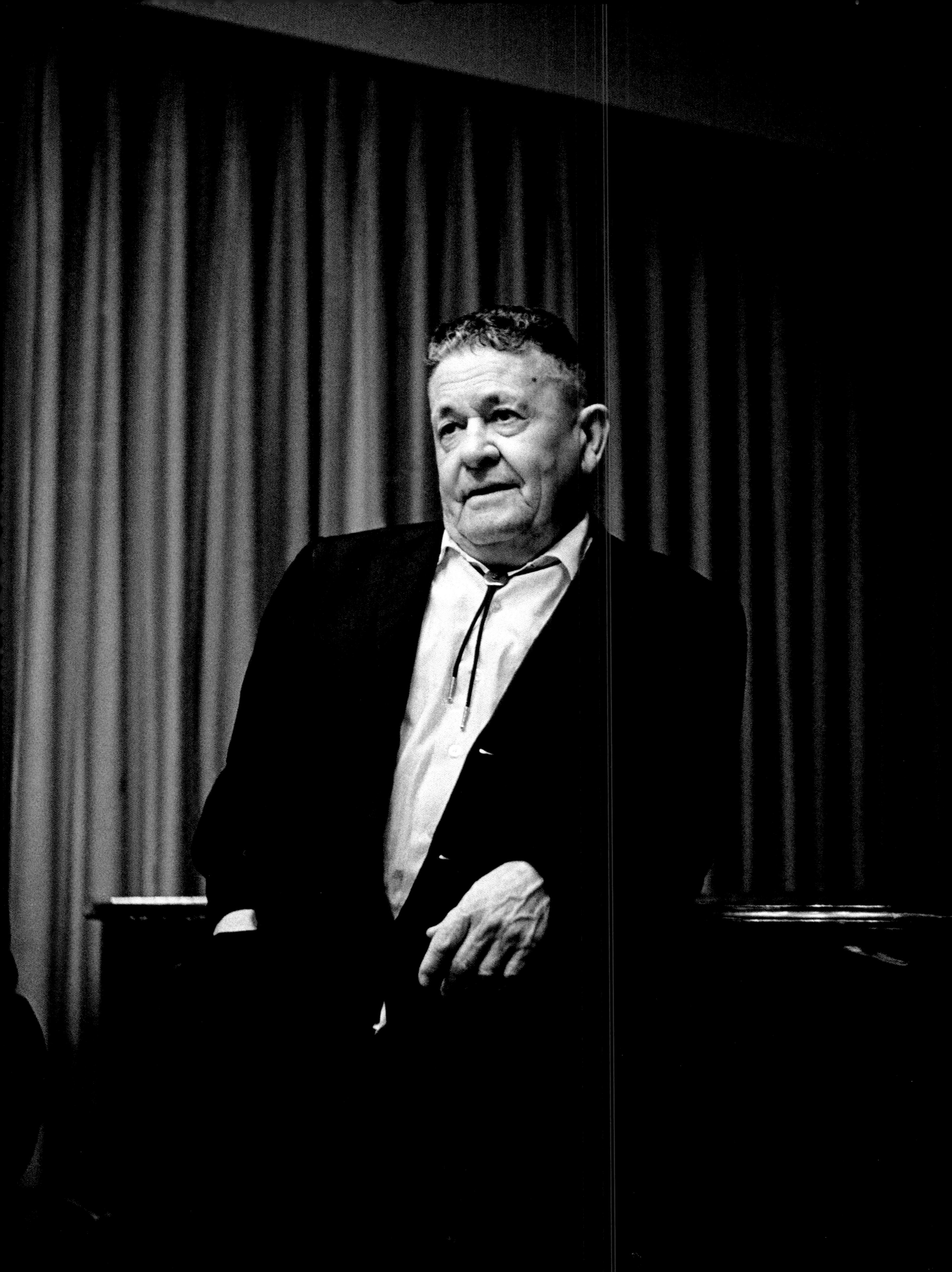

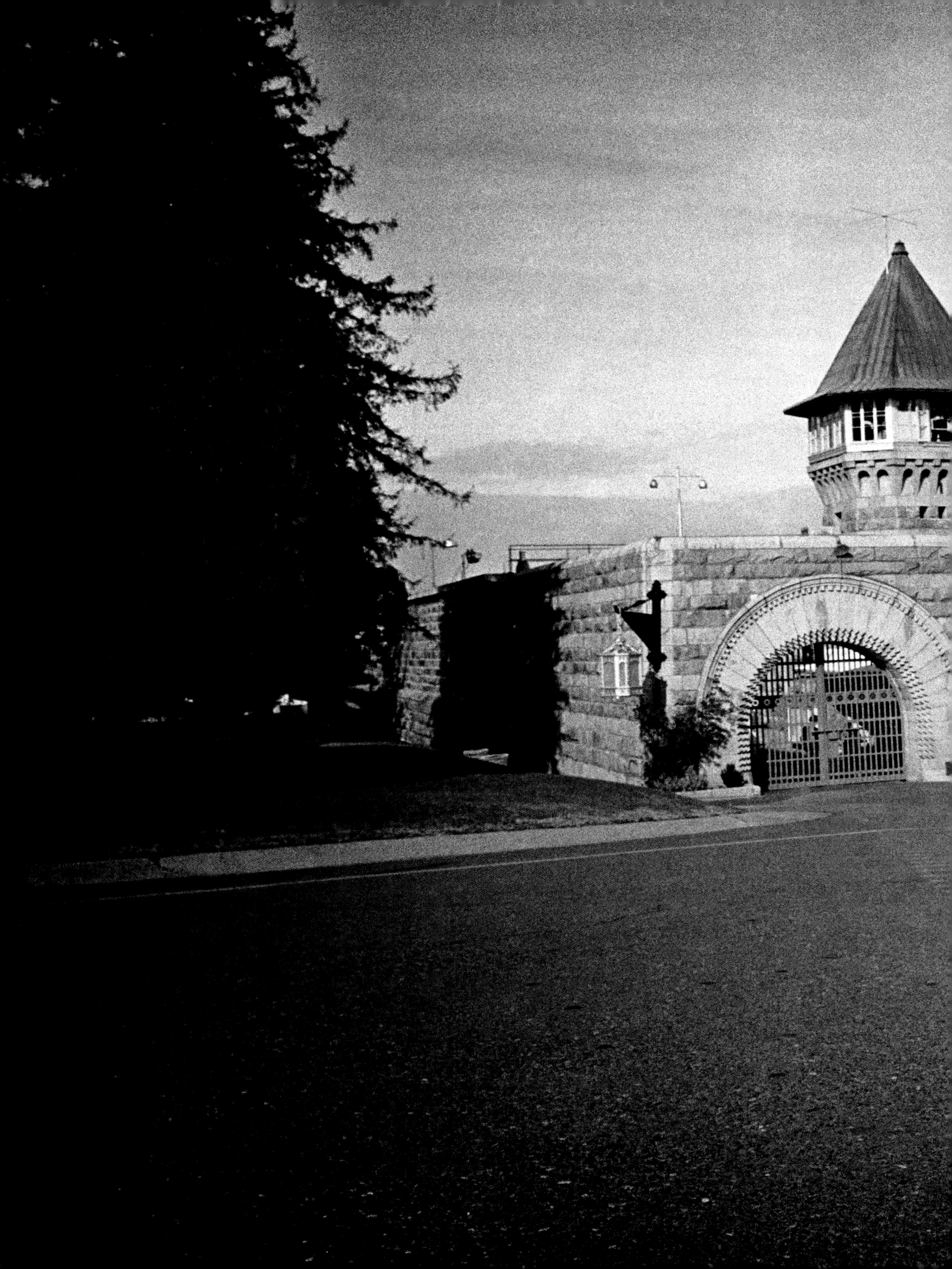

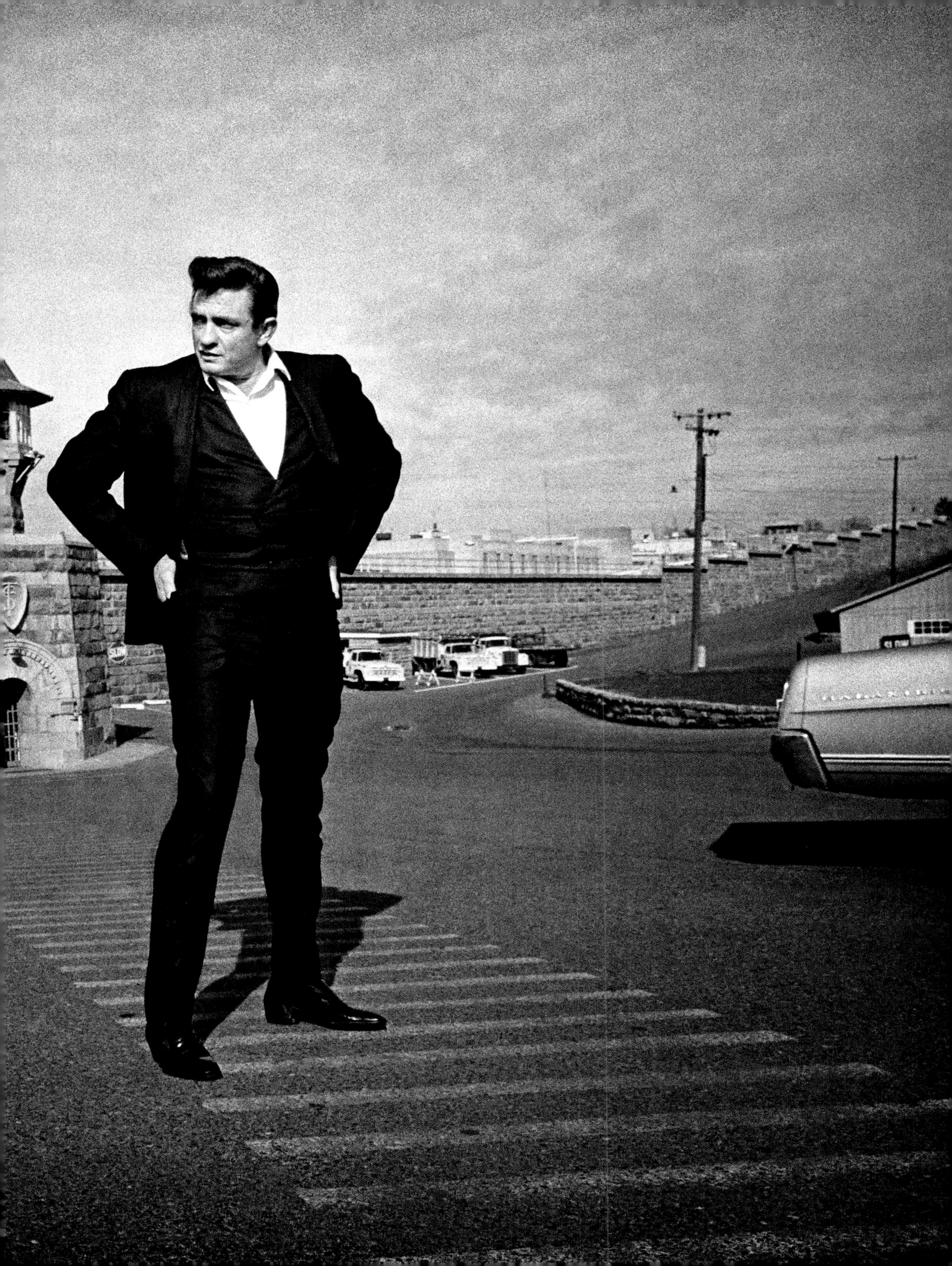

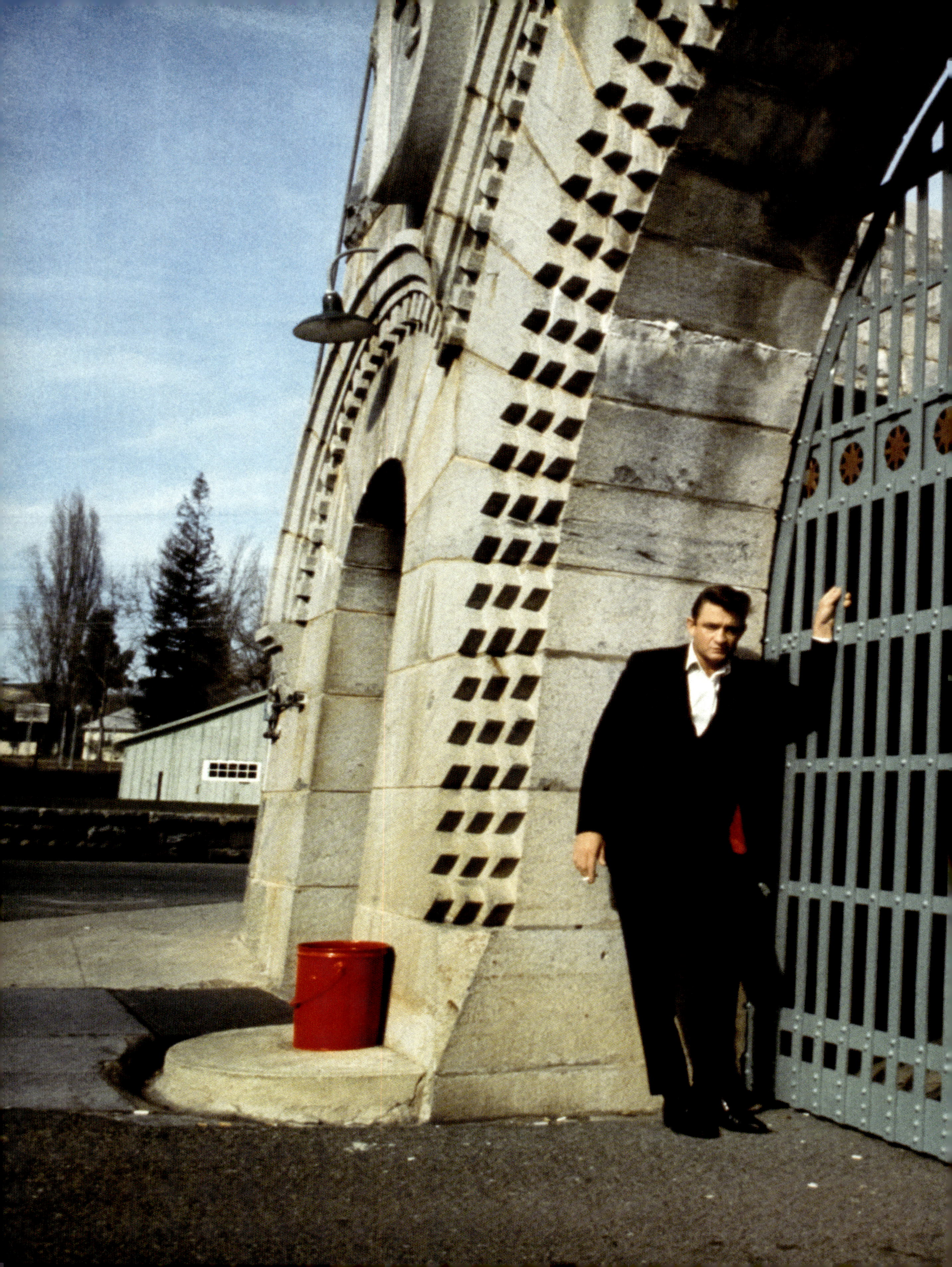

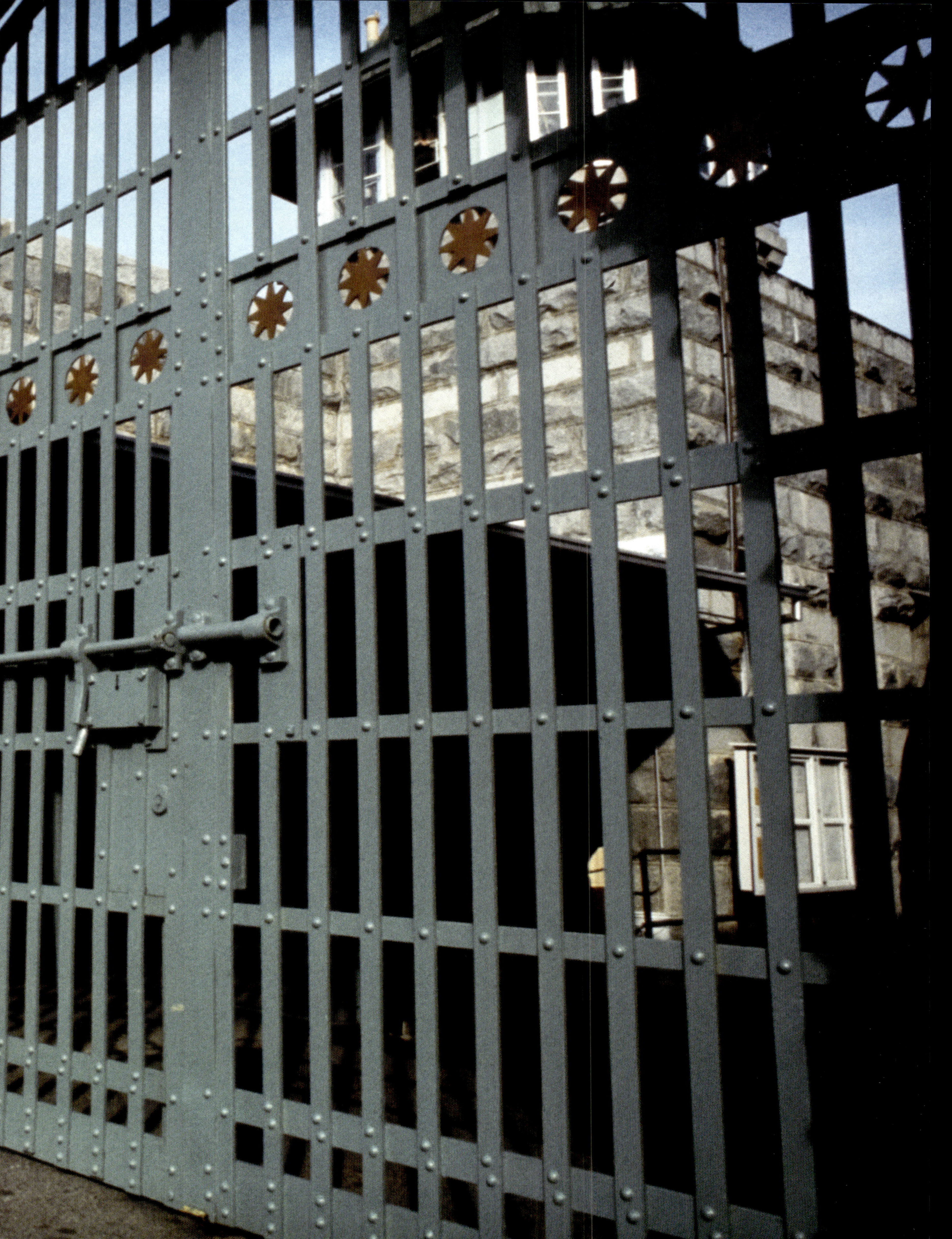

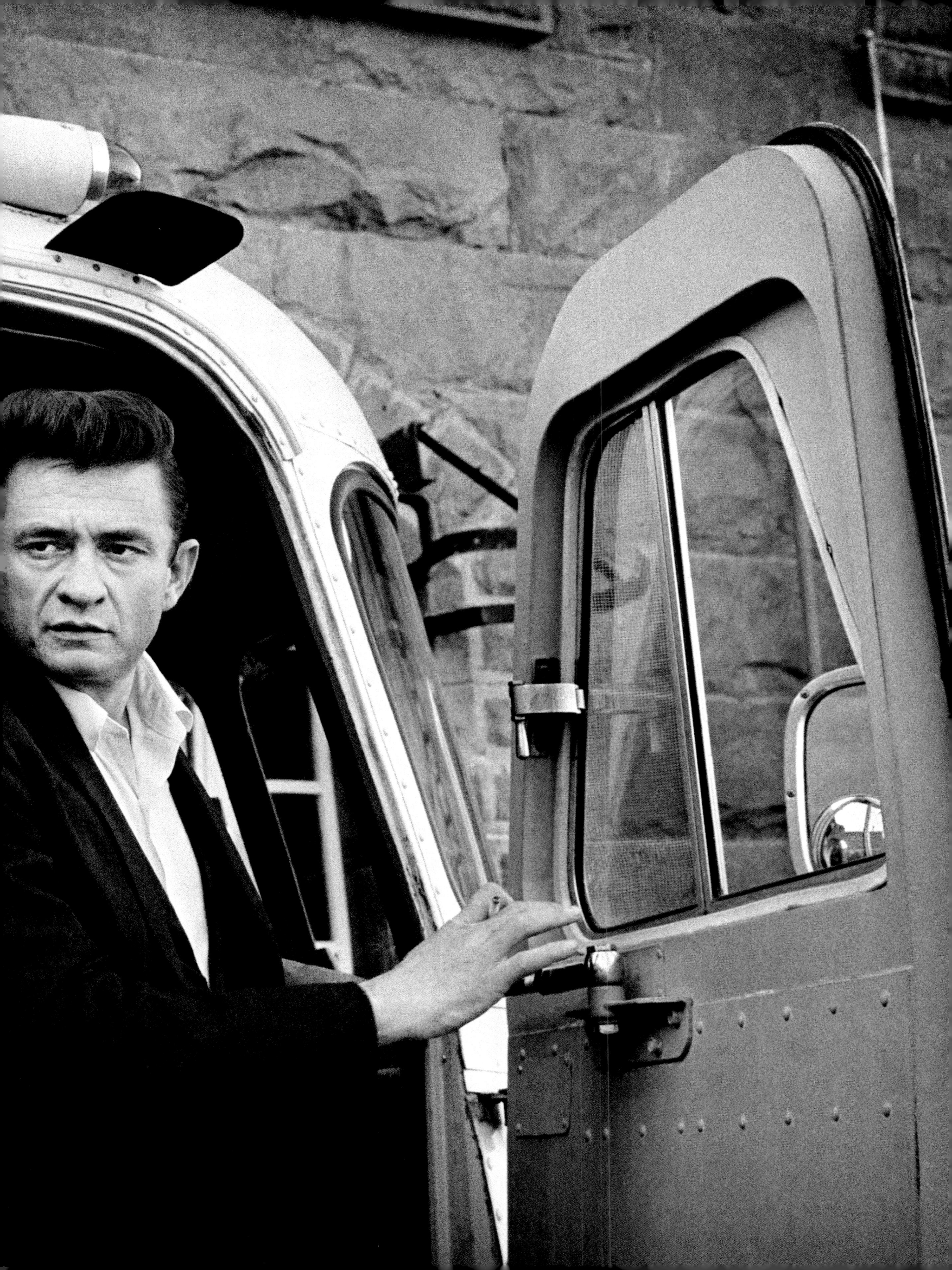

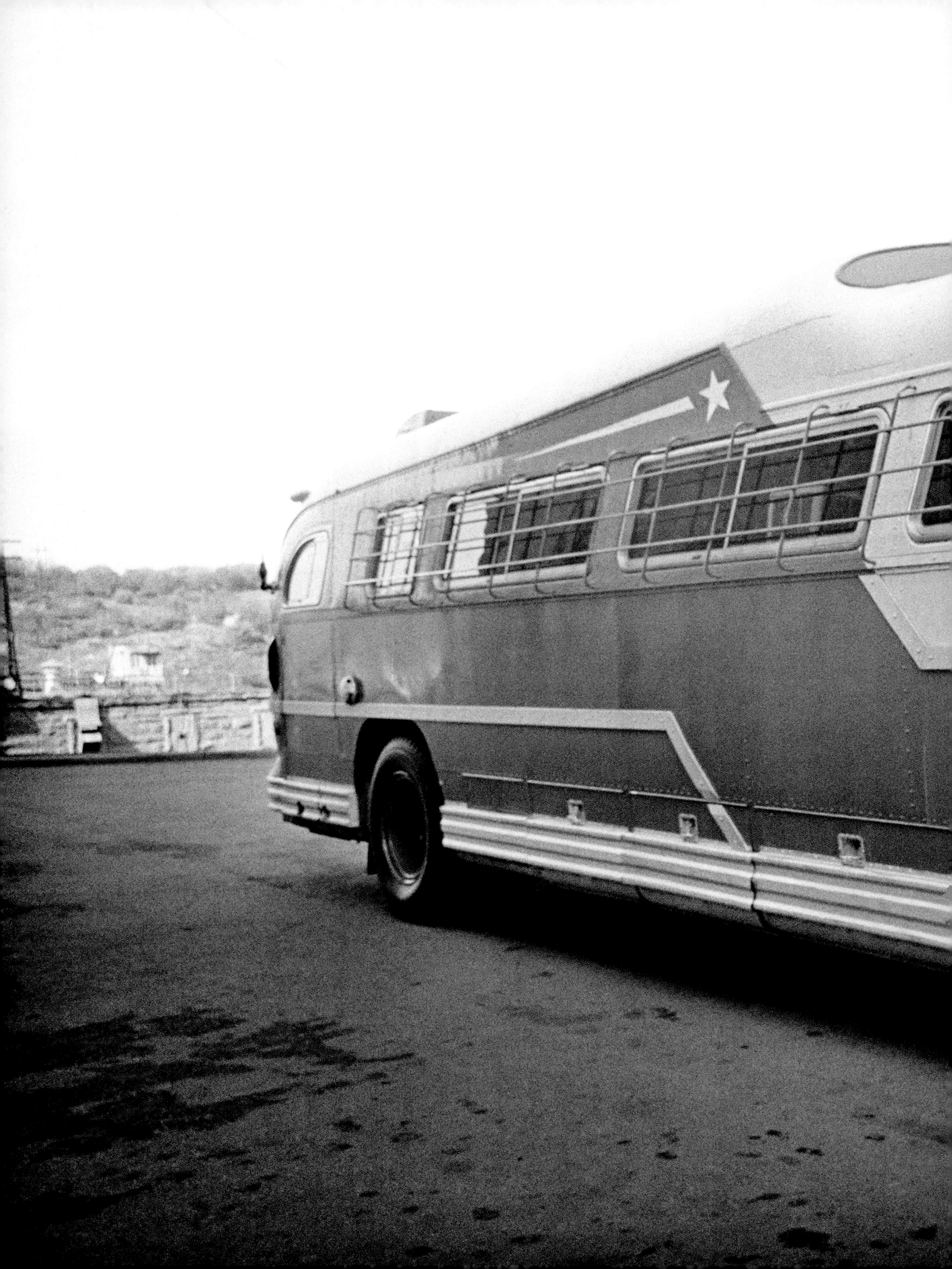

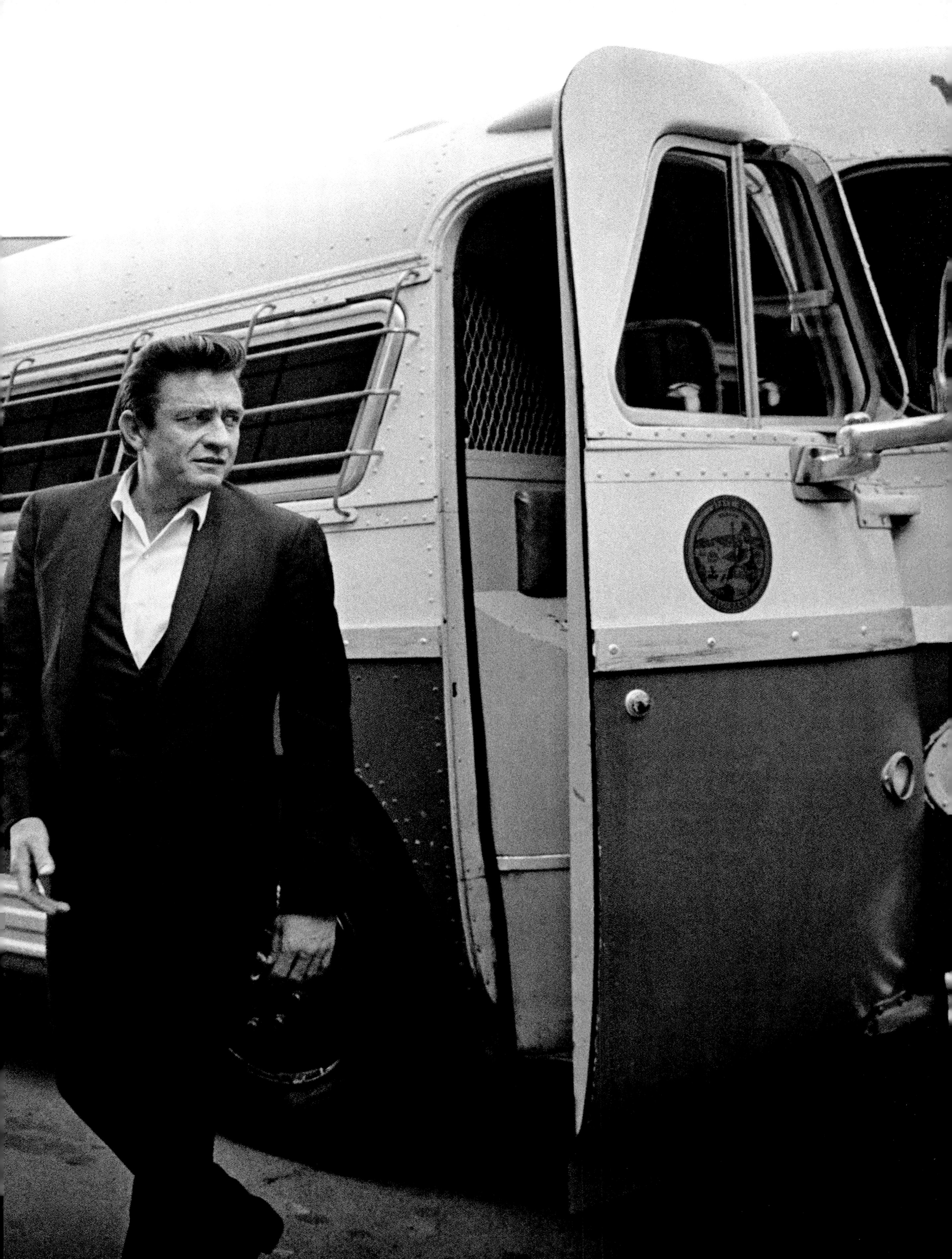

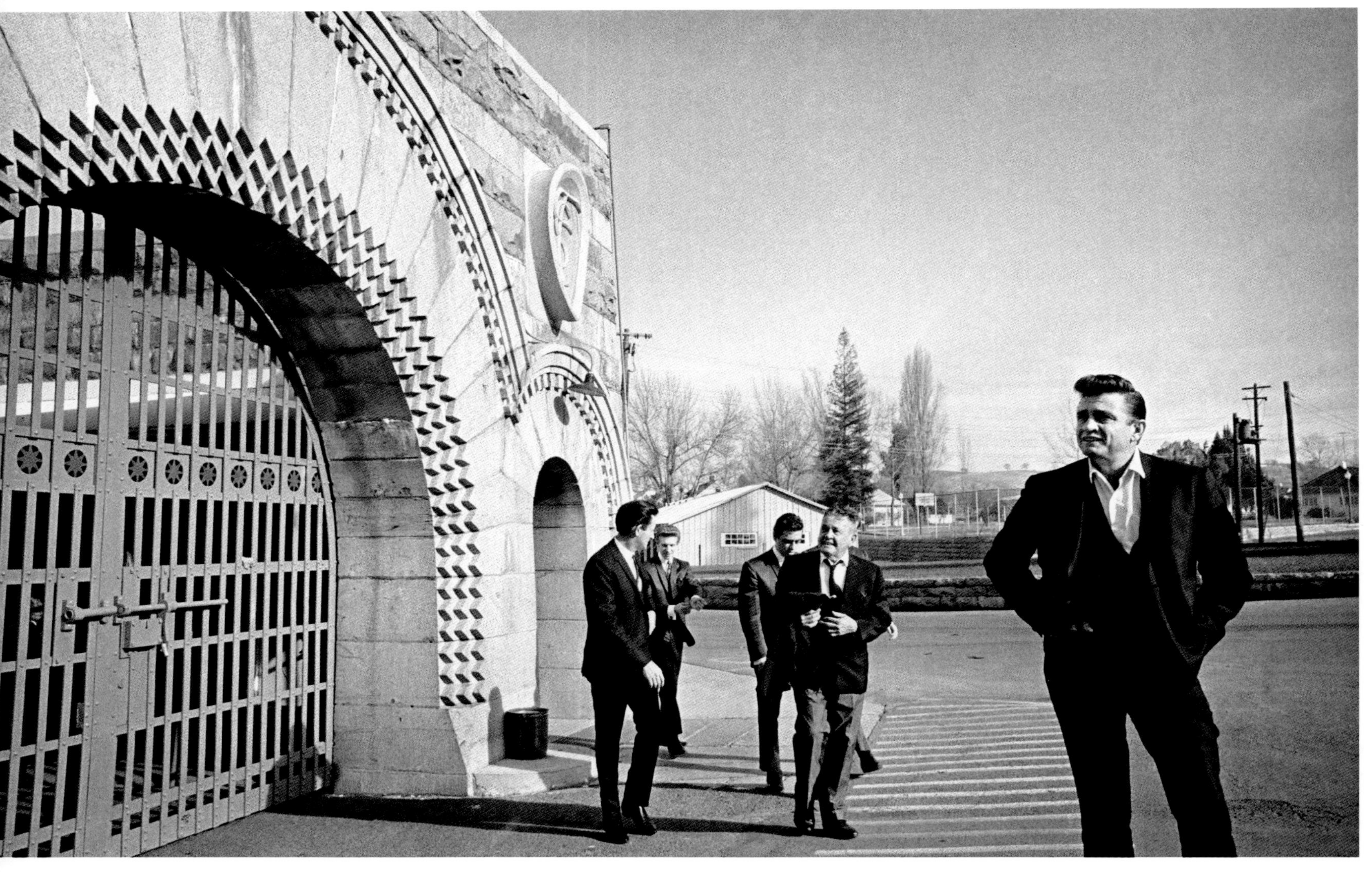

Johnny Cash was up early the next morning. He and his entourage were driven the 25 miles from the El Rancho Hotel to Folsom State Prison where they gathered outside the gates around 7:30 or 8:00 AM. In addition to everyone who'd gathered in the hotel banquet room the night before, they were joined by several prison officials, DJ Hugh Cherry (who would serve as the emcee for the event), and the young bespectacled *Los Angeles Times* music critic Robert Hilburn (who would go on to write the definitive Cash biography in 2013). After a few photos outside, it was time to travel beyond the prison walls.

"The limos were parked in the prison parking lot," Gene Beley recalled, "and we boarded a school bus. The huge gates of Folsom opened to allow the bus inside. A second set had to be opened after the first was shut behind us." There was a quiet sense of foreboding among everyone present. "The granite walls in Folsom are about eight feet thick," Jim Marshall later remembered, "and we had just gotten off the bus and gone through one giant gate into a holding area. Then we went through a second gate, and, when it clanked shut, John said, 'Jim, there's a feeling of permanence in that sound.' After that, I started wondering when we were going to get out of there."

Marshall's photographs capture the somber expressions on everyone's faces once inside the prison walls. Those who were there described the walk to Dining Hall #2, where the shows would be

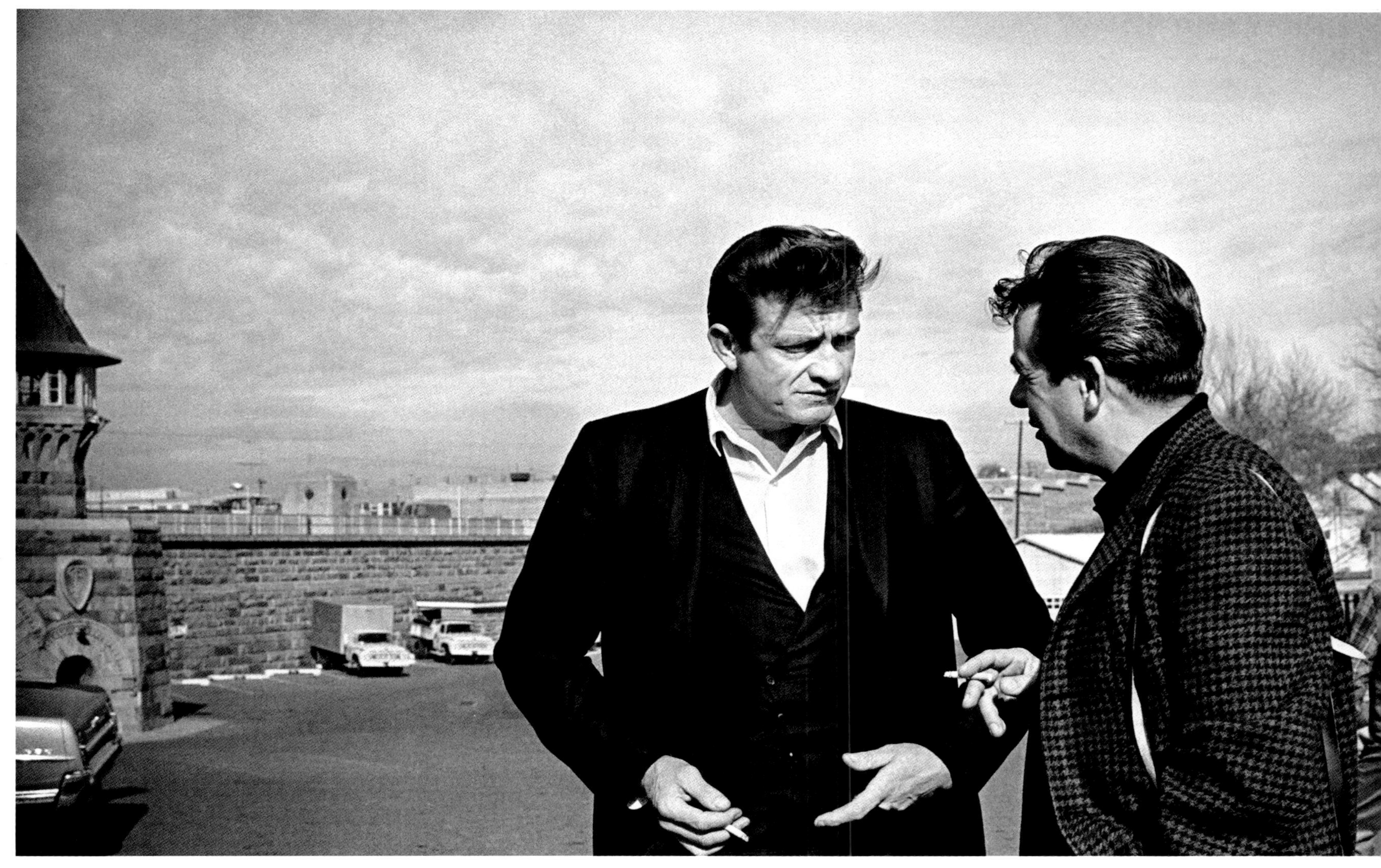

performed, as something akin to a funeral march. The air was thick with tension and Johnny was nervous. "The authorities had made every effort to protect us," Marshall Grant recalled years later, "but as we know from past experience, anytime you go into a maximum-security penitentiary filled with hardened criminals, there was always the potential for violence. Despite the precautions, it was pretty scary at Folsom, especially since June was with us, and she was pretty uptight about being there."

Grant elaborated further in the documentary film *Johnny Cash at Folsom Prison*: "The pictures that Jim Marshall taken [sic] wasn't exaggerated at all. He got those things just the way that we all looked and the way that we all felt. It was a very, very somber atmosphere."

While he'd gotten his drug habit largely under control, Cash was not yet completely clean. He later confessed to Bob Johnston that he'd popped a handful of pills to calm his nerves. "He said, 'I took more pills that morning than I ever had in my life,'" Johnston recounted to Robert Hilburn. "He was scared."

***Above:** Cash confers with emcee Hugh Cherry. It was decided that, rather than giving him a big introduction, Cherry would have the headliner take the stage and simply announce, "Hello, I'm Johnny Cash."*

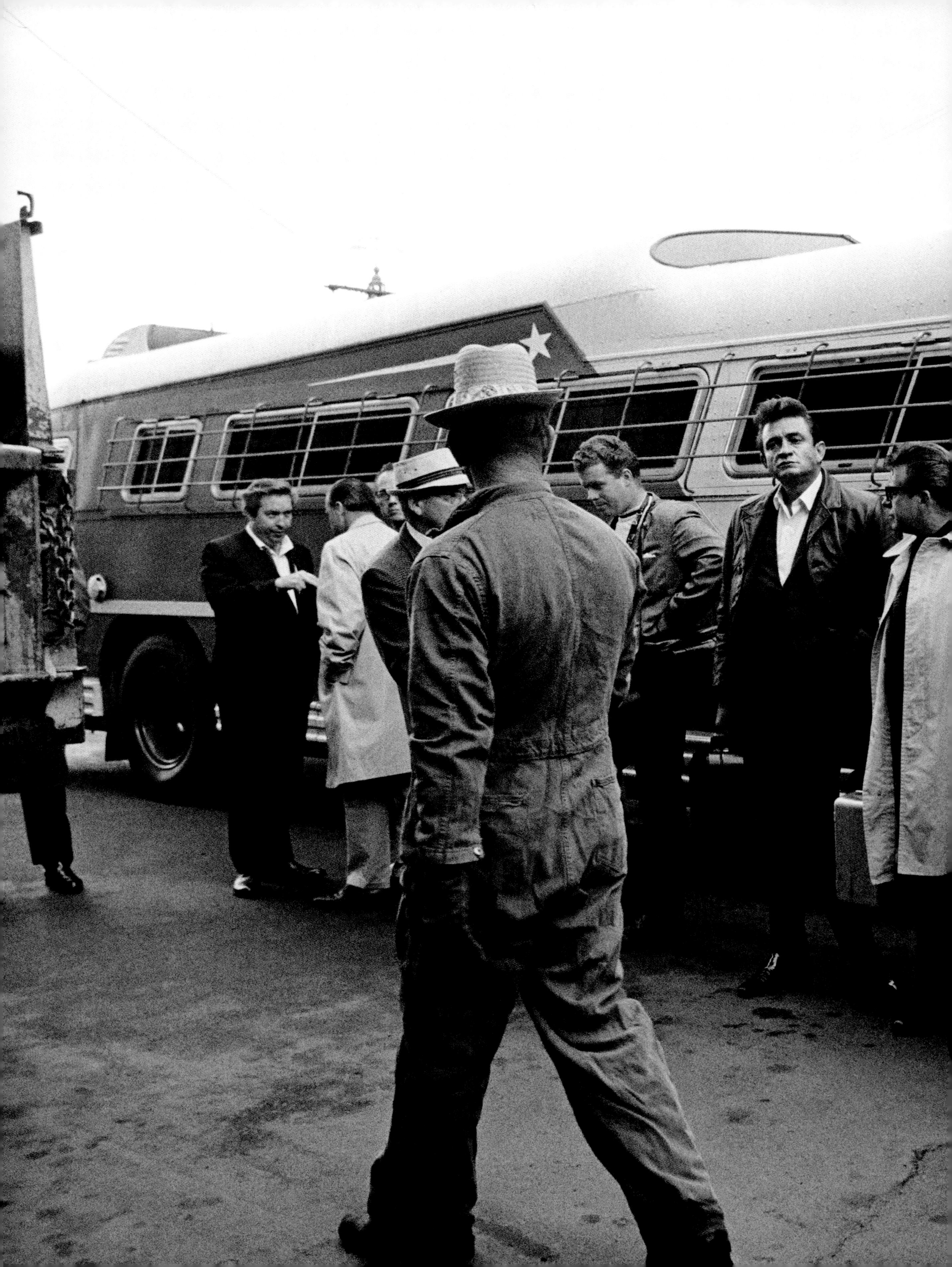

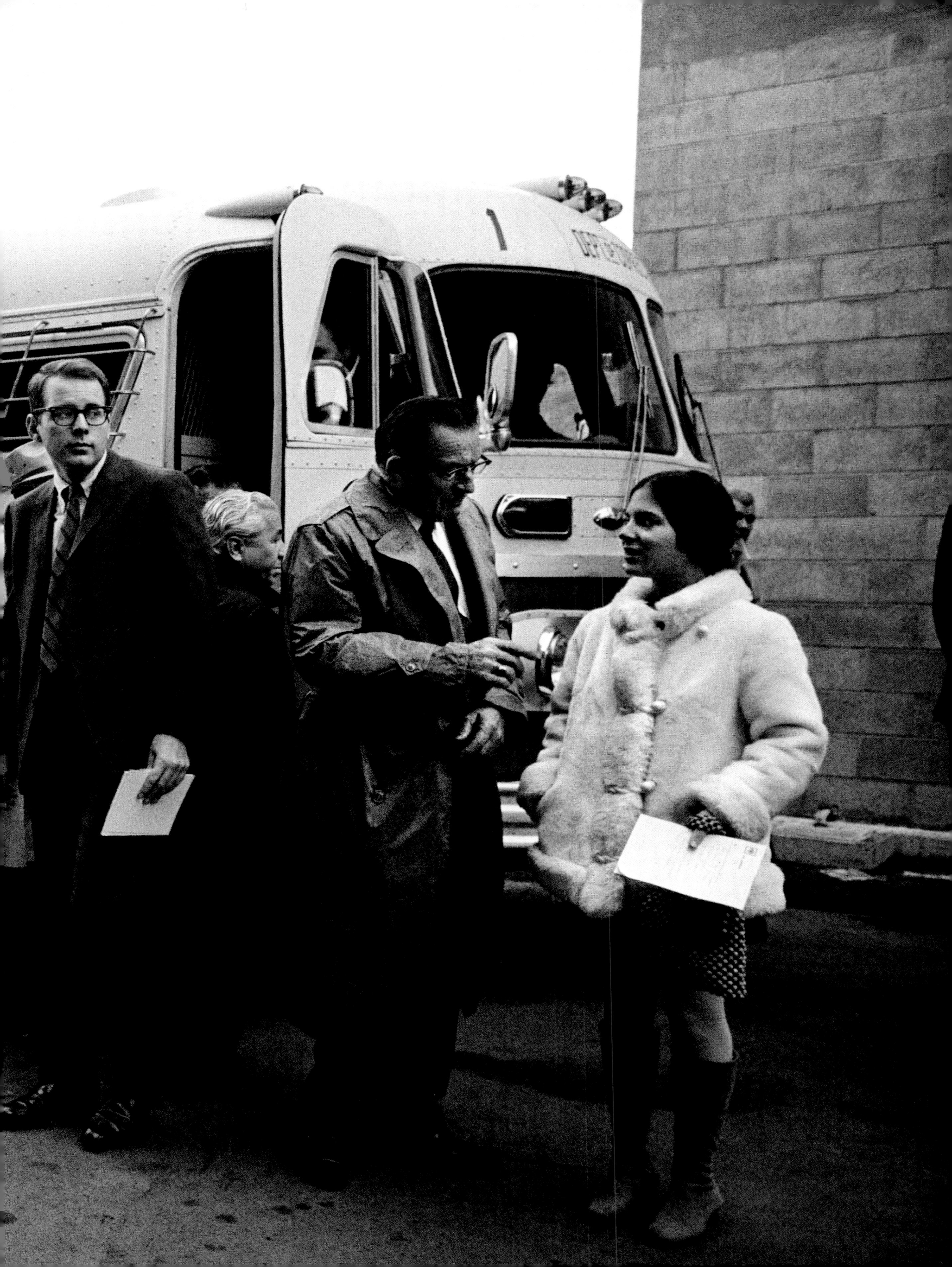

John asked Columbia Records to have me come with them to Folsom Prison in 1968. I had been busted a few months before for shooting a guy so it was really a bit weird for me. When those gates banged shut I wondered when we were gonna get out again. Obviously it was very different from any other show … you had to sign a release, if you were taken hostage or anything they wouldn't negotiate for you! They weren't expecting any trouble but they had armed guards up in the towers. It was a real treat, the audience was great, respectful. Not all of them would have been Johnny Cash fans before but by the end they certainly were. If Johnny would've said, "C'mon, let's crash out of here right now," they'd have done it.

JIM MARSHALL

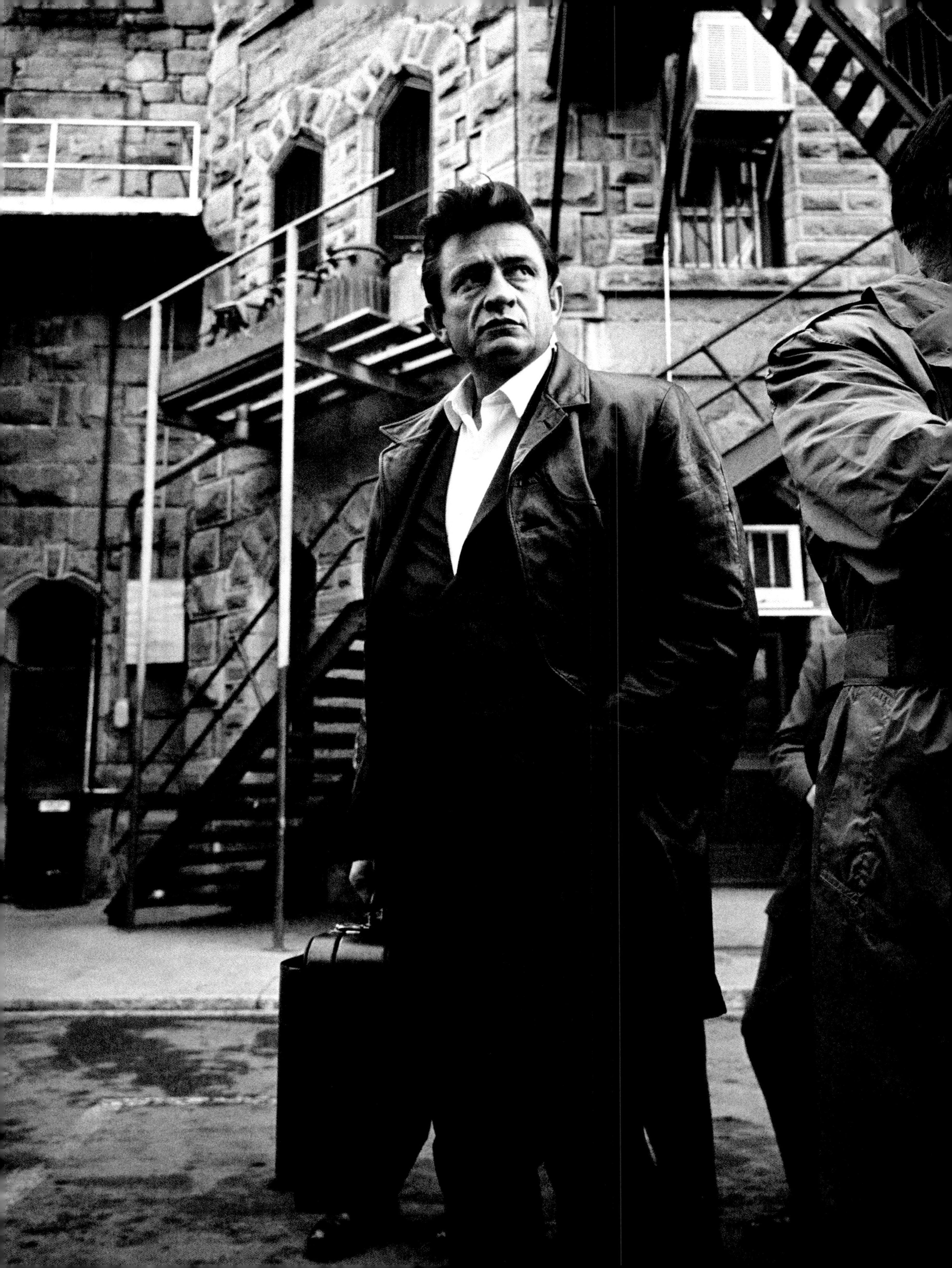

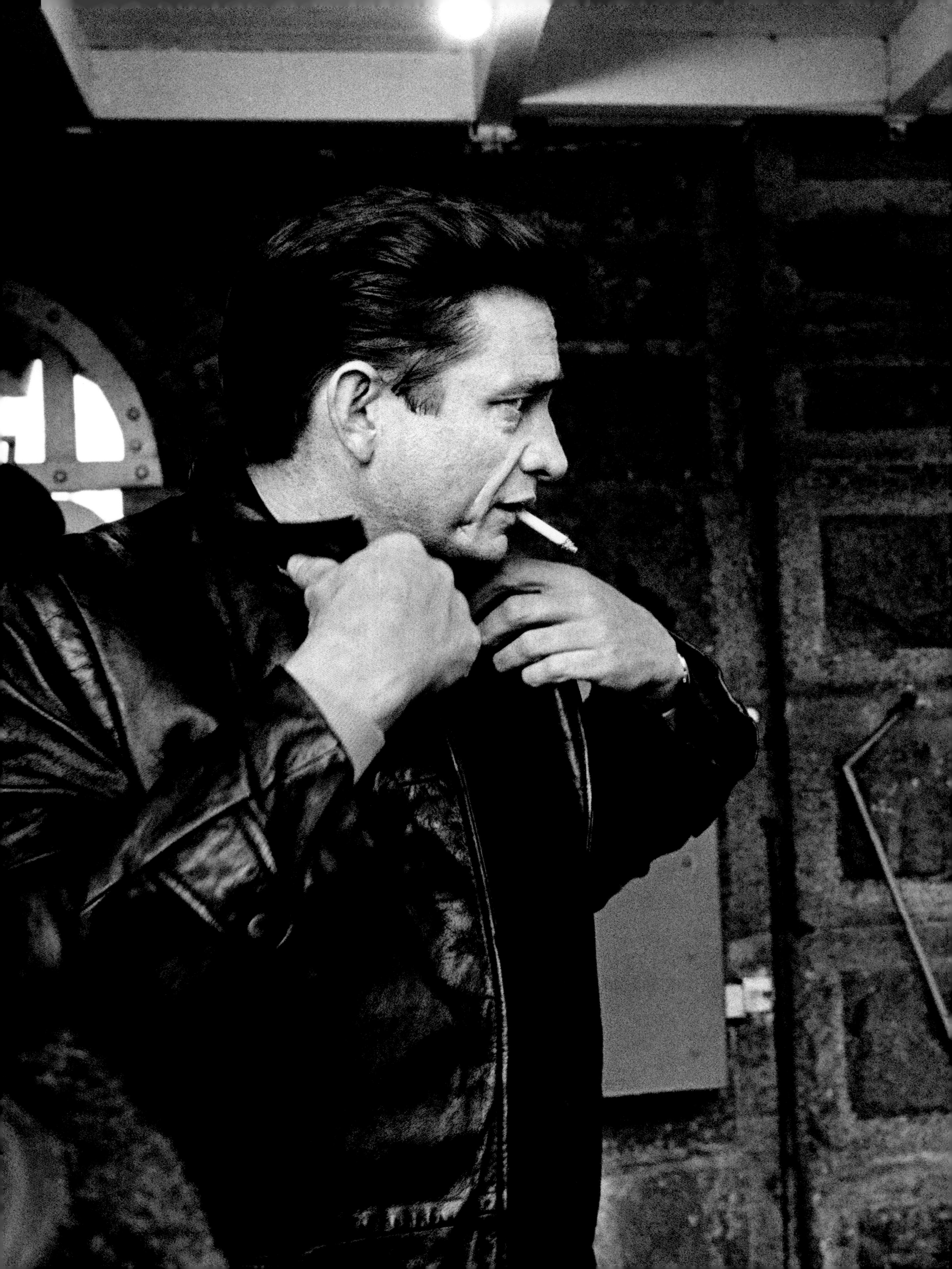

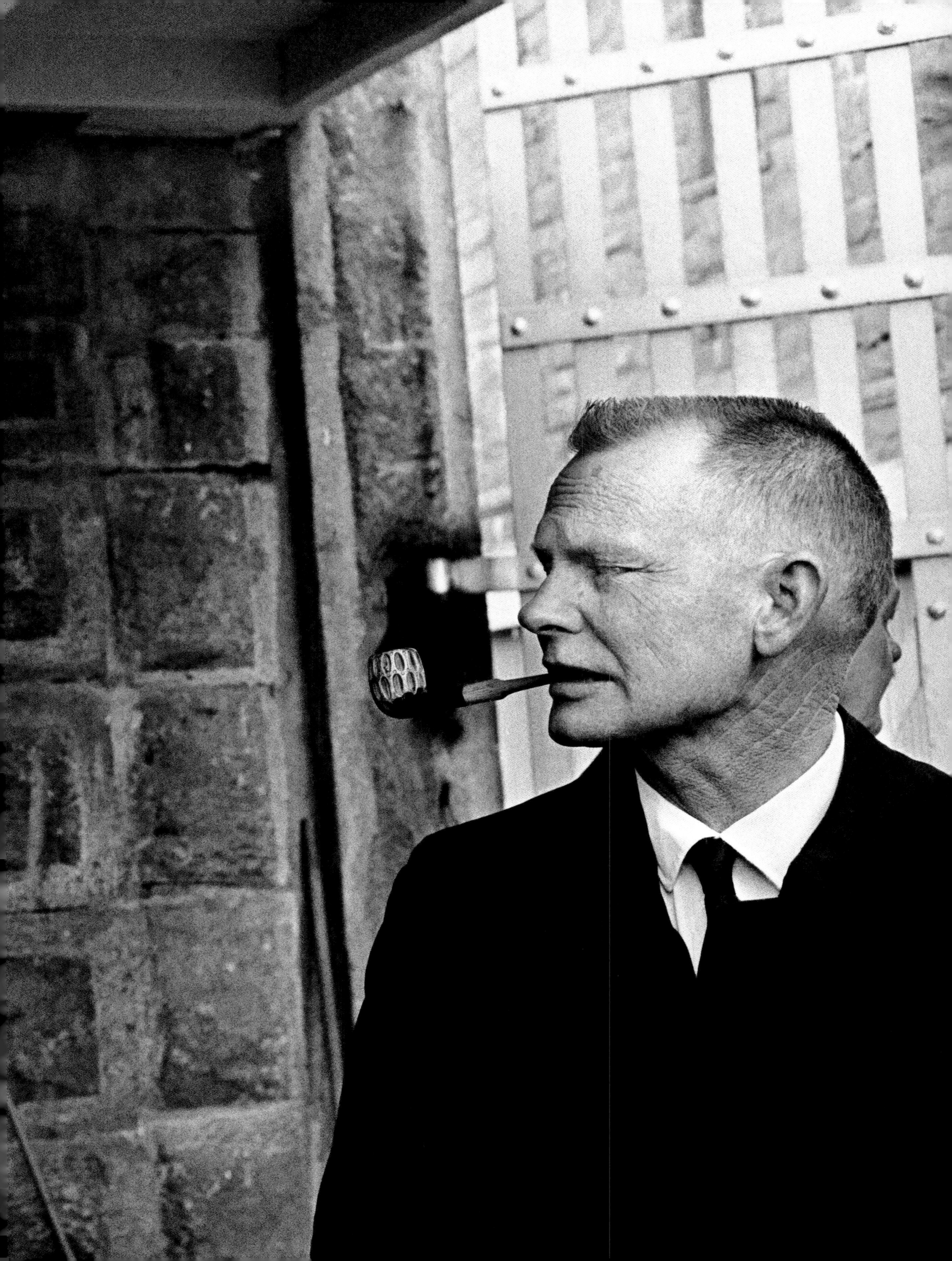

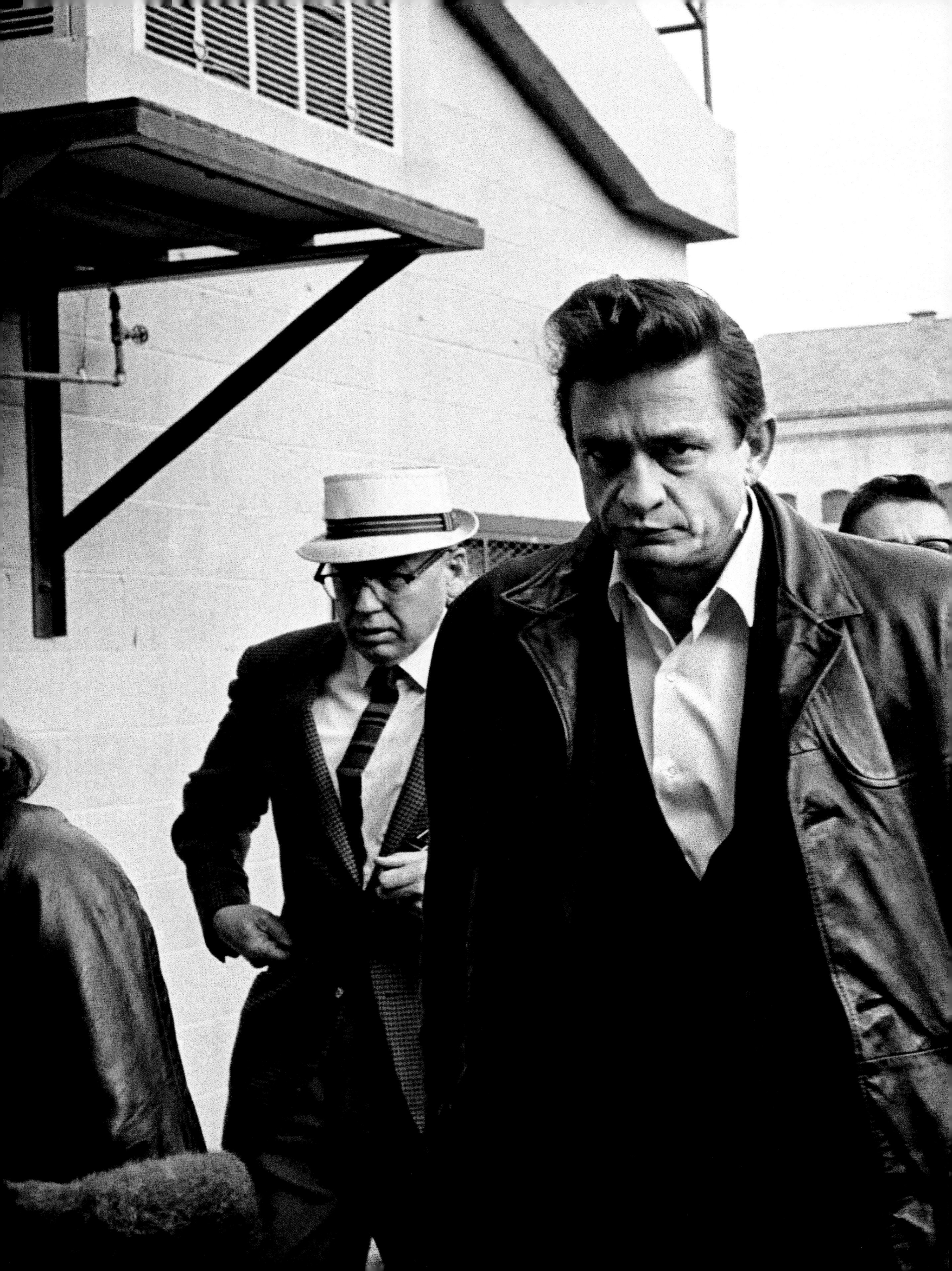

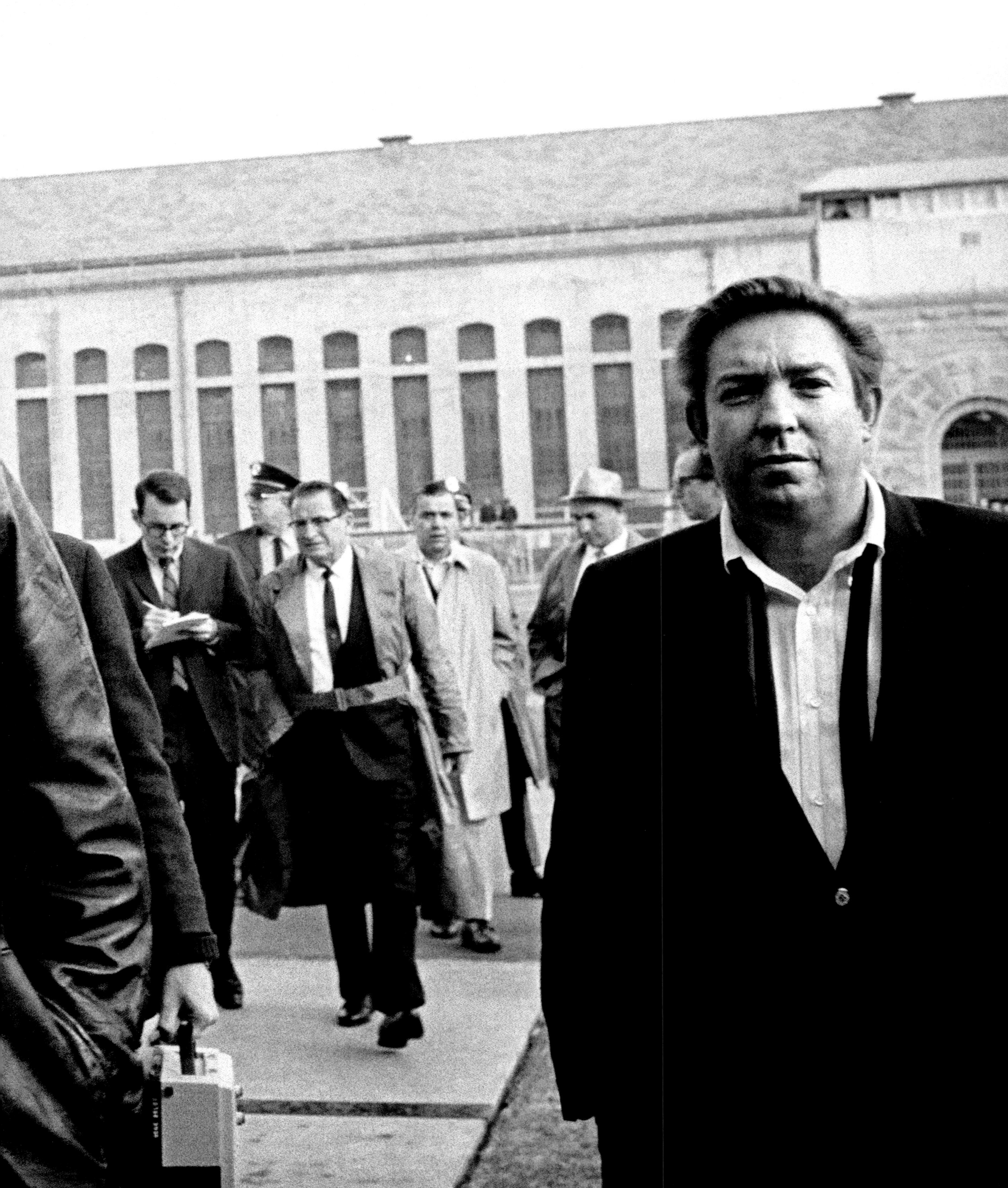

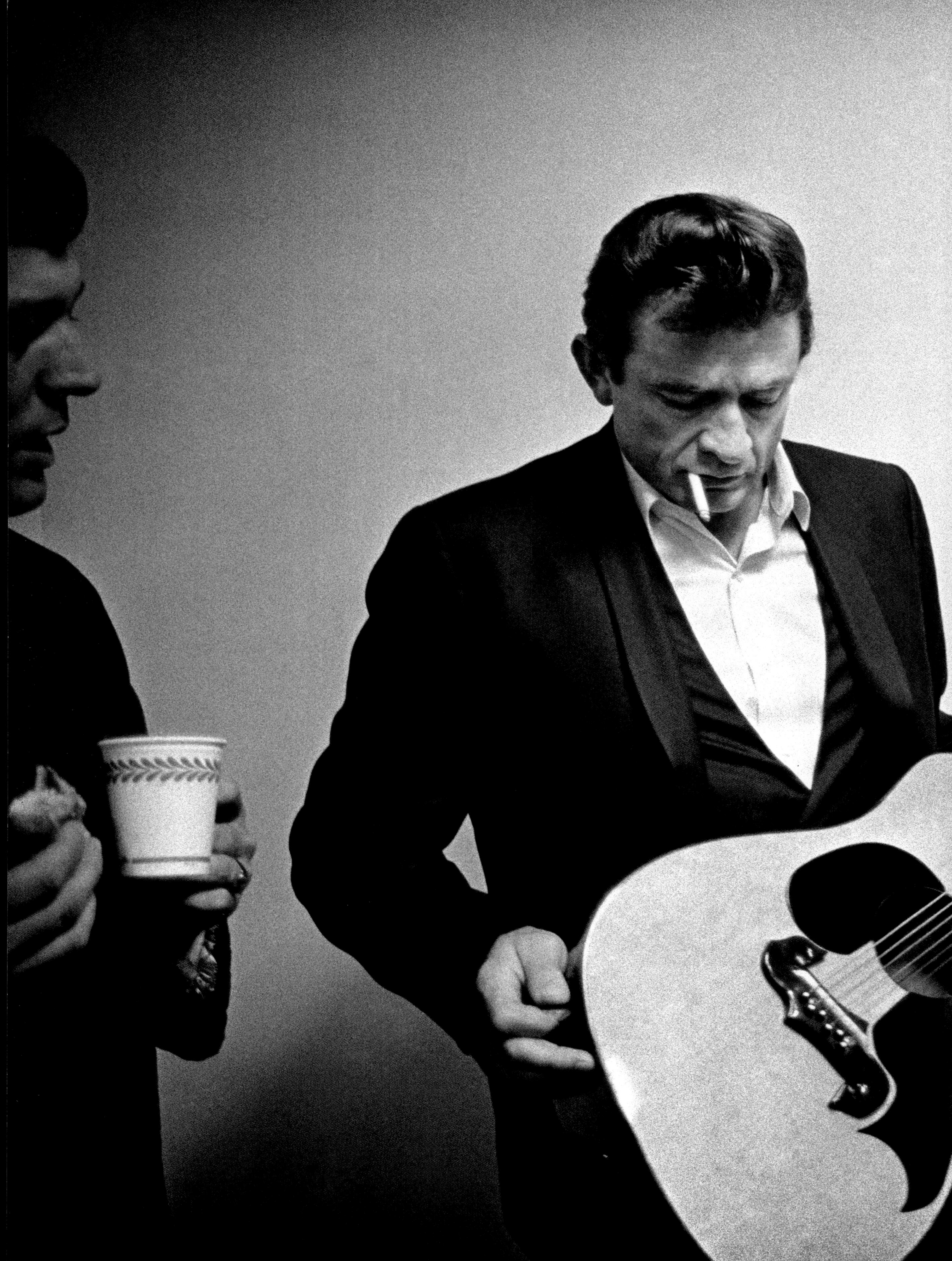

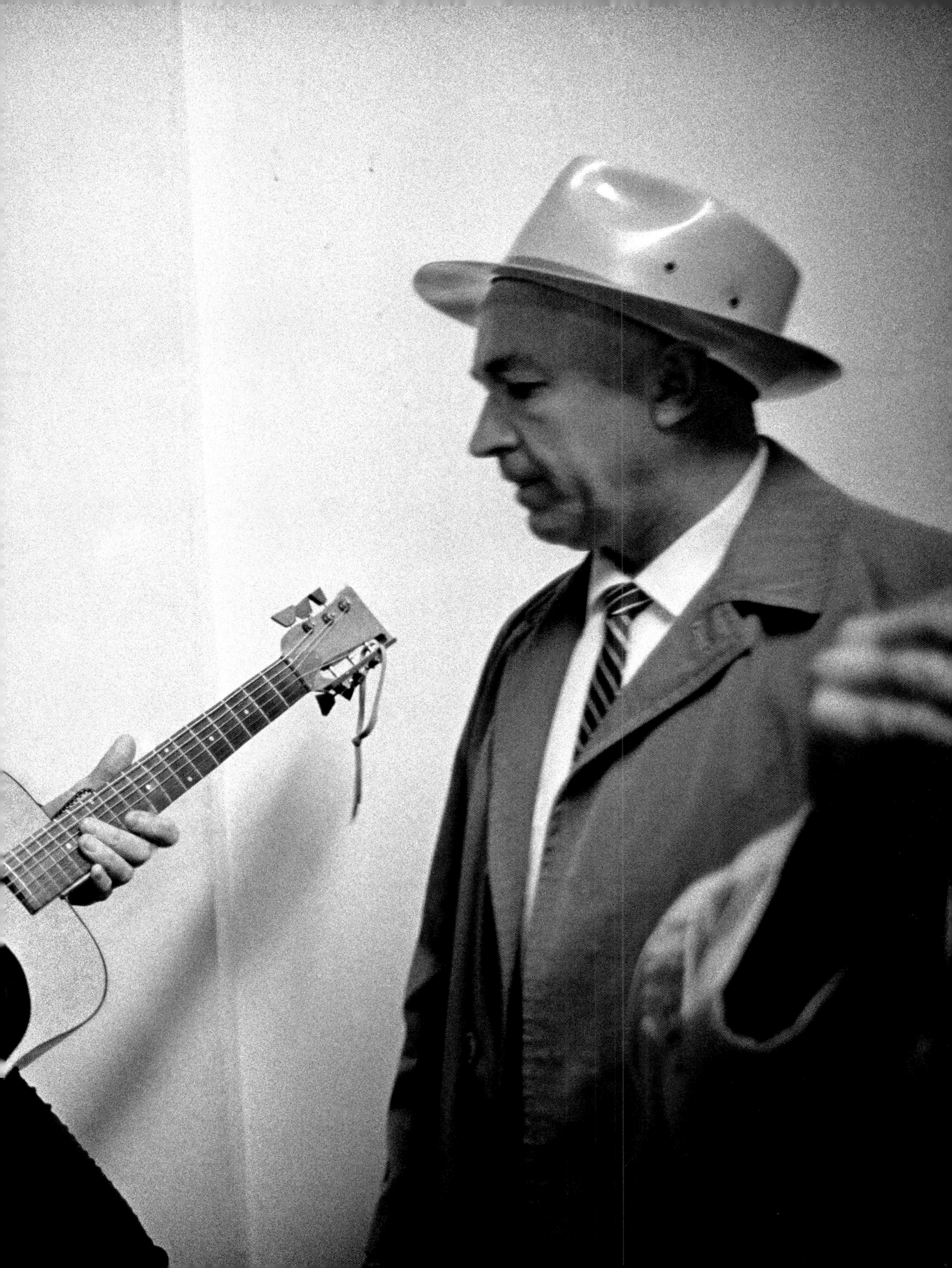

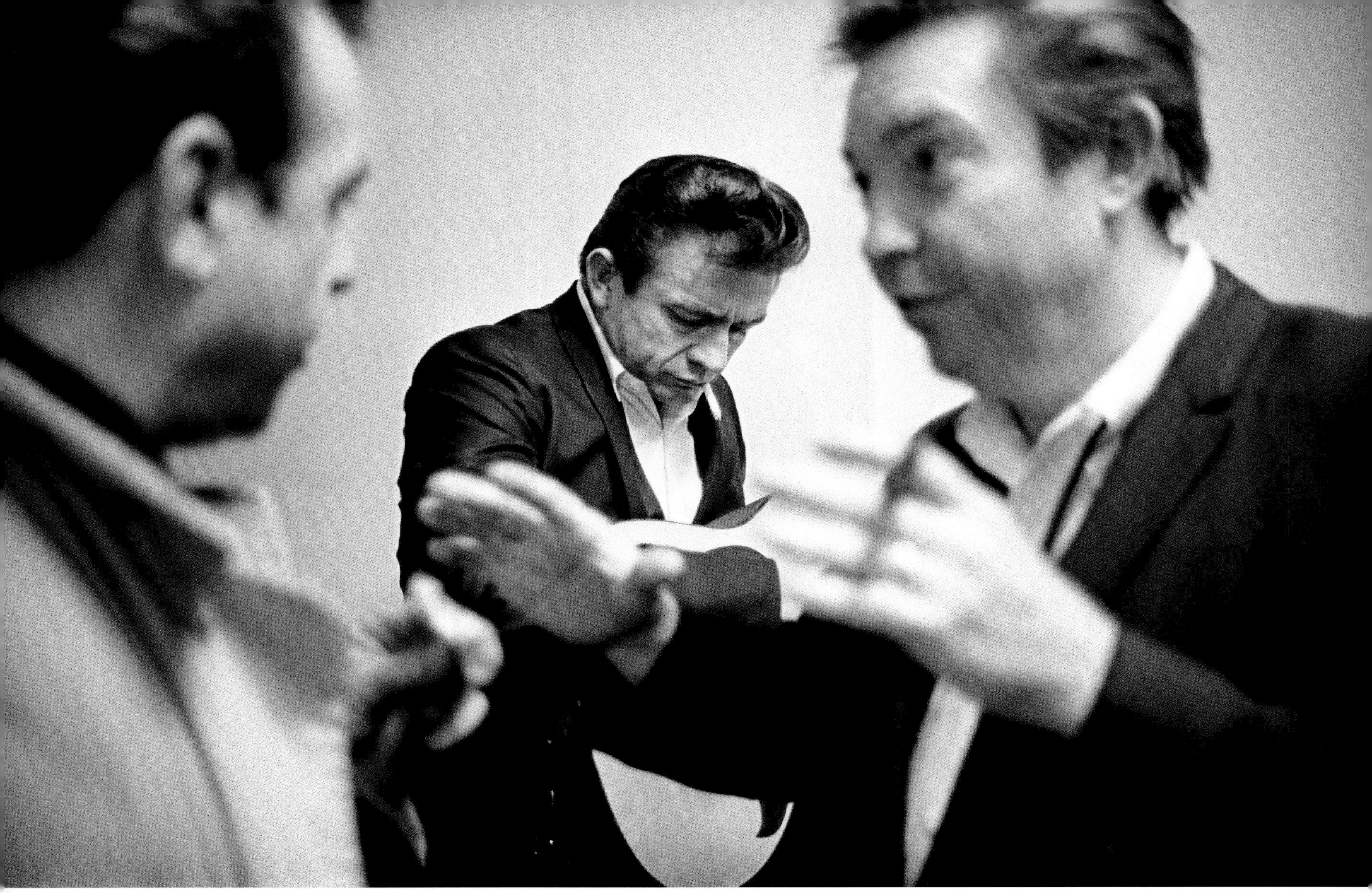

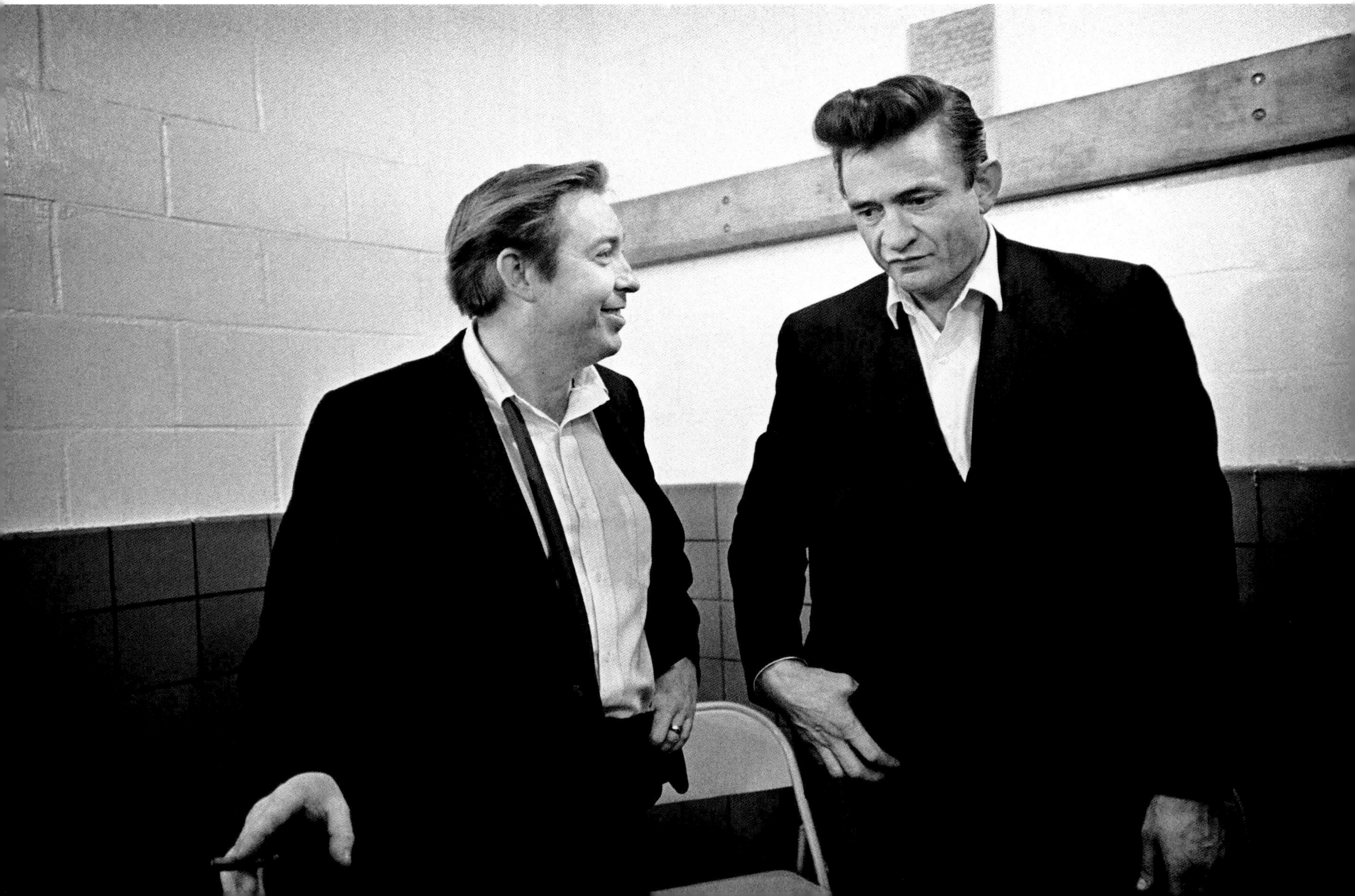

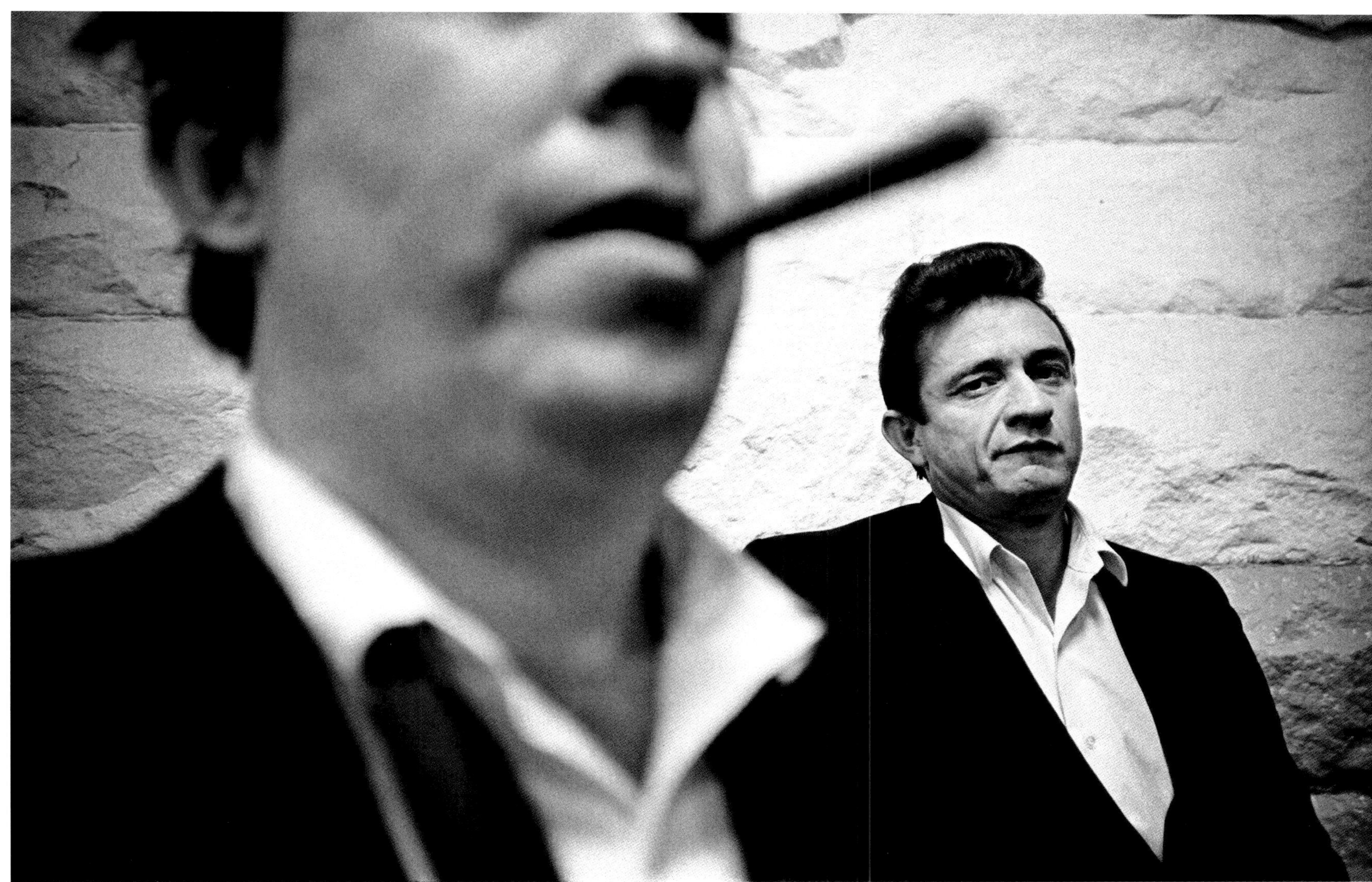

Bob Johnston's arrival in Nashville was the start of an important relationship that would see Cash through his most successful period as a recording artist. He was a brash Texan with little use for authority who established his career producing independent rockabilly records and writing songs that were recorded by Elvis, Bill Haley, and others. He was hired by Columbia Records in New York and, in 1965, became Bob Dylan's producer. After producing *Highway 61 Revisited*, he took Dylan to Nashville to record *Blonde on Blonde*. Working as a producer for Dylan, Simon & Garfunkel, Marty Robbins, Flatt and Scruggs, The Byrds, Leonard Cohen, and others, Johnston became an important bridge between the worlds of country, folk, and rock. His adventurous sensibilities were the perfect match for Cash and the seven albums they would record together. "He helped me understand I needed to put everything I had into the *Folsom* album," Cash said of his producer years later.

Previous pages: *Carl Perkins and Cash chat backstage with Folsom's Recreation Supervisor, Lloyd Kelley.*
Opposite and above: *Producer Bob Johnston goes over the final plans with Cash and emcee Hugh Cherry.*

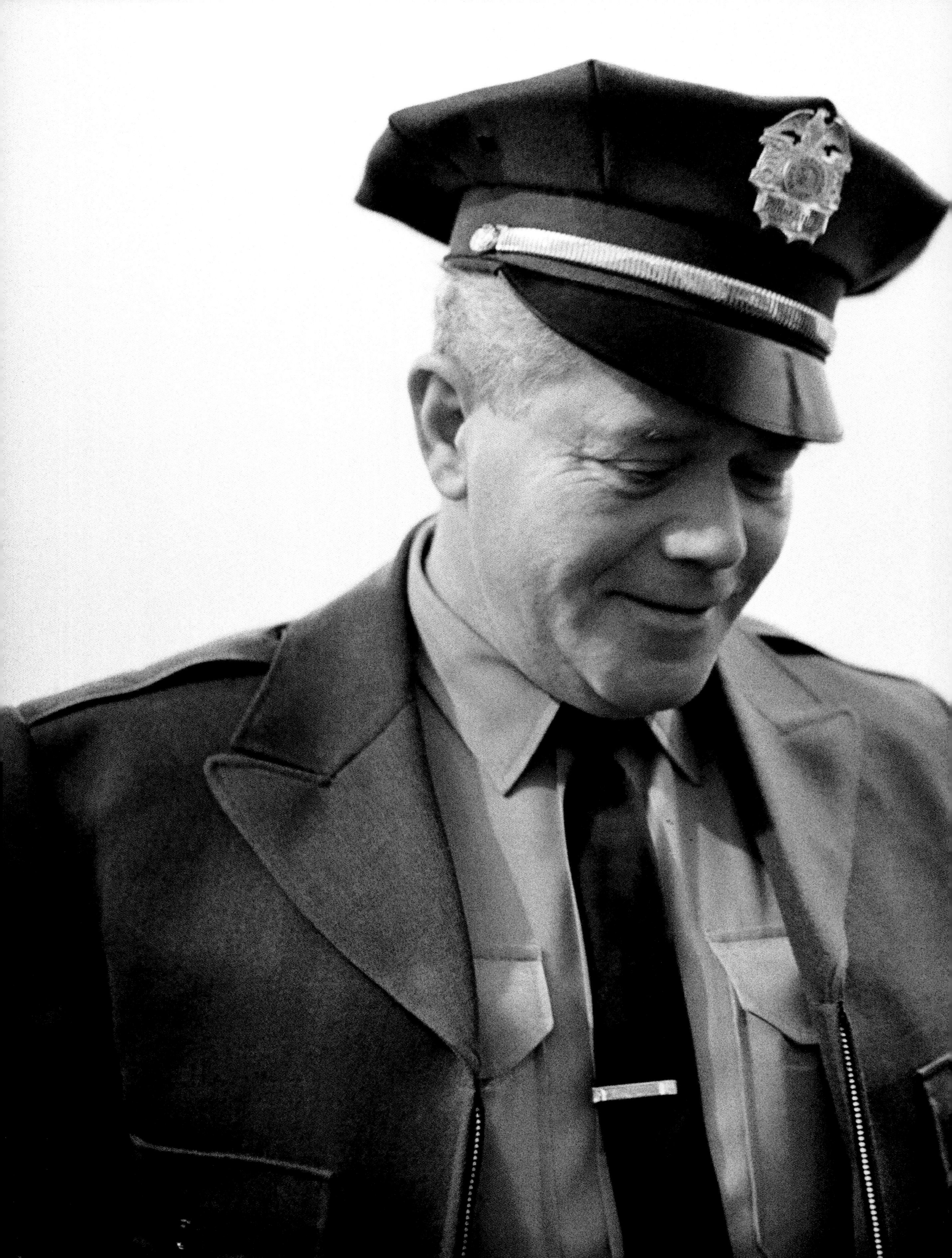

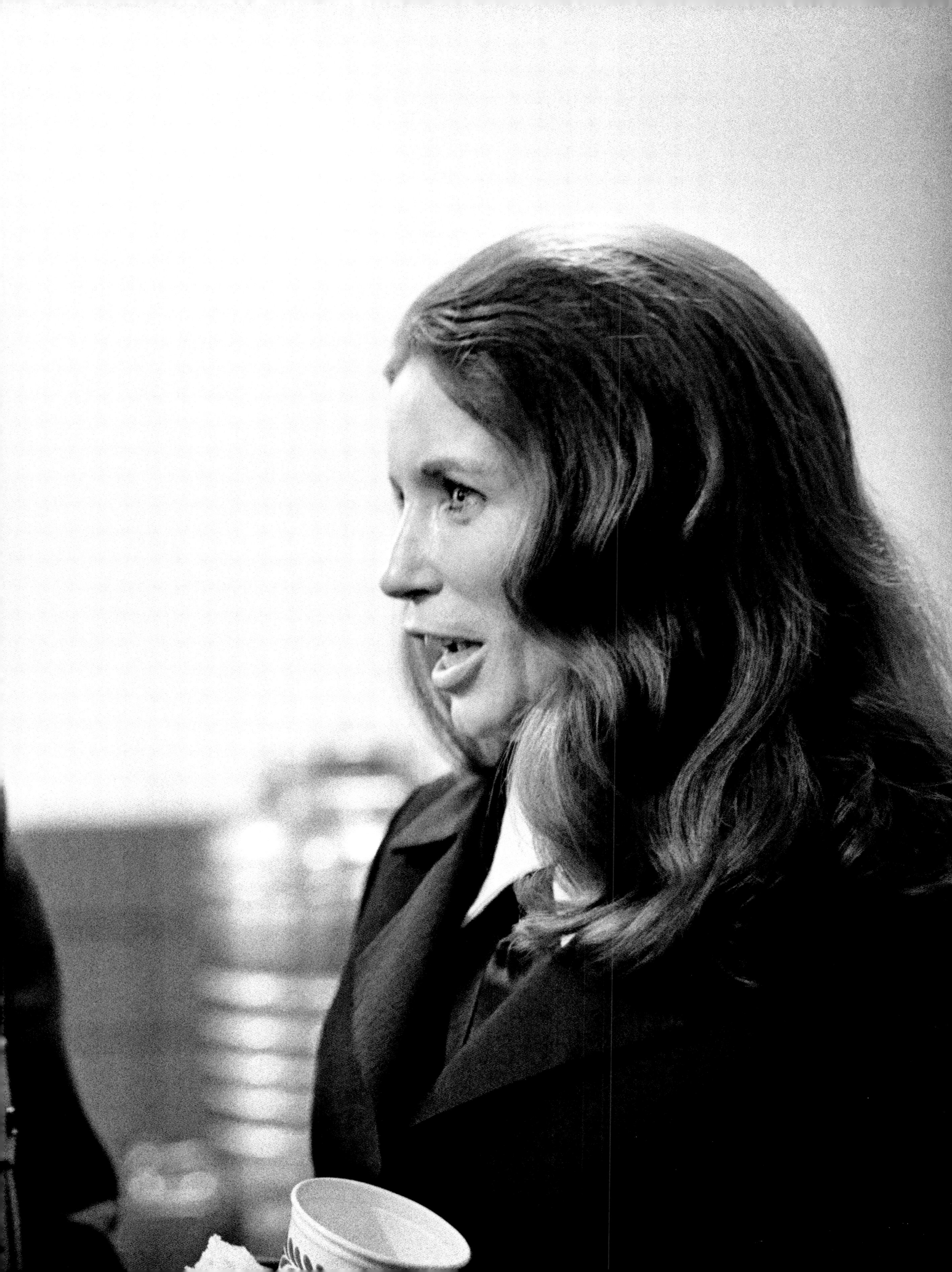

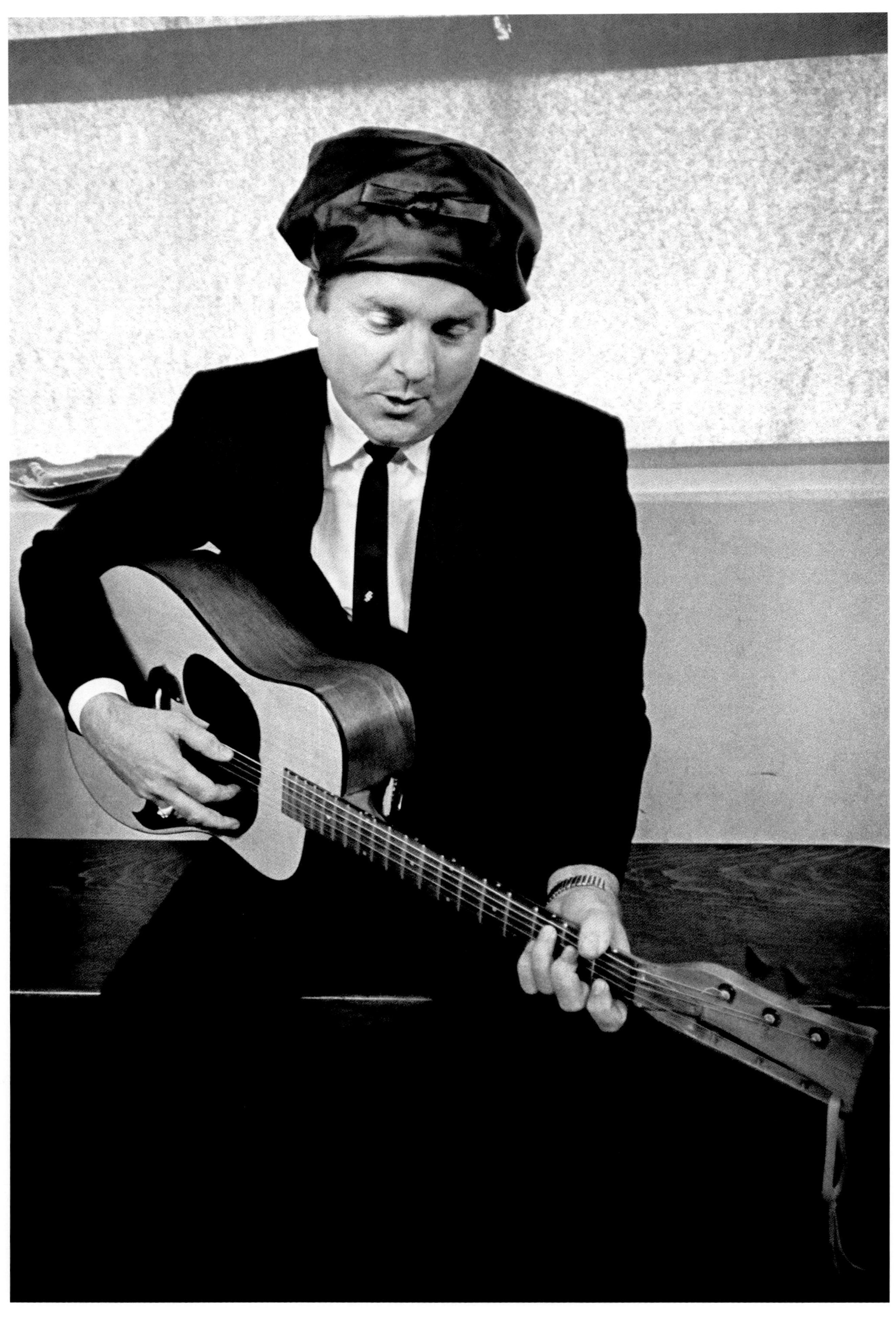

Above: Marshall Grant lightens the mood by donning June Carter's hat and serenading his colleagues.
Opposite: Statler Brother Harold Reid adjusts his sock as June and the rest of the Statlers anxiously await the start of the show.
Following pages: Guitarist Luther Perkins takes it all in stride.

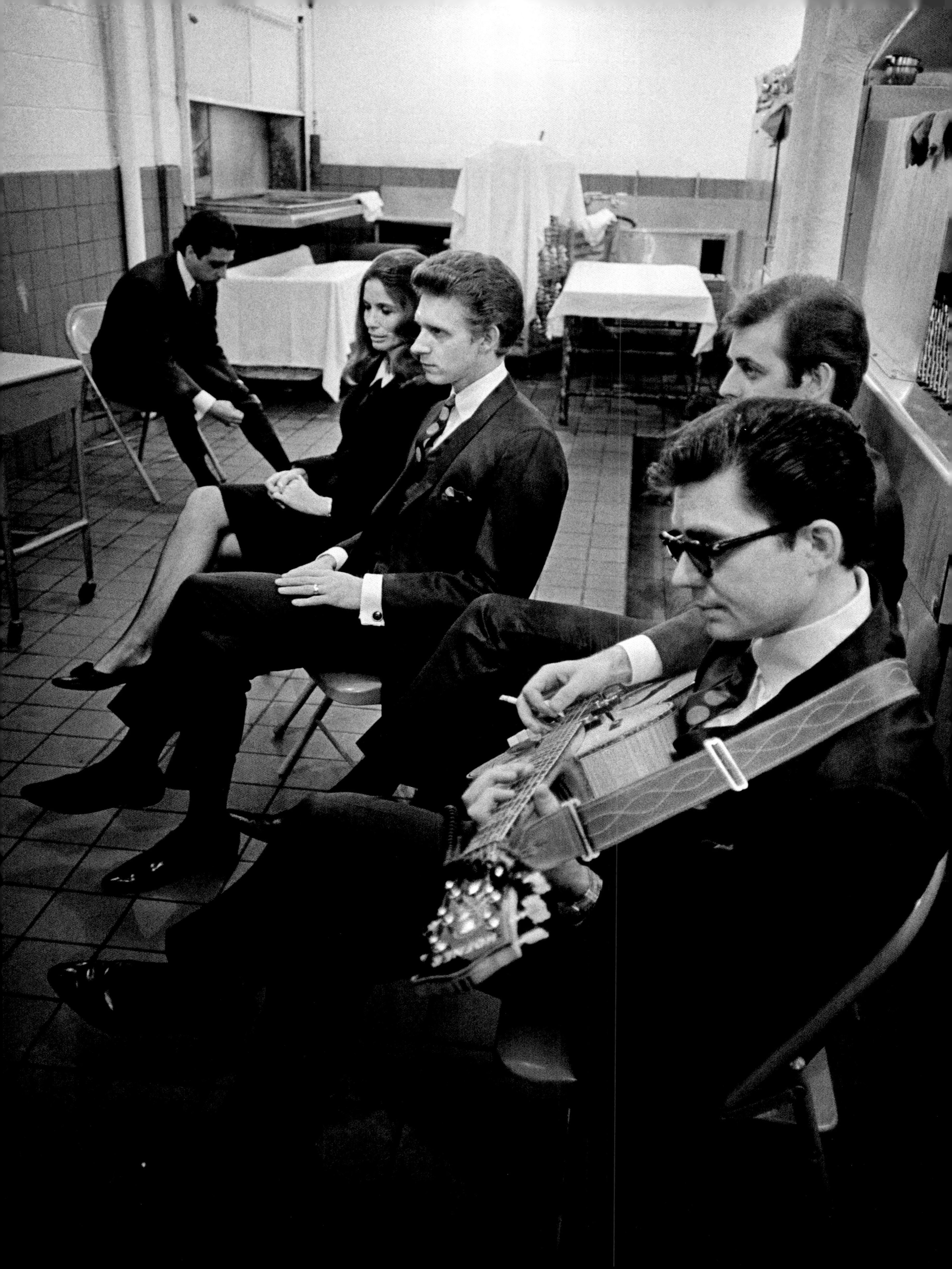

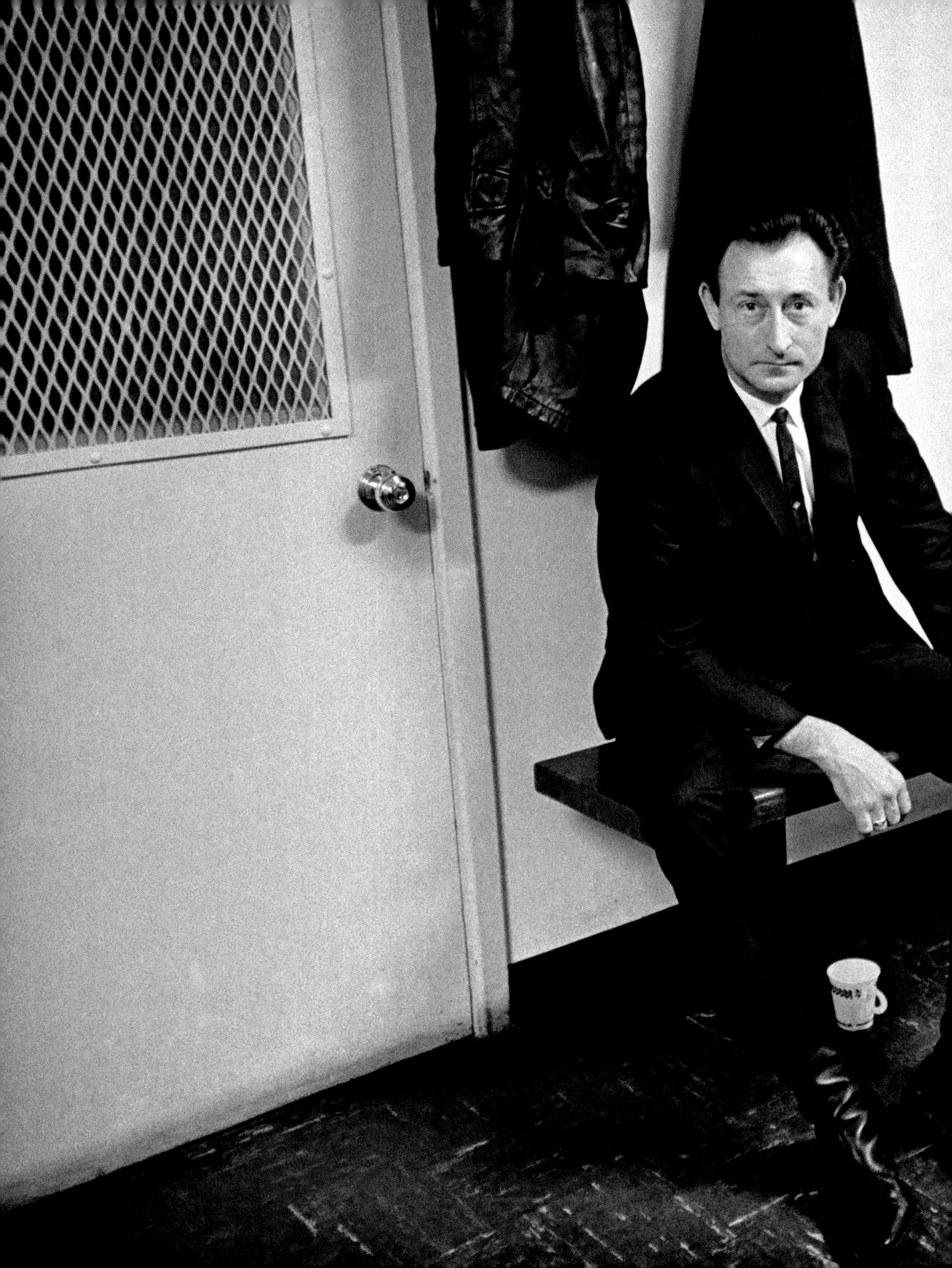

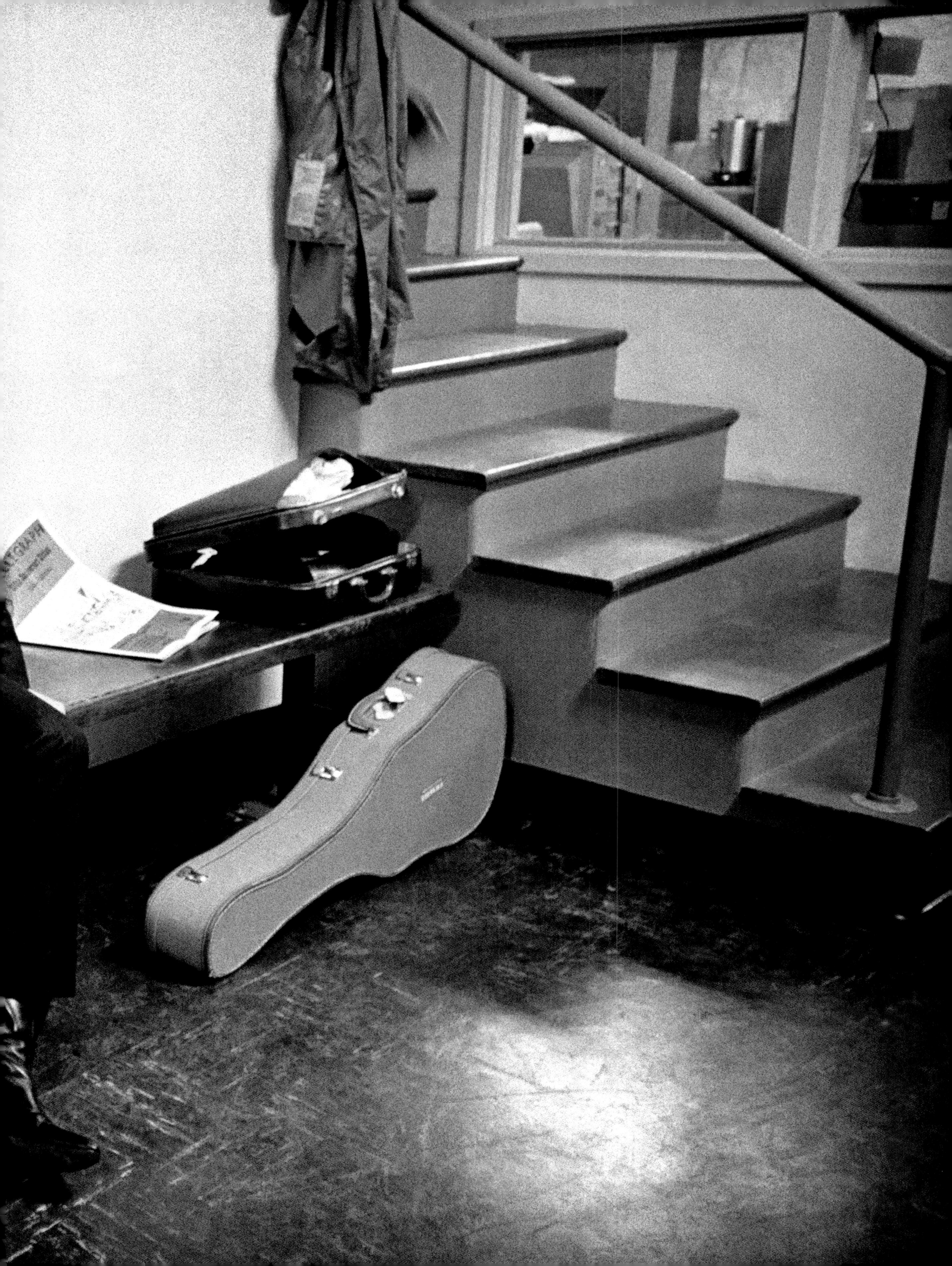

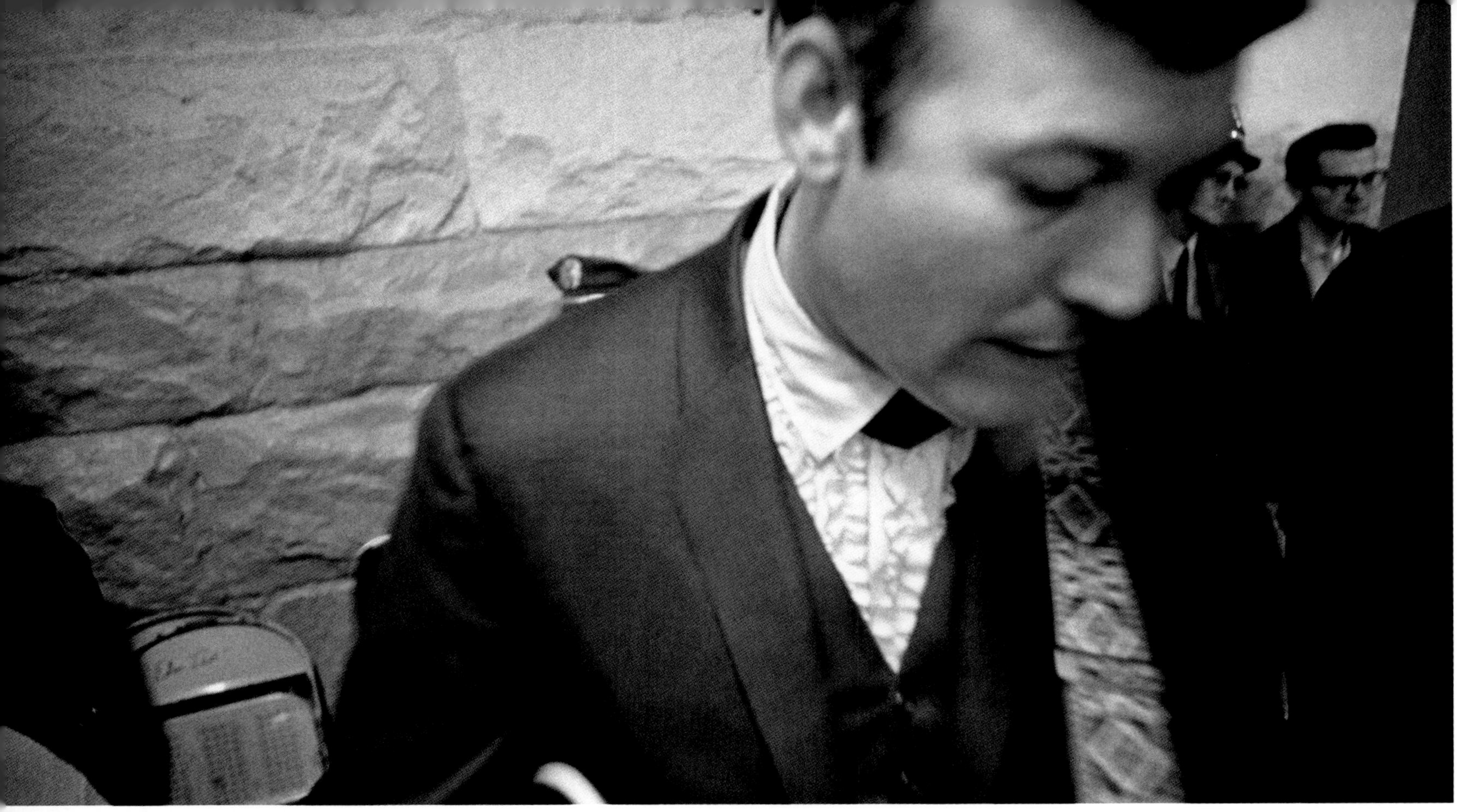

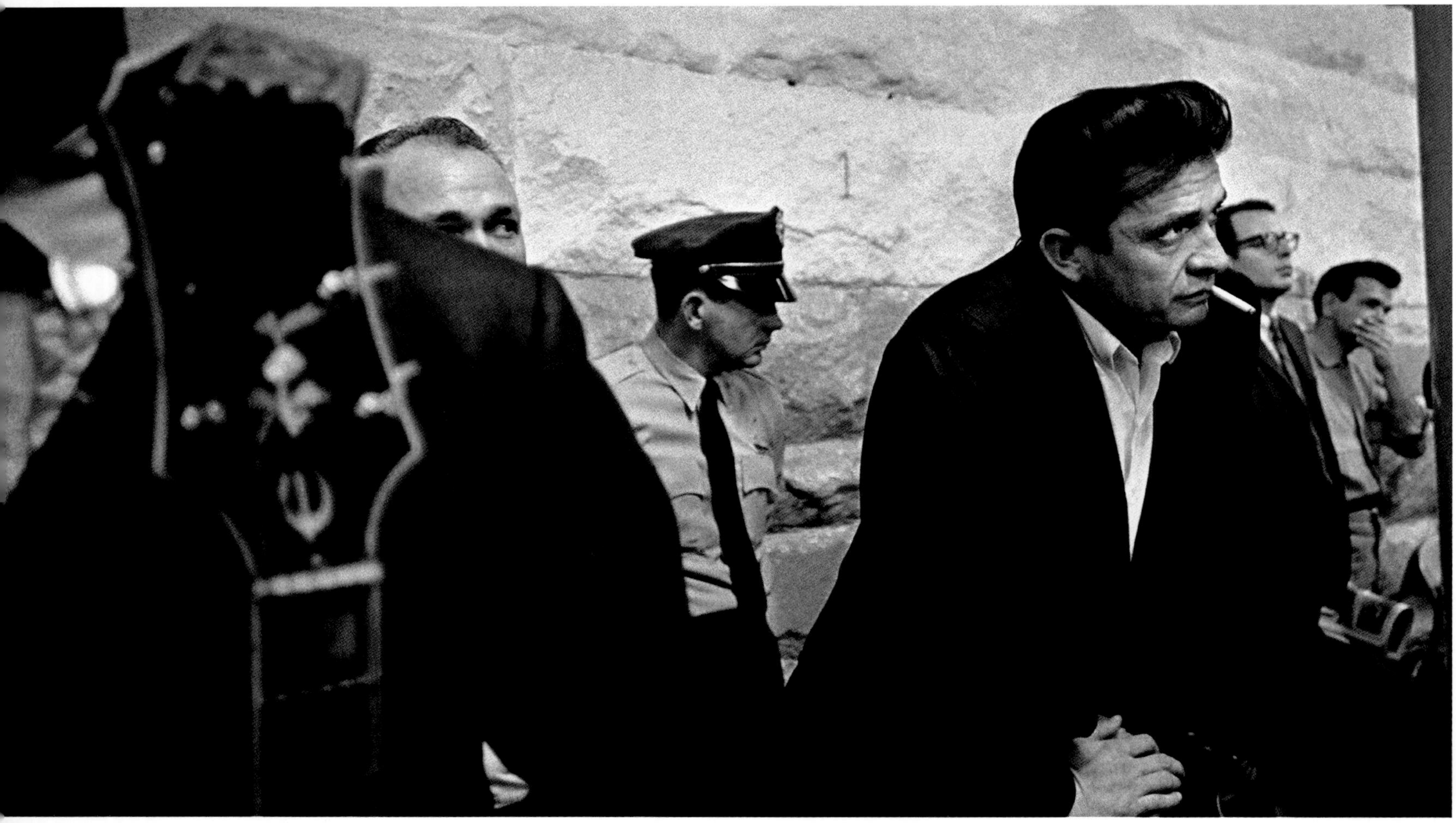

The first performance was scheduled for 9:40 AM. Carl Perkins took the stage with the Tennessee Three to start the show with his hit "Blue Suede Shoes." Johnny stood off to the side to watch his friend perform when a sense of peace washed over him. "I knew this was it," he told Hilburn, "my chance to make up for all the times when I had messed up. Then I suddenly felt calm. I could see the men looking over at me. There was something in their eyes that made me realize everything was going to be okay. I felt I had something they needed."

After "Blue Suede Shoes," The Statlers performed "This Ole House." Then Johnny took the stage and introduced himself with that now-legendary greeting, "Hello, I'm Johnny Cash." "I don't think I've ever seen as much excitement in a room as when we launched into 'Folsom Prison Blues,'" Grant would later write in his memoir, *I Was There When It Happened*. Hilburn, too, was struck by what he witnessed over the next hour: "The atmosphere was electric as Cash prowled the stage between verses with the pent-up tension of a caged panther."

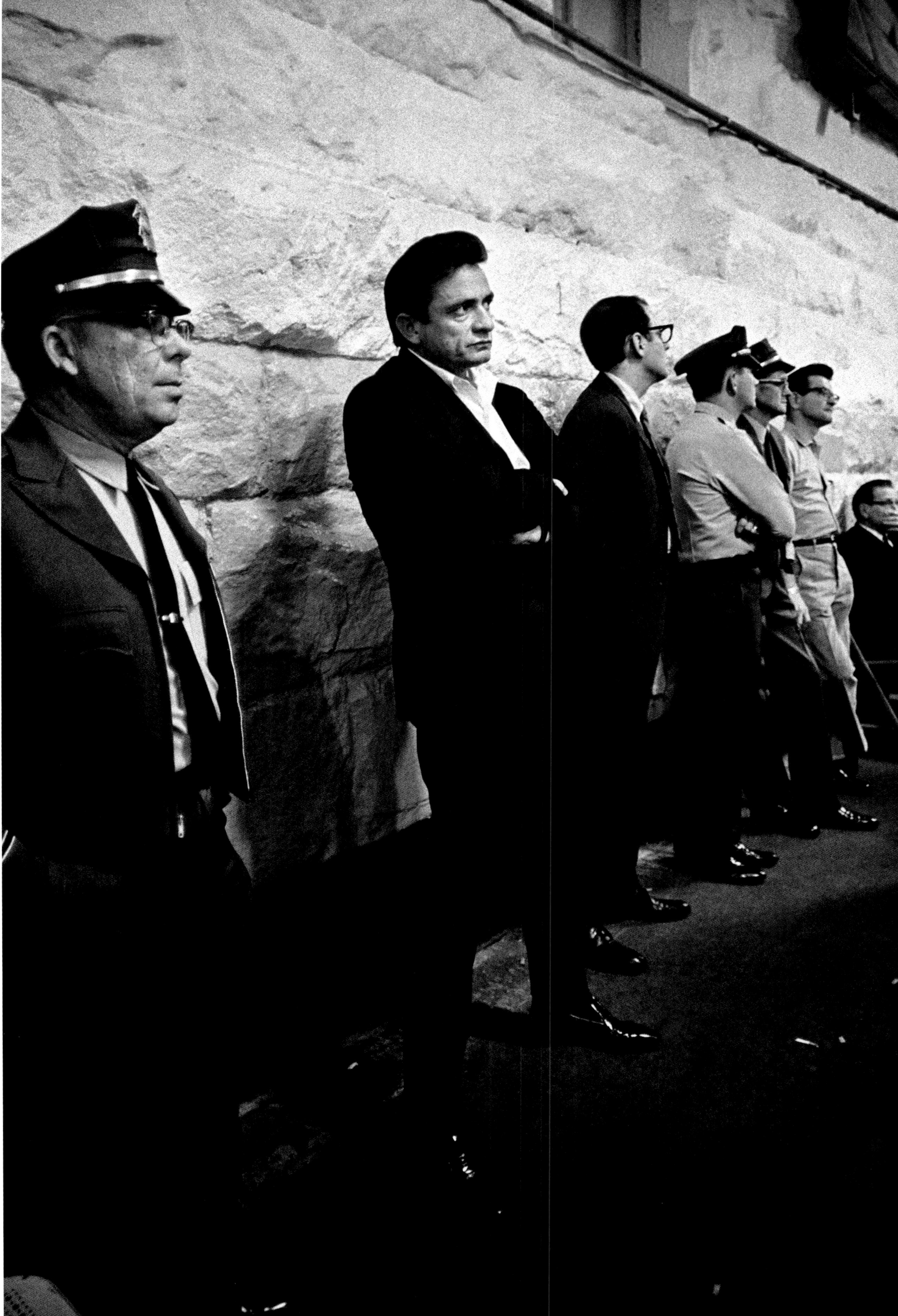

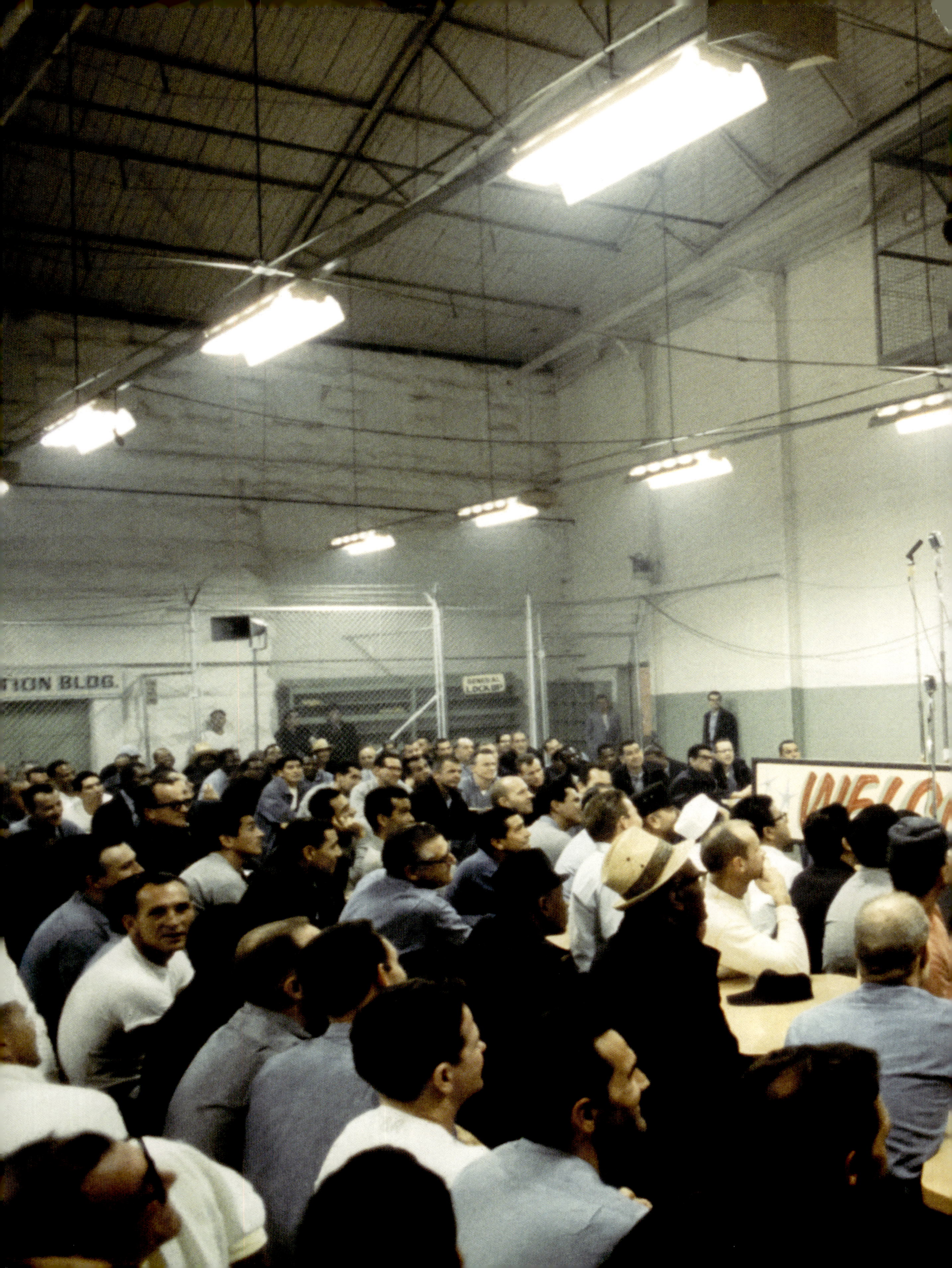
TION BLDG.
WELC

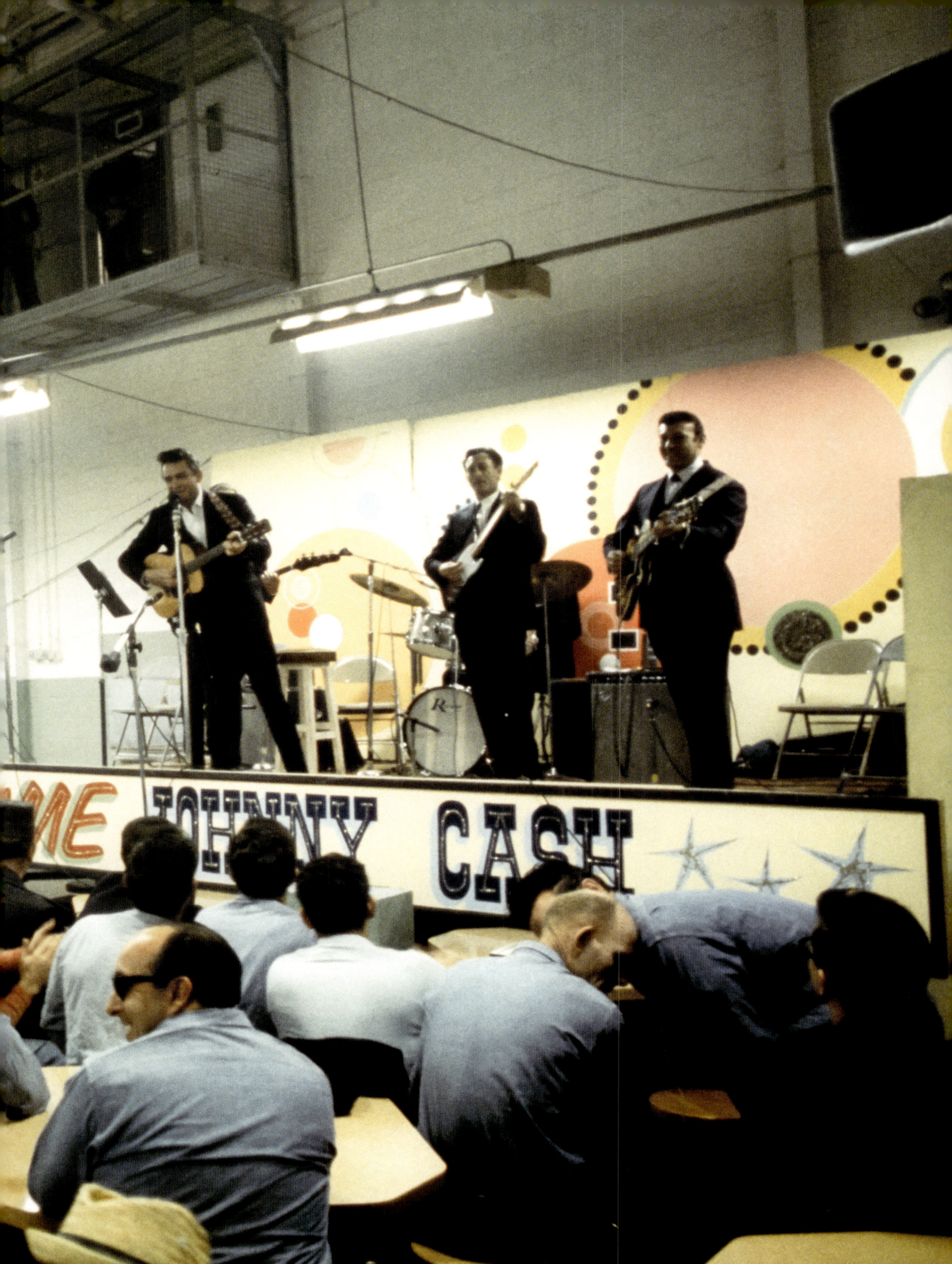
THE JOHNNY CASH

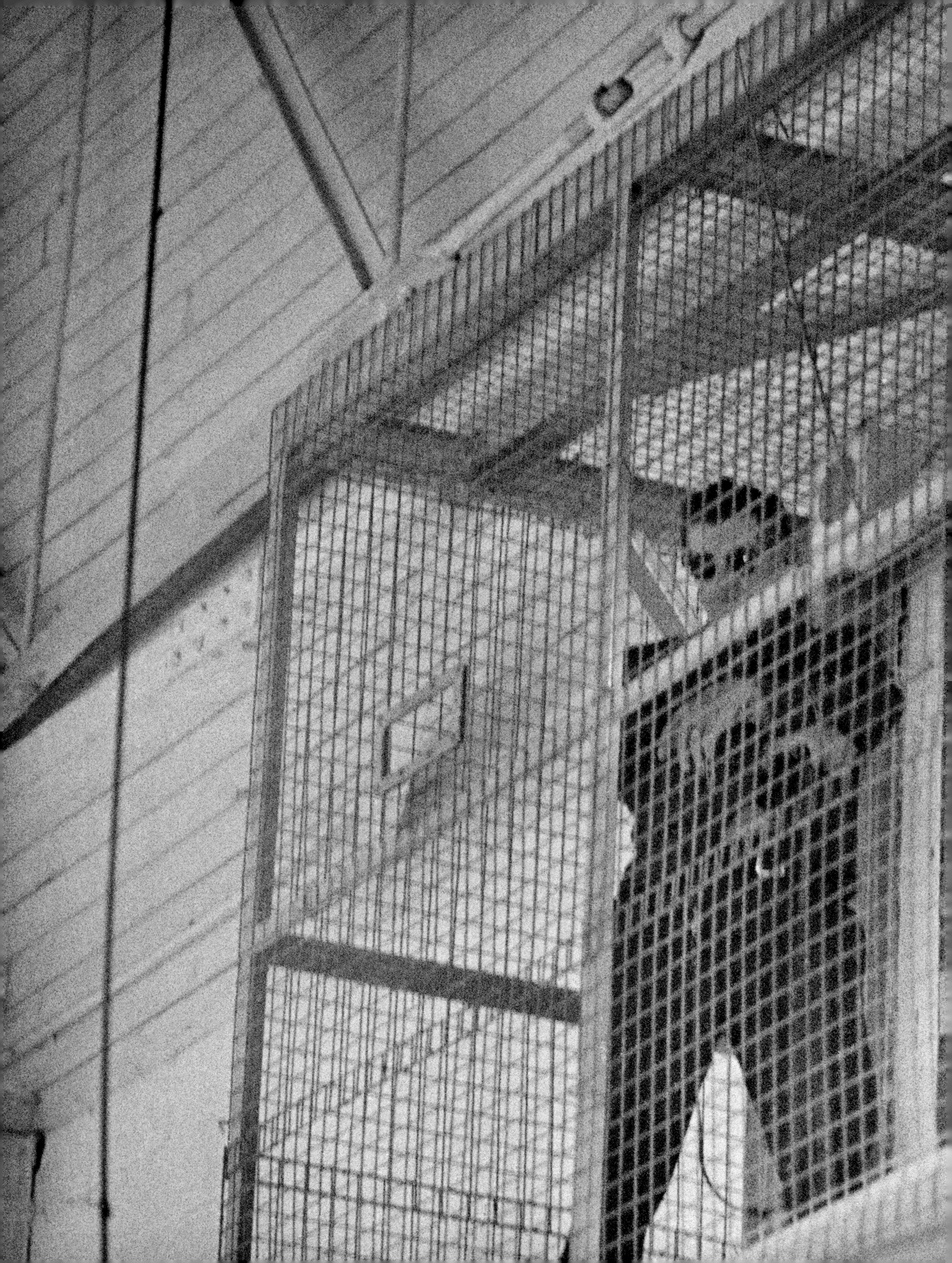

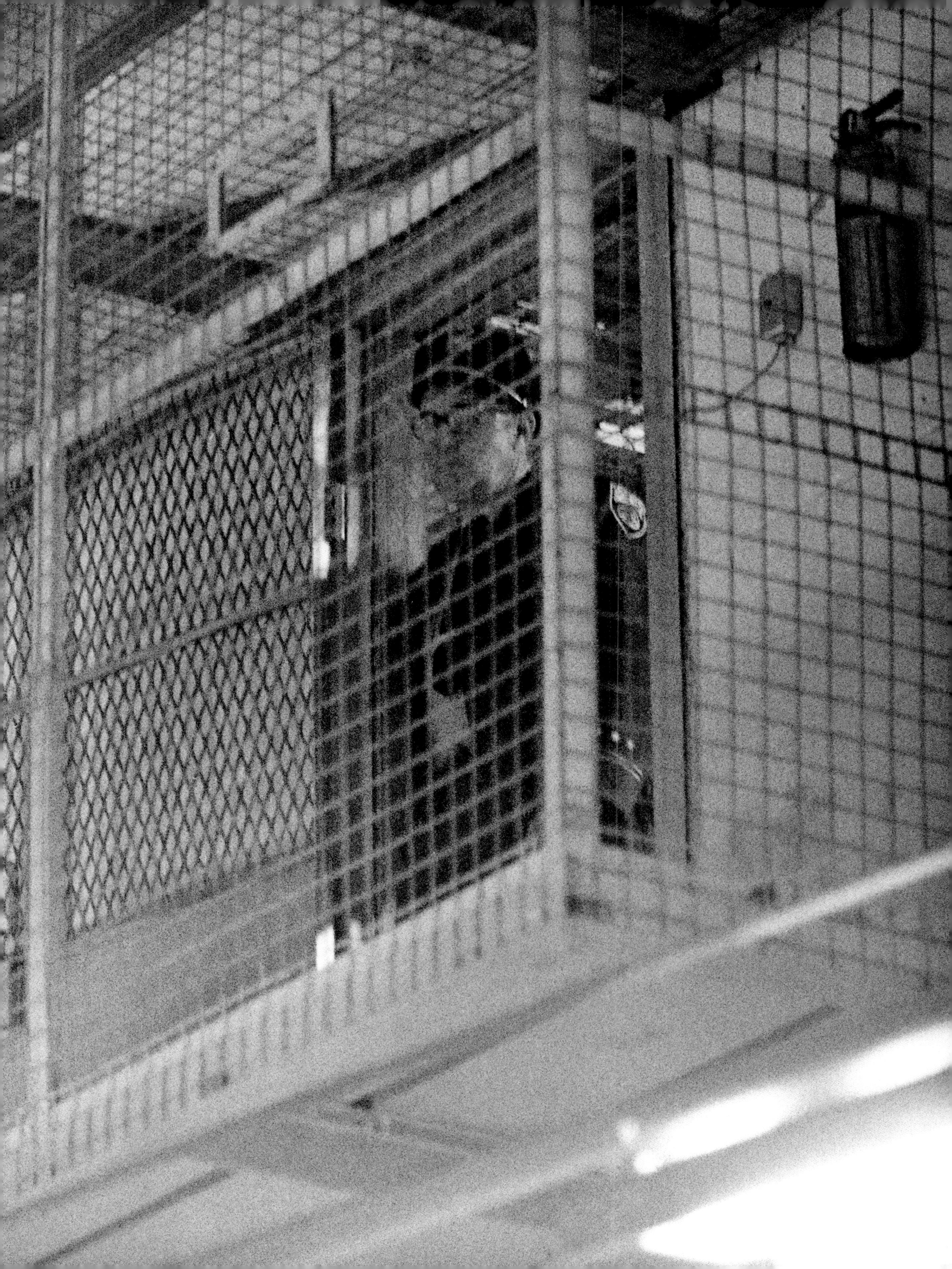

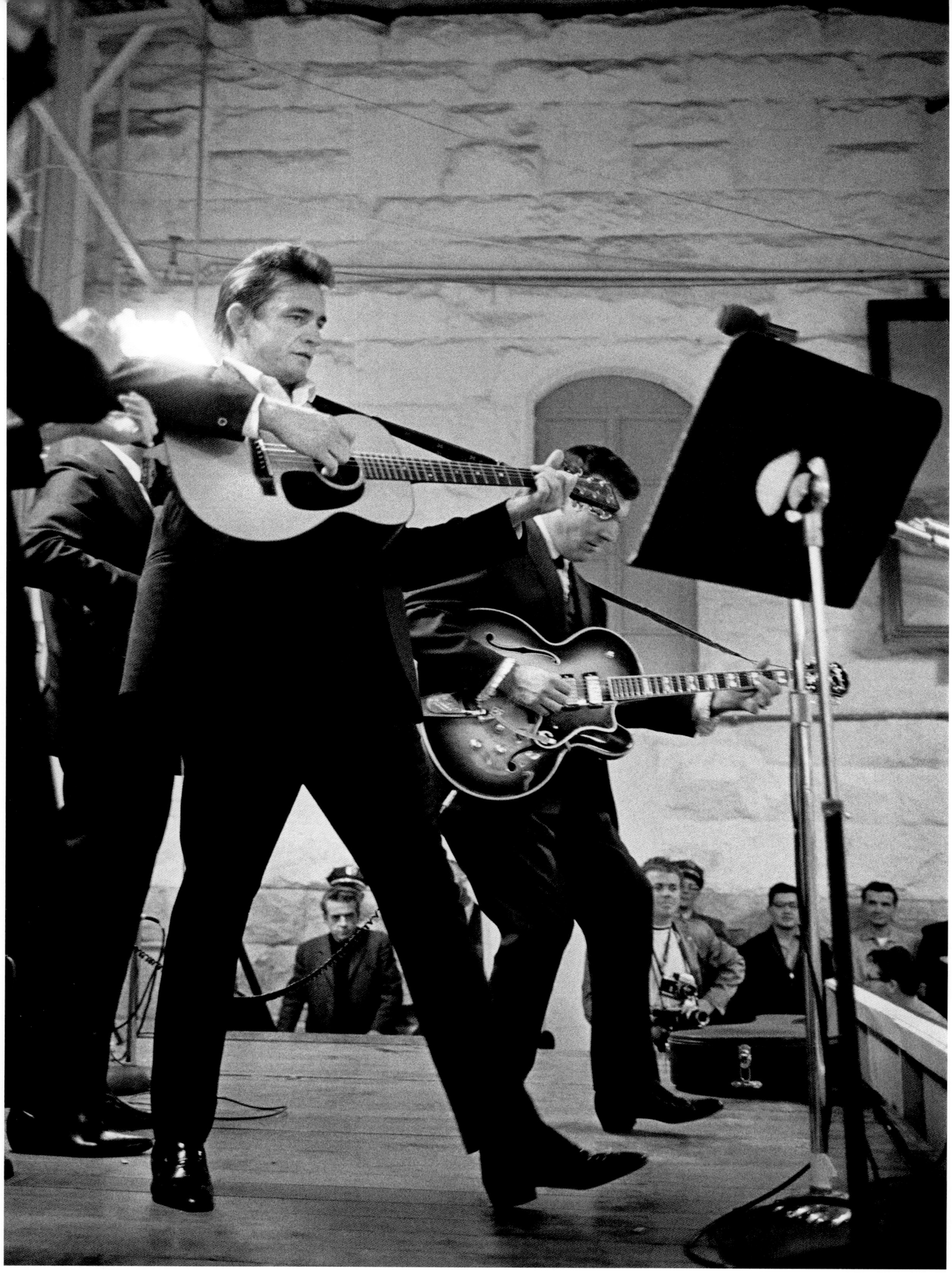

Johnny and the band played more than a half dozen songs before he sat down for an intimate solo acoustic performance of "The Long Black Veil," "Send a Picture of Mother," and "The Wall." After bringing the band back up for a handful of novelty songs he introduced June Carter, who joined him onstage for the rest of the show.

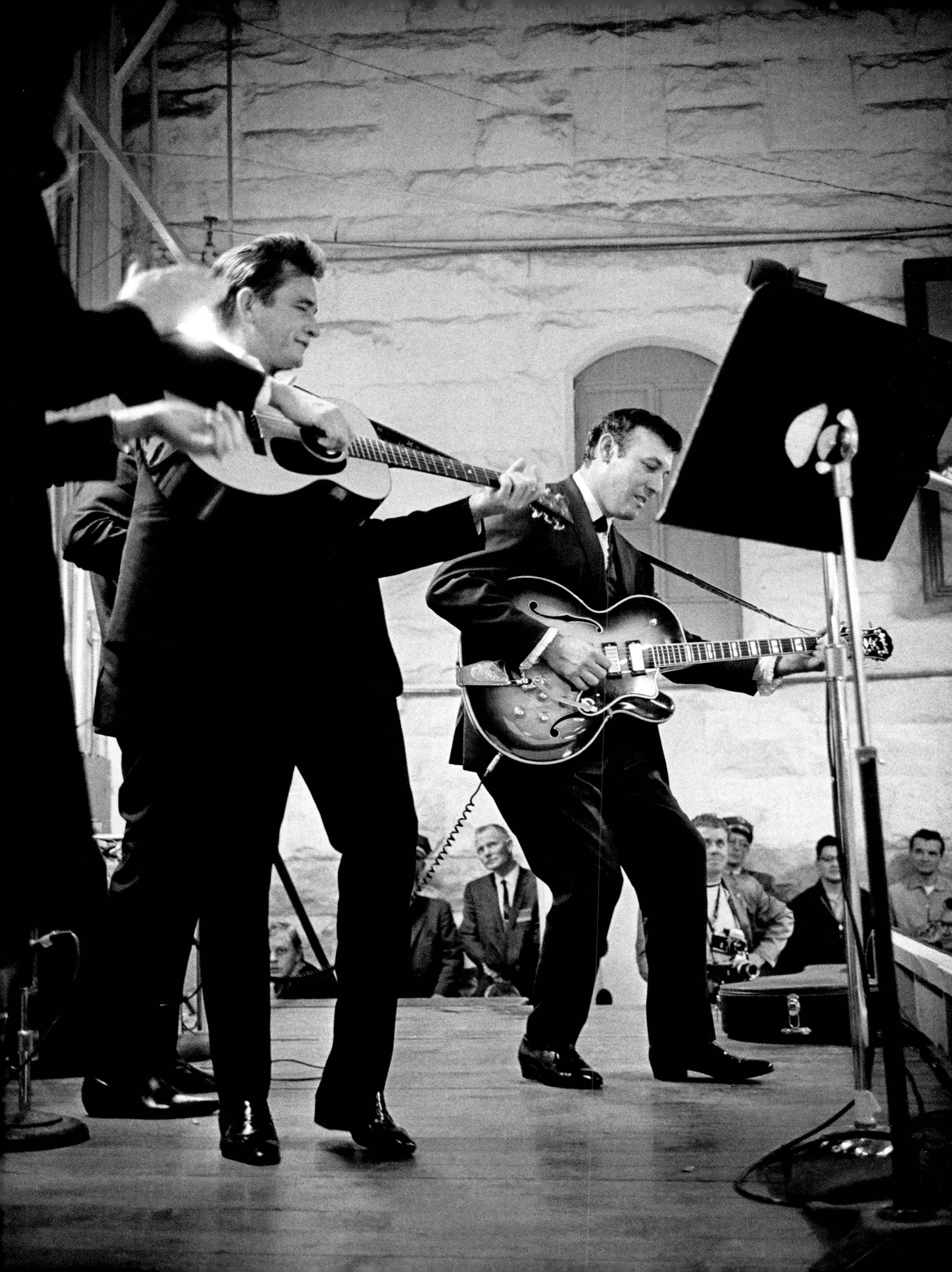

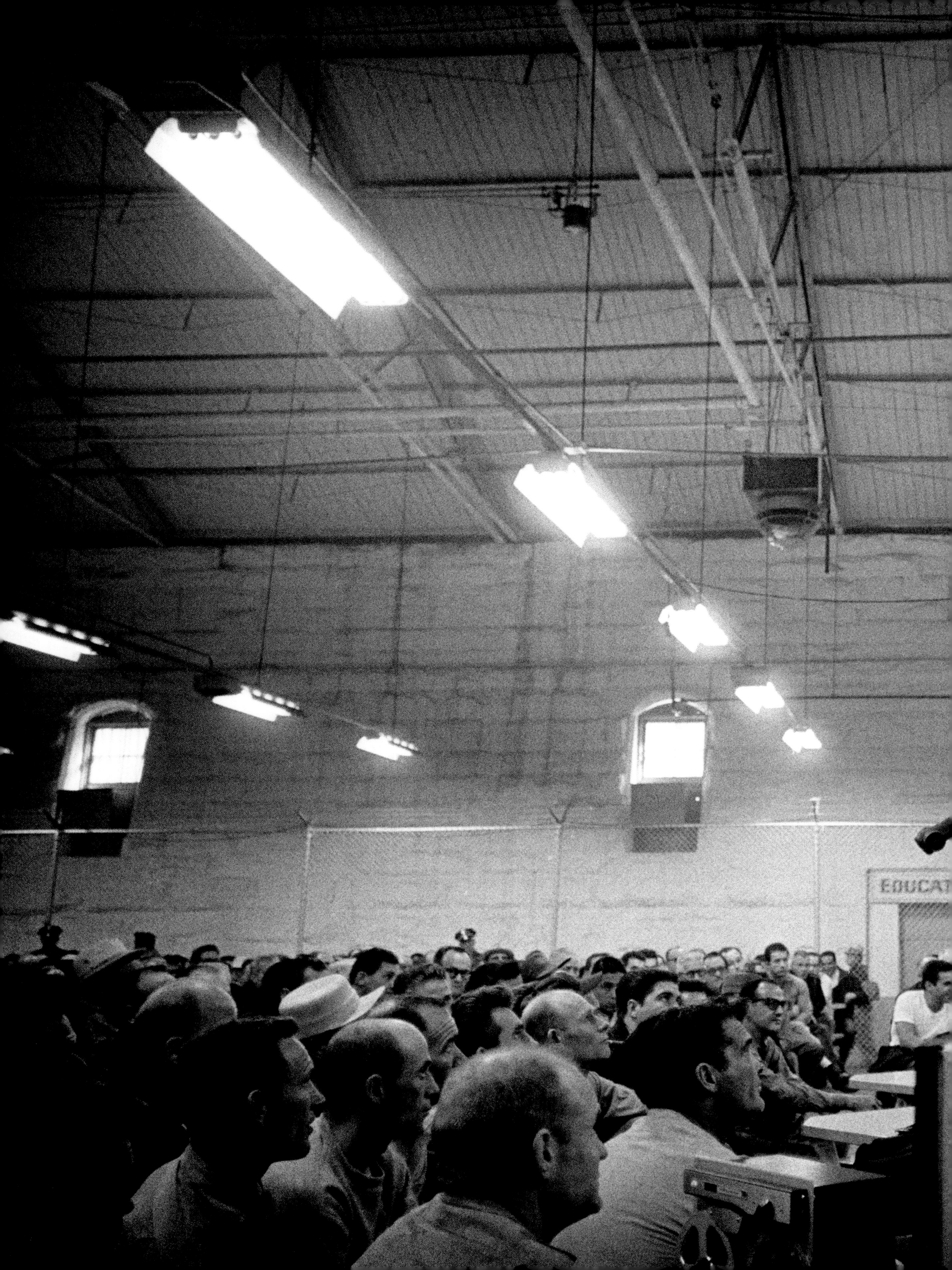
EDUCAT

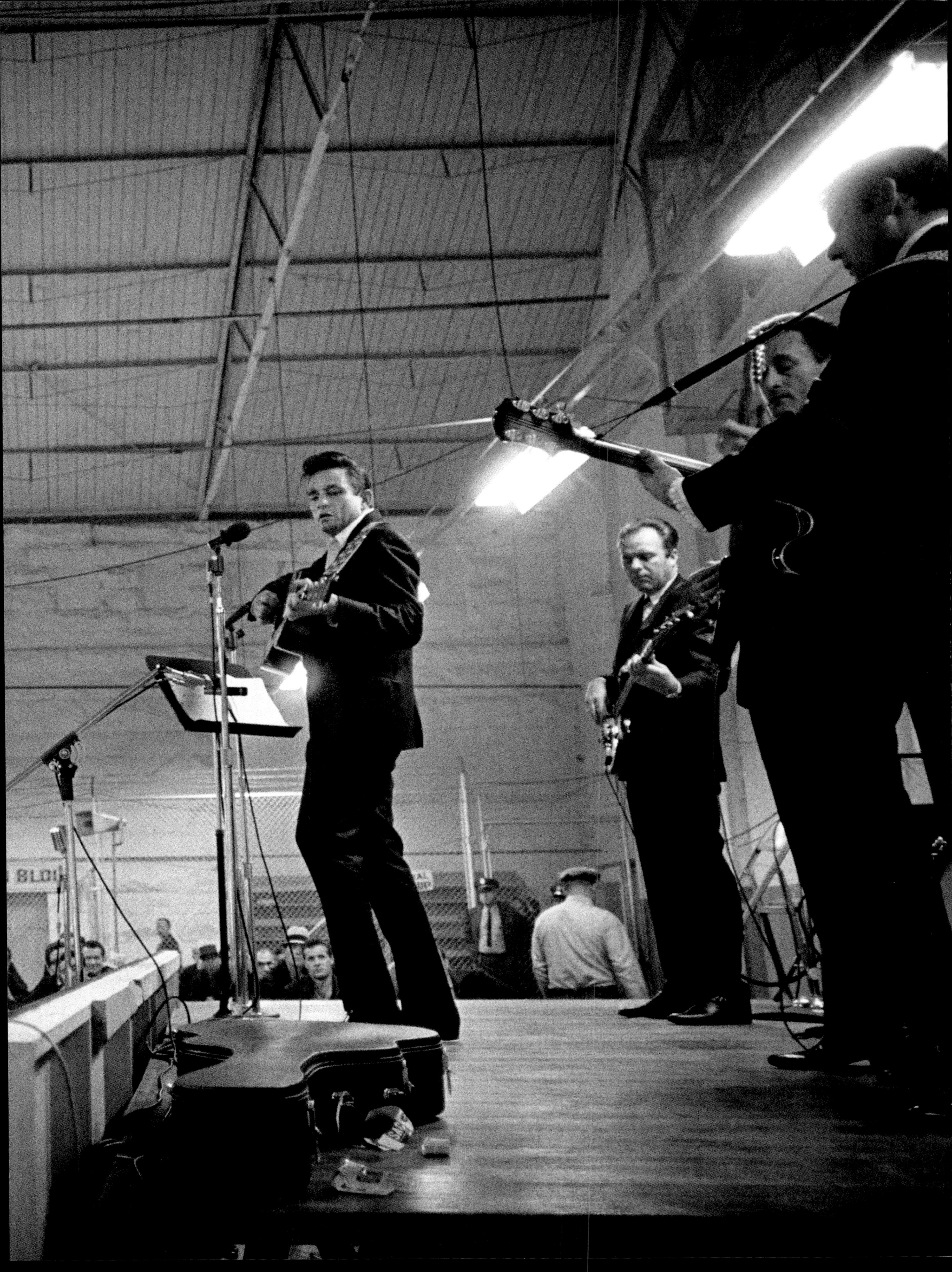

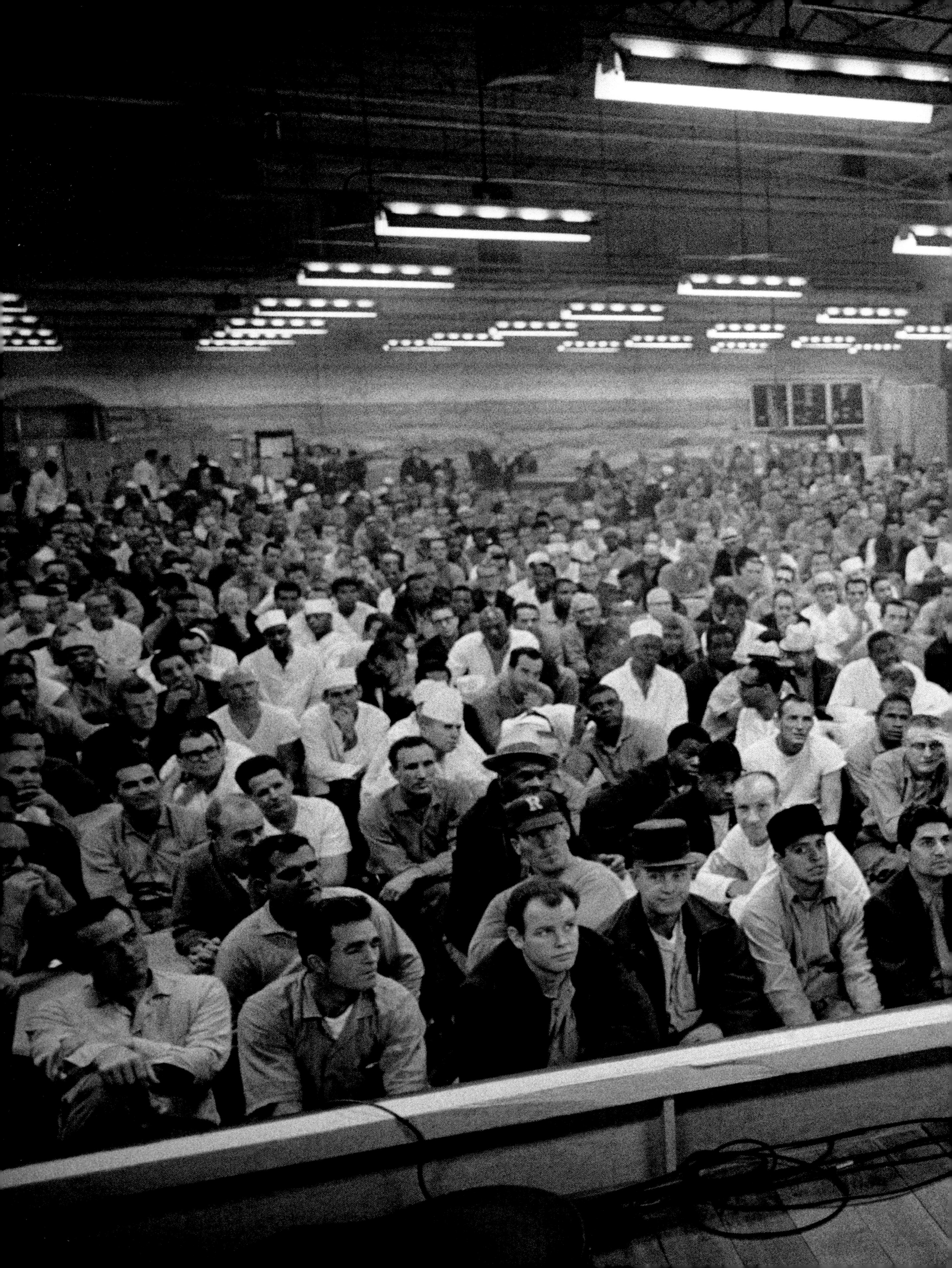

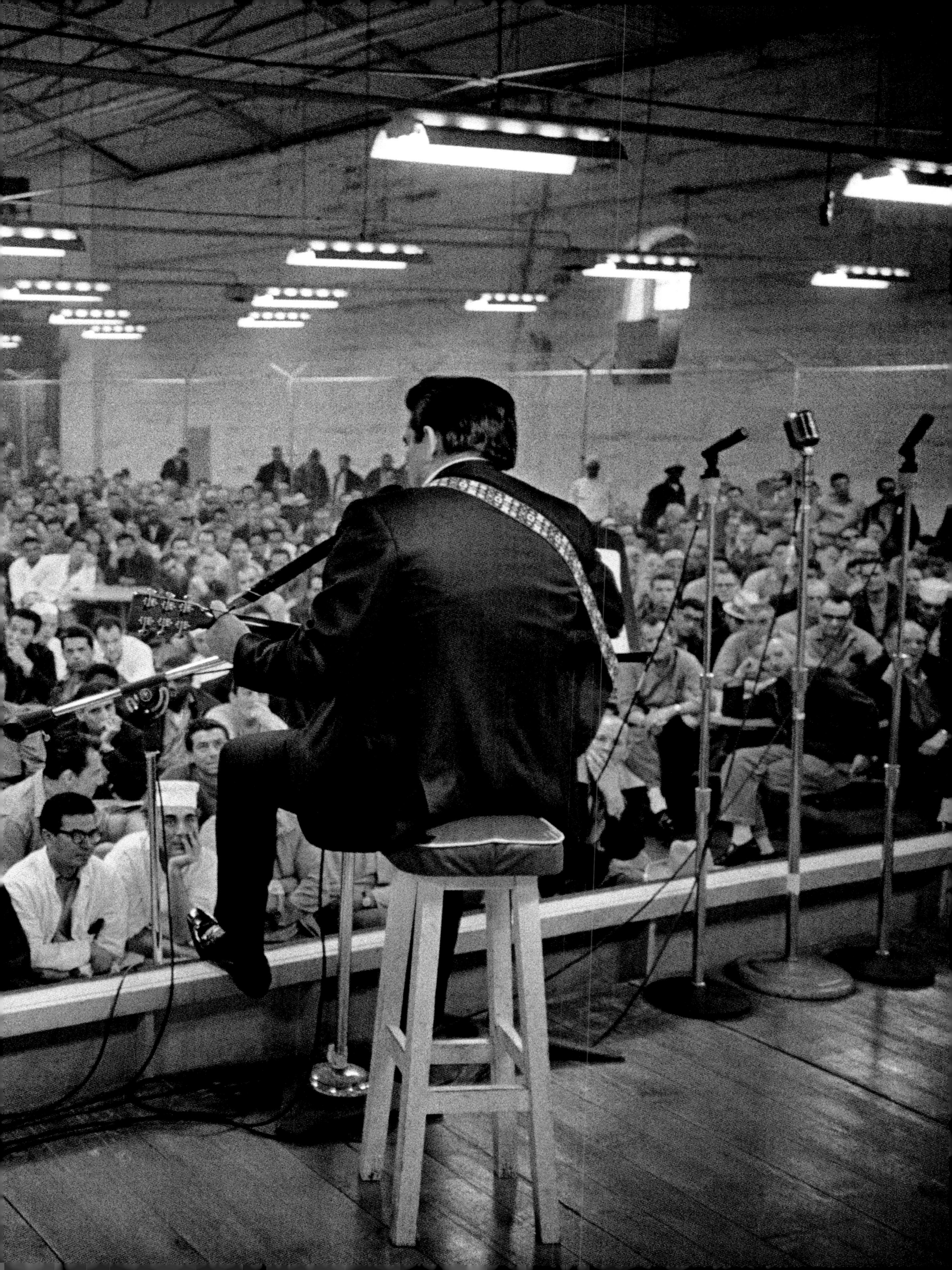

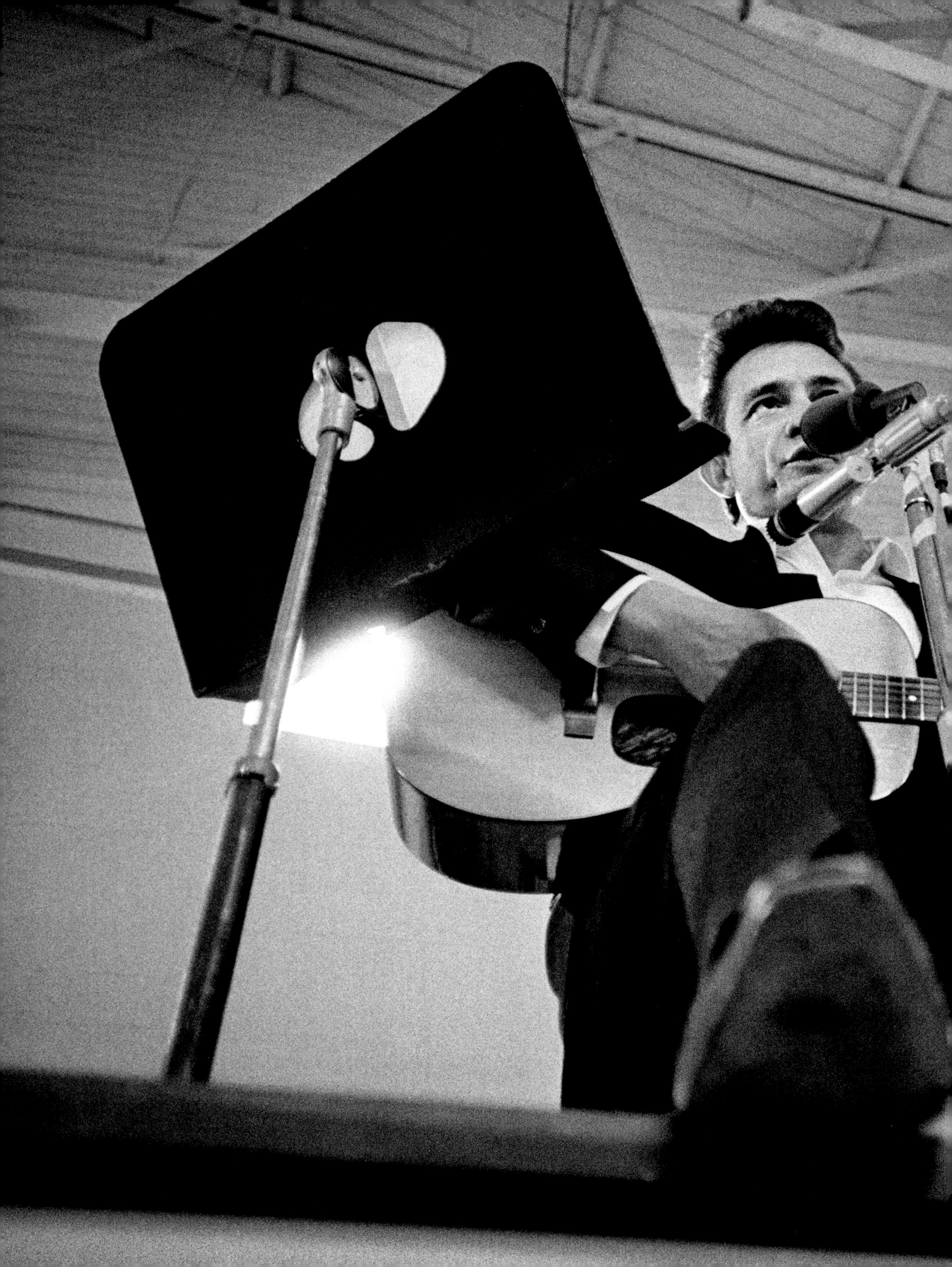

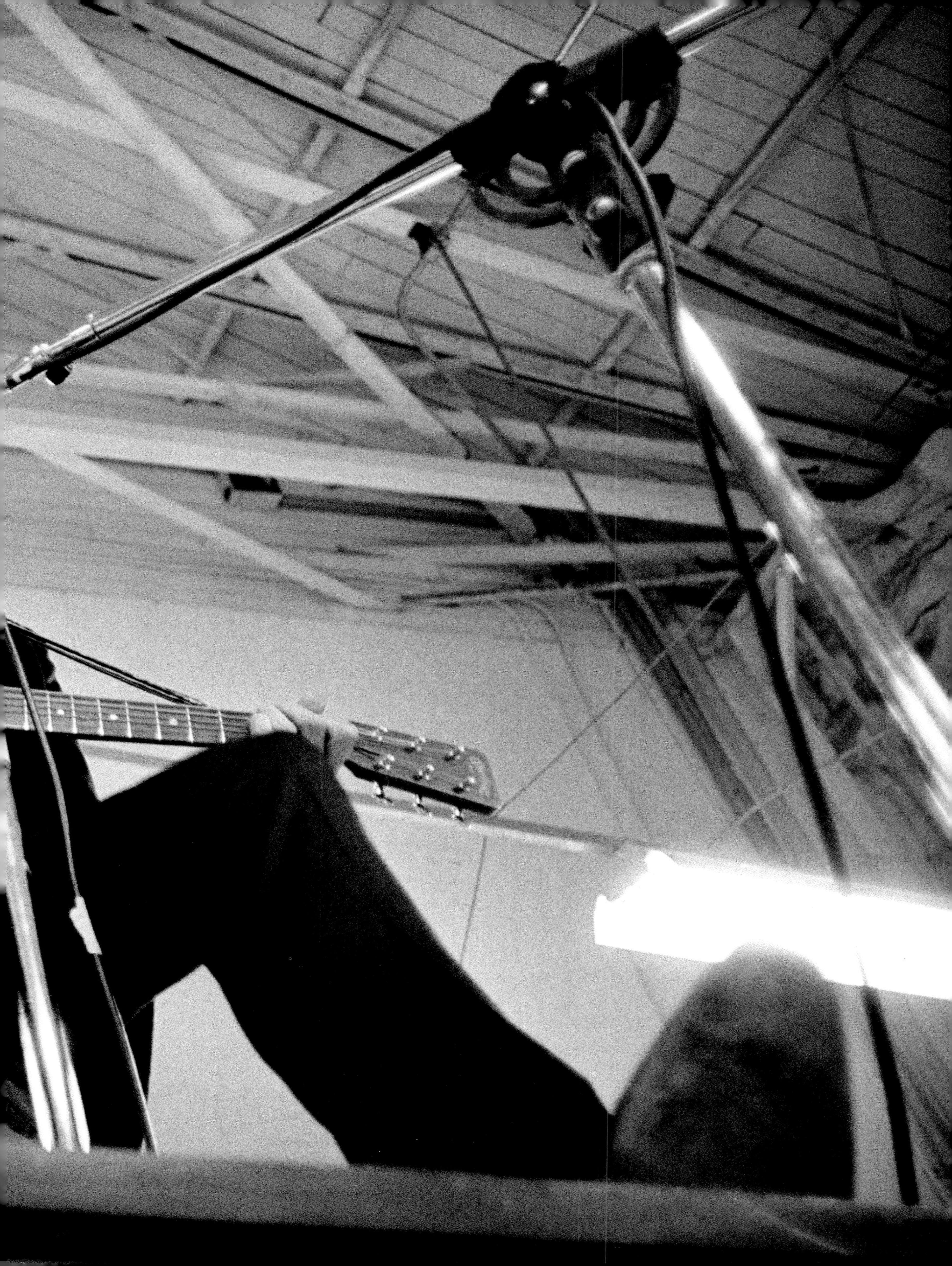

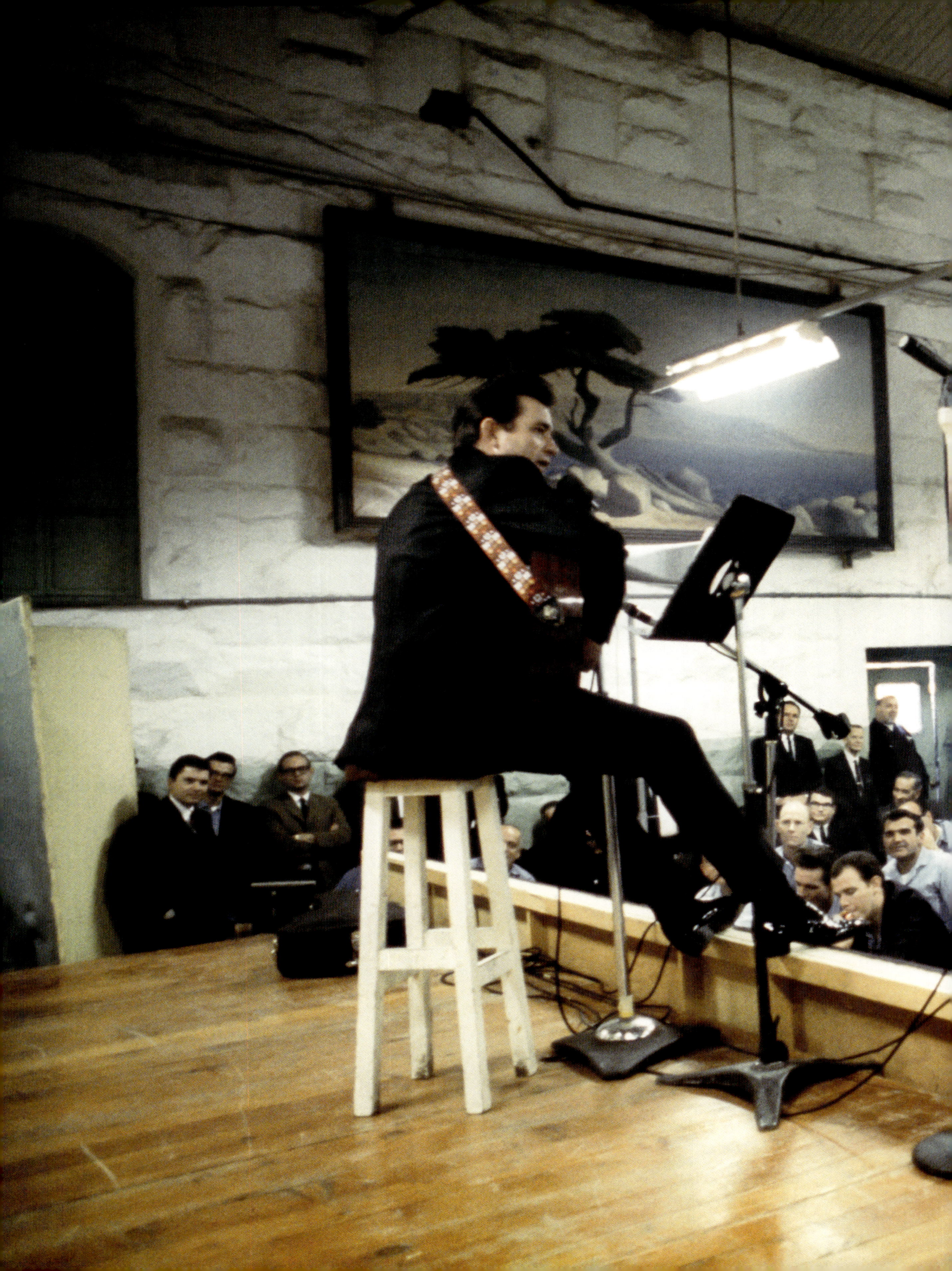

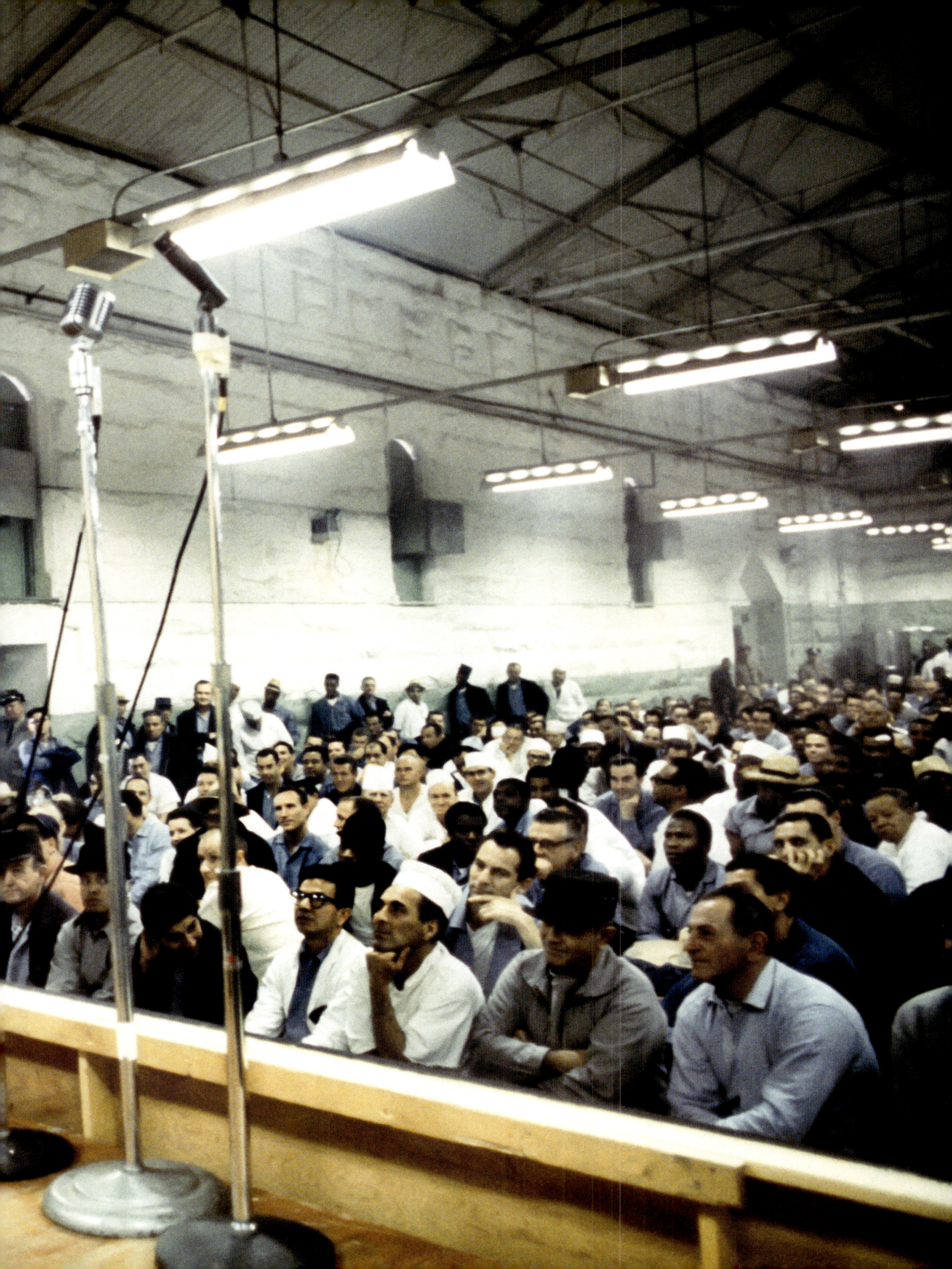

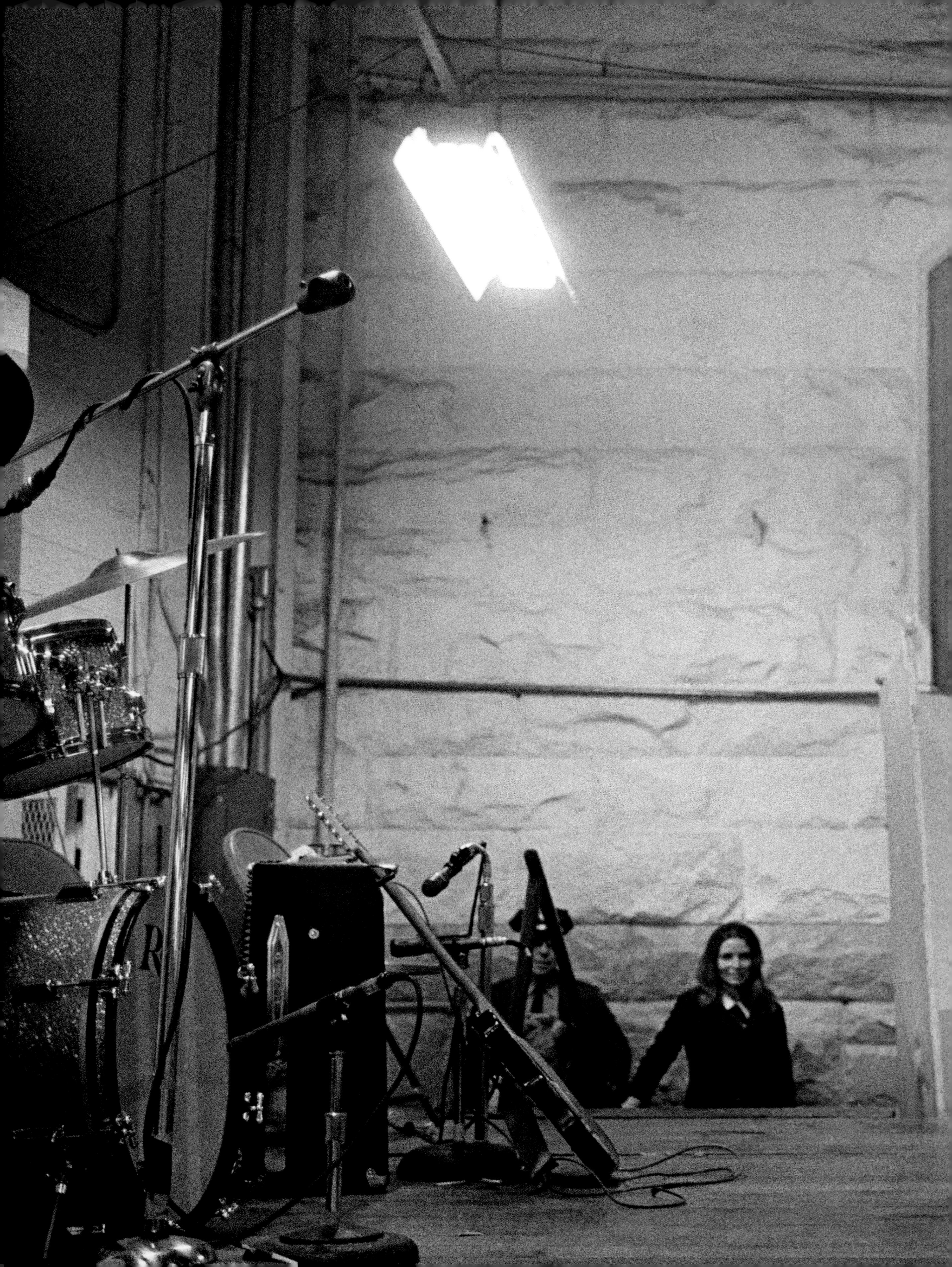

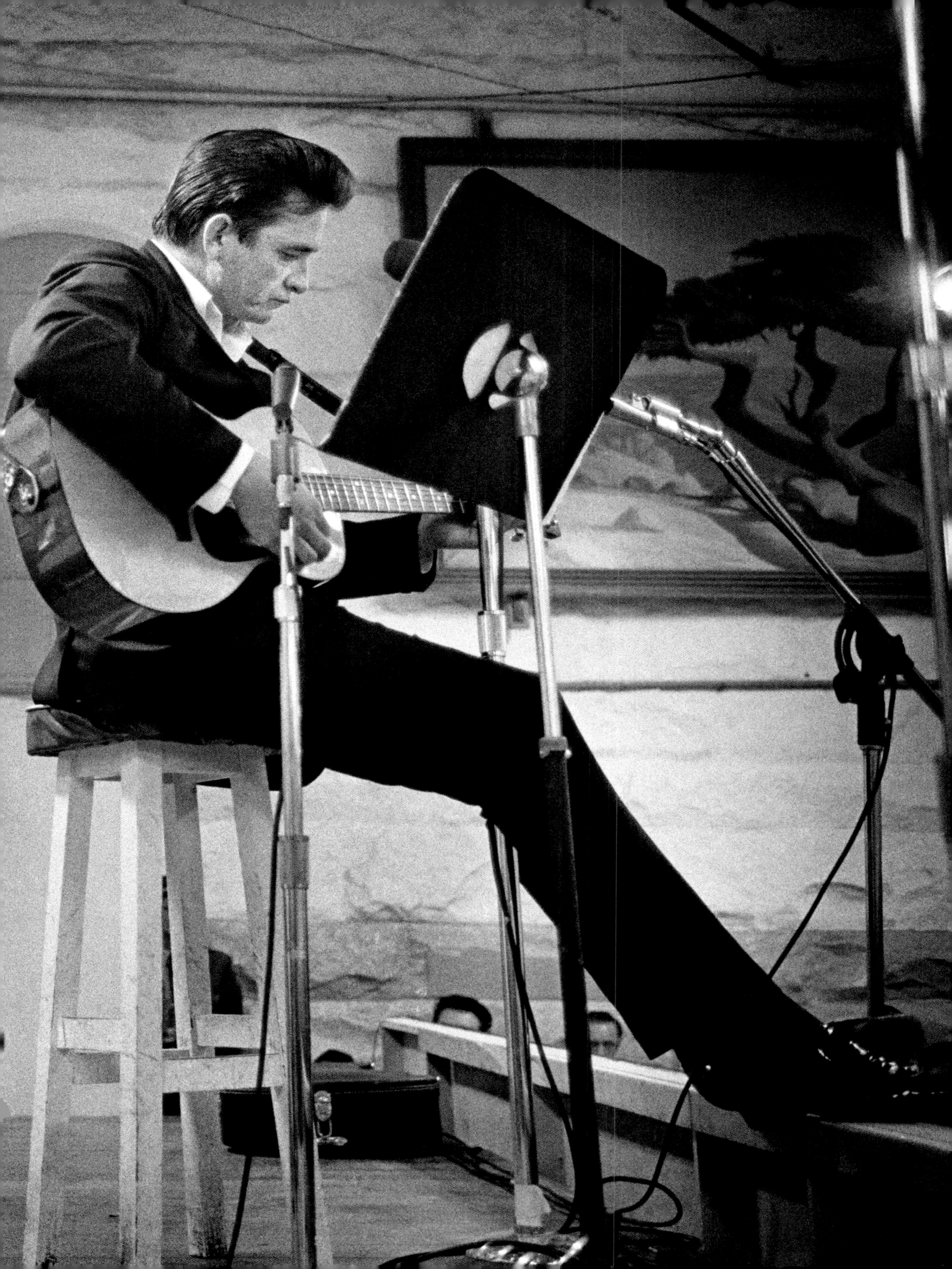

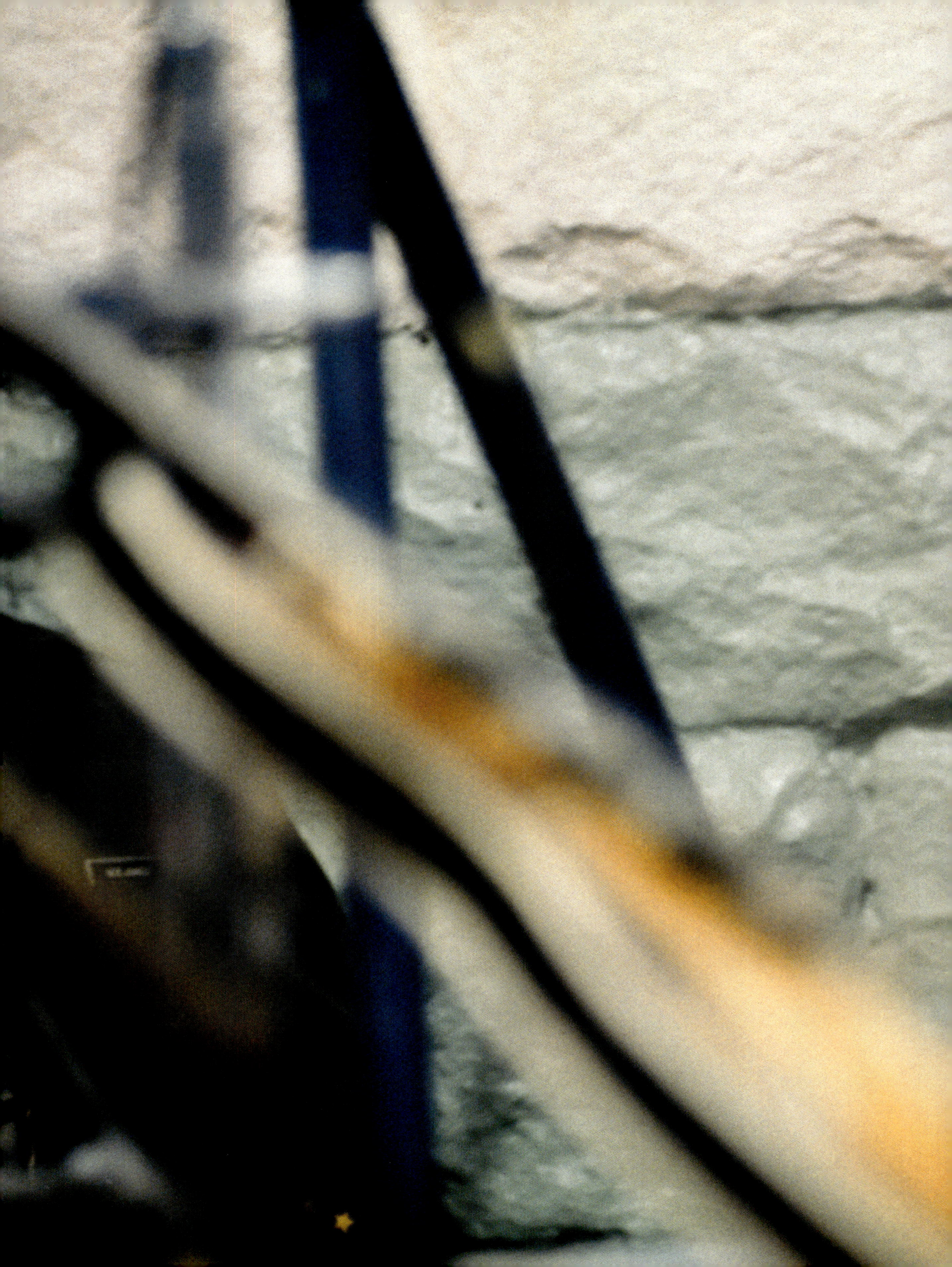

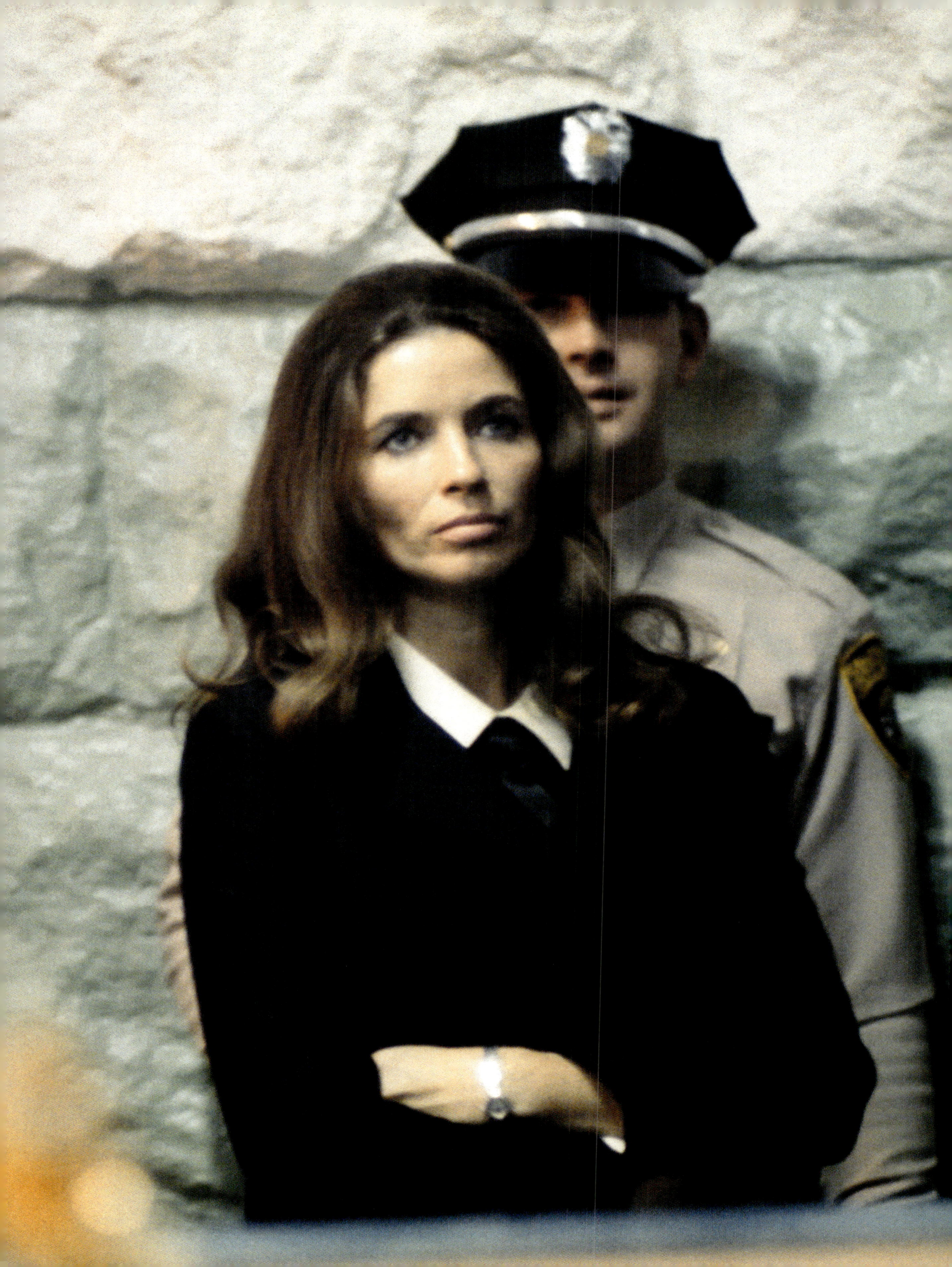

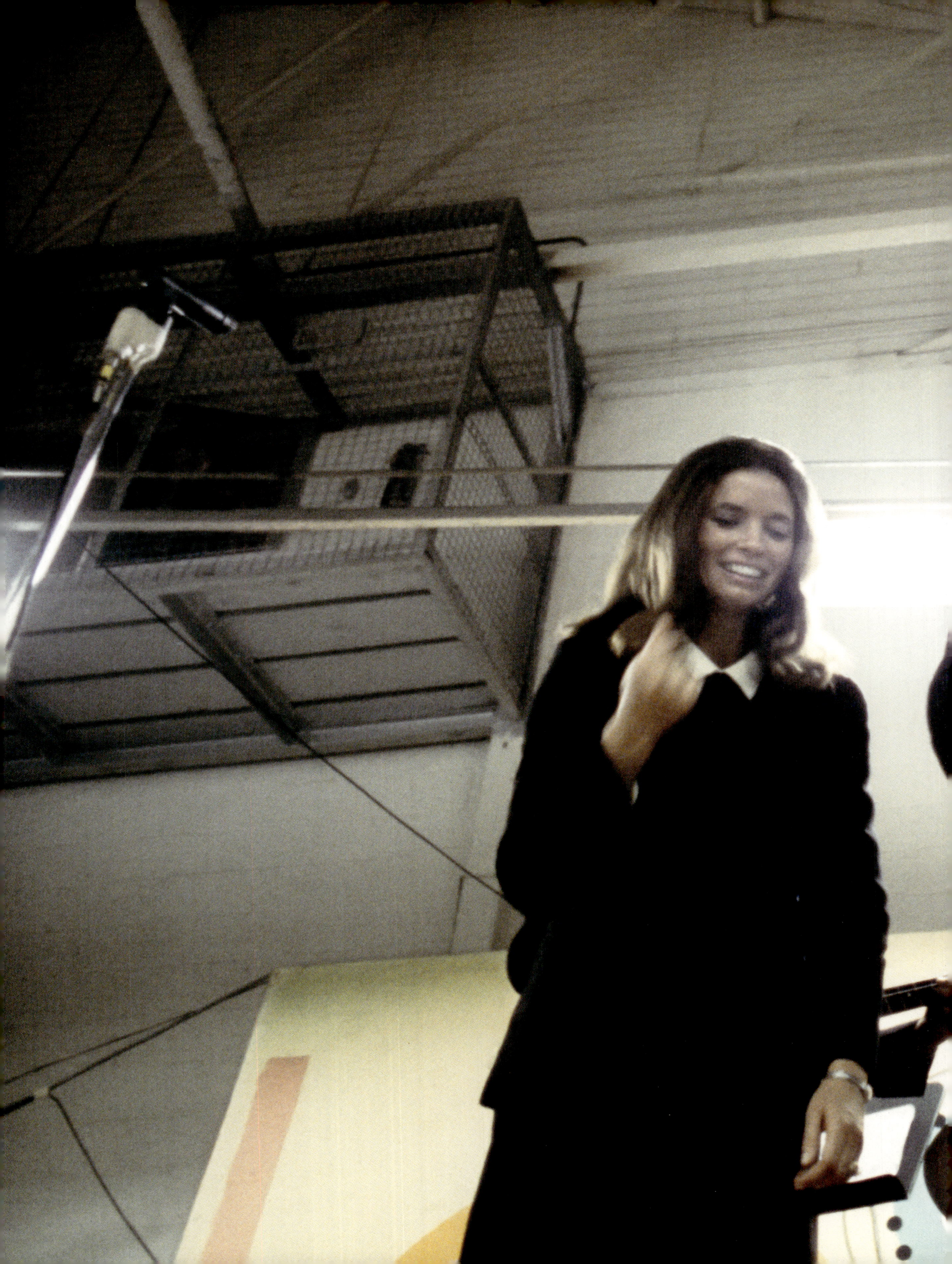

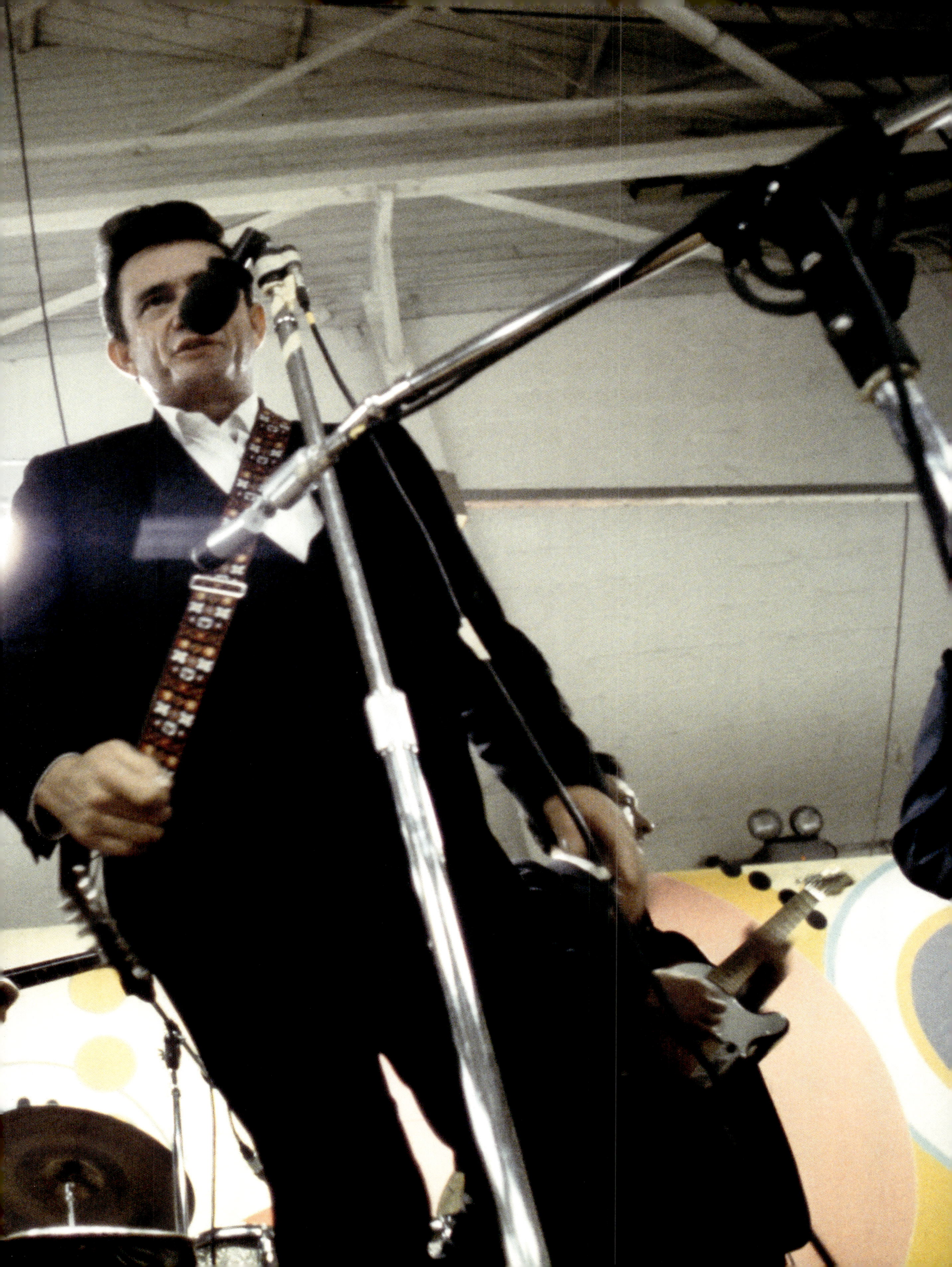

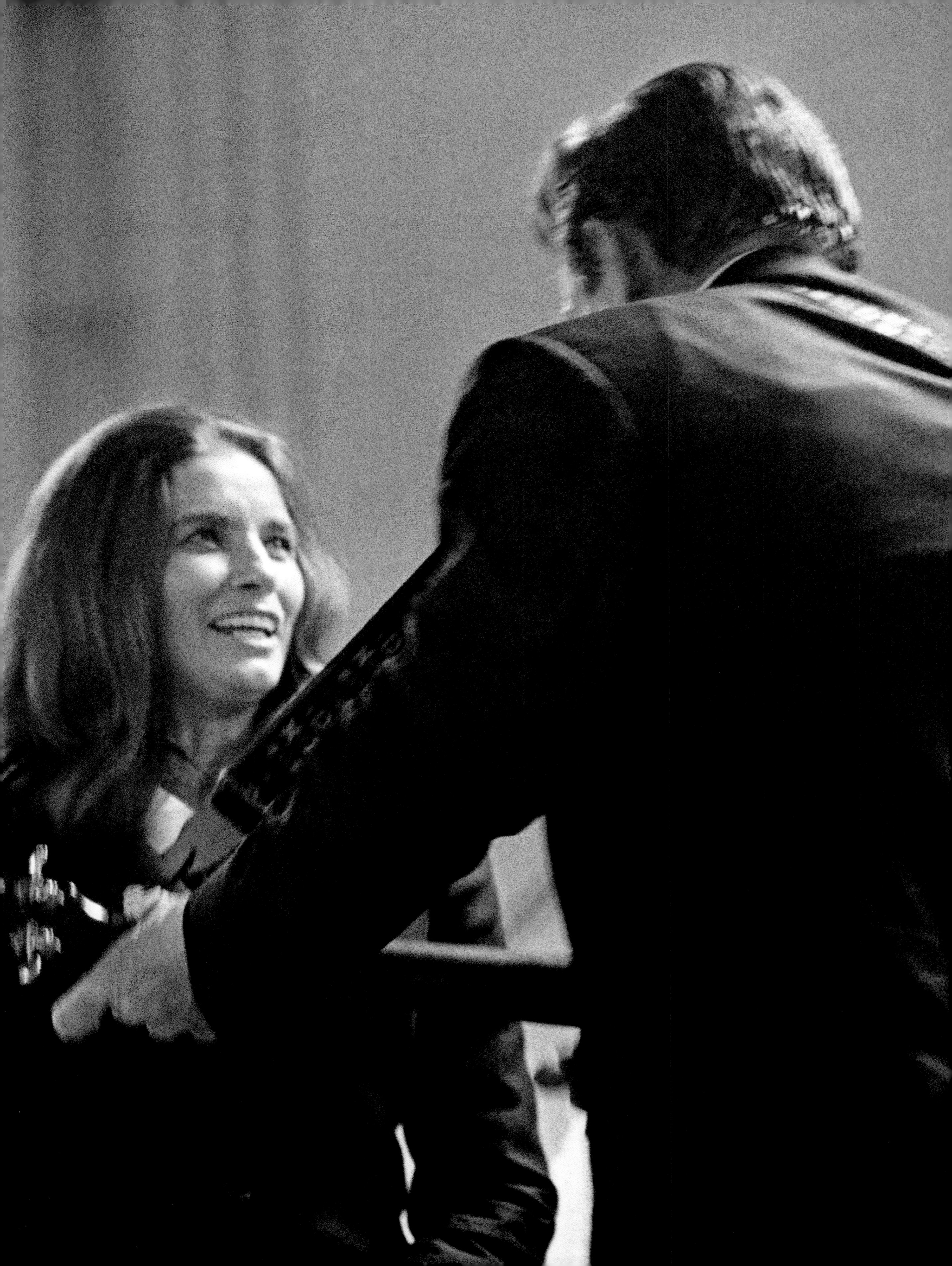

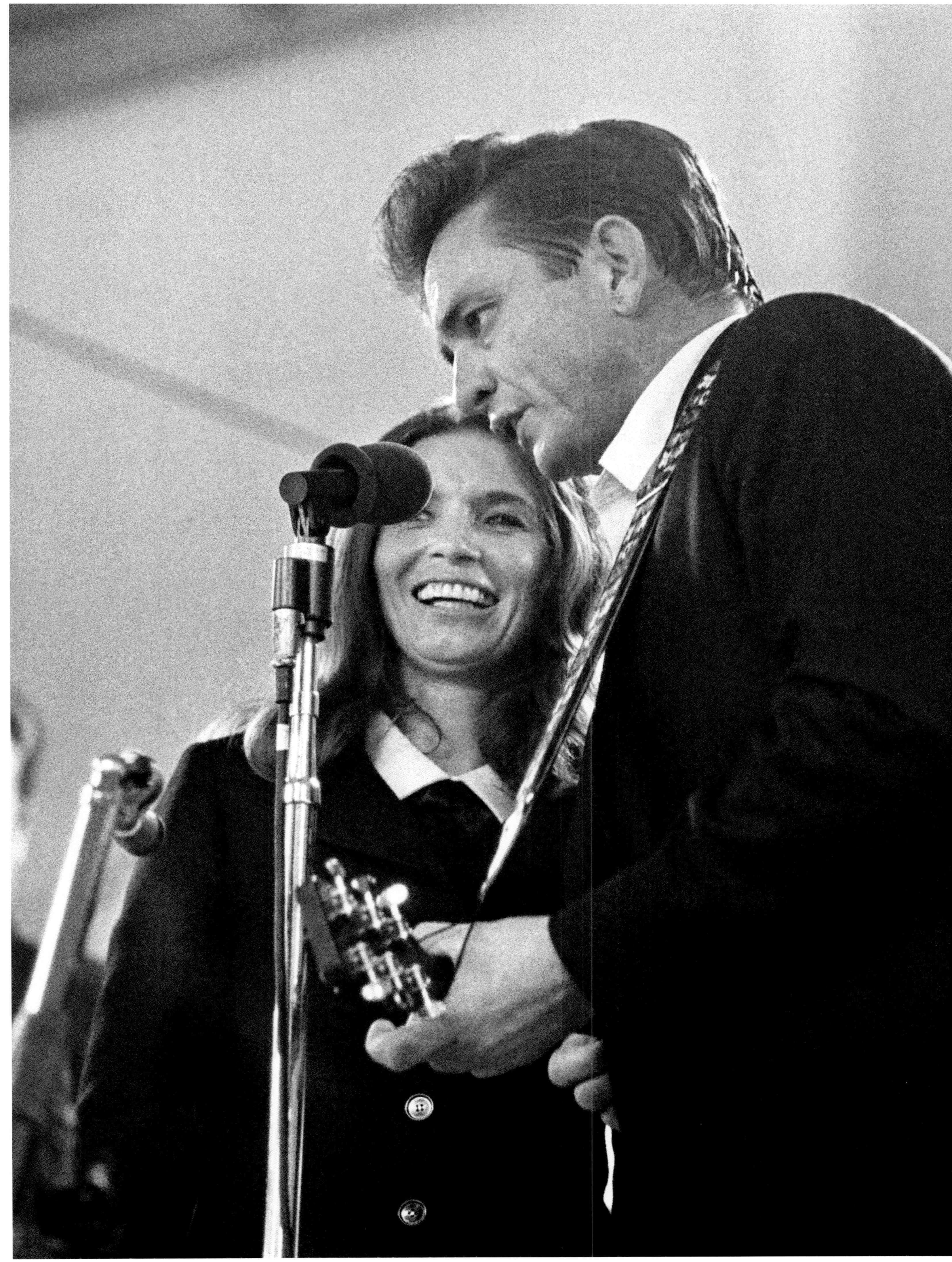

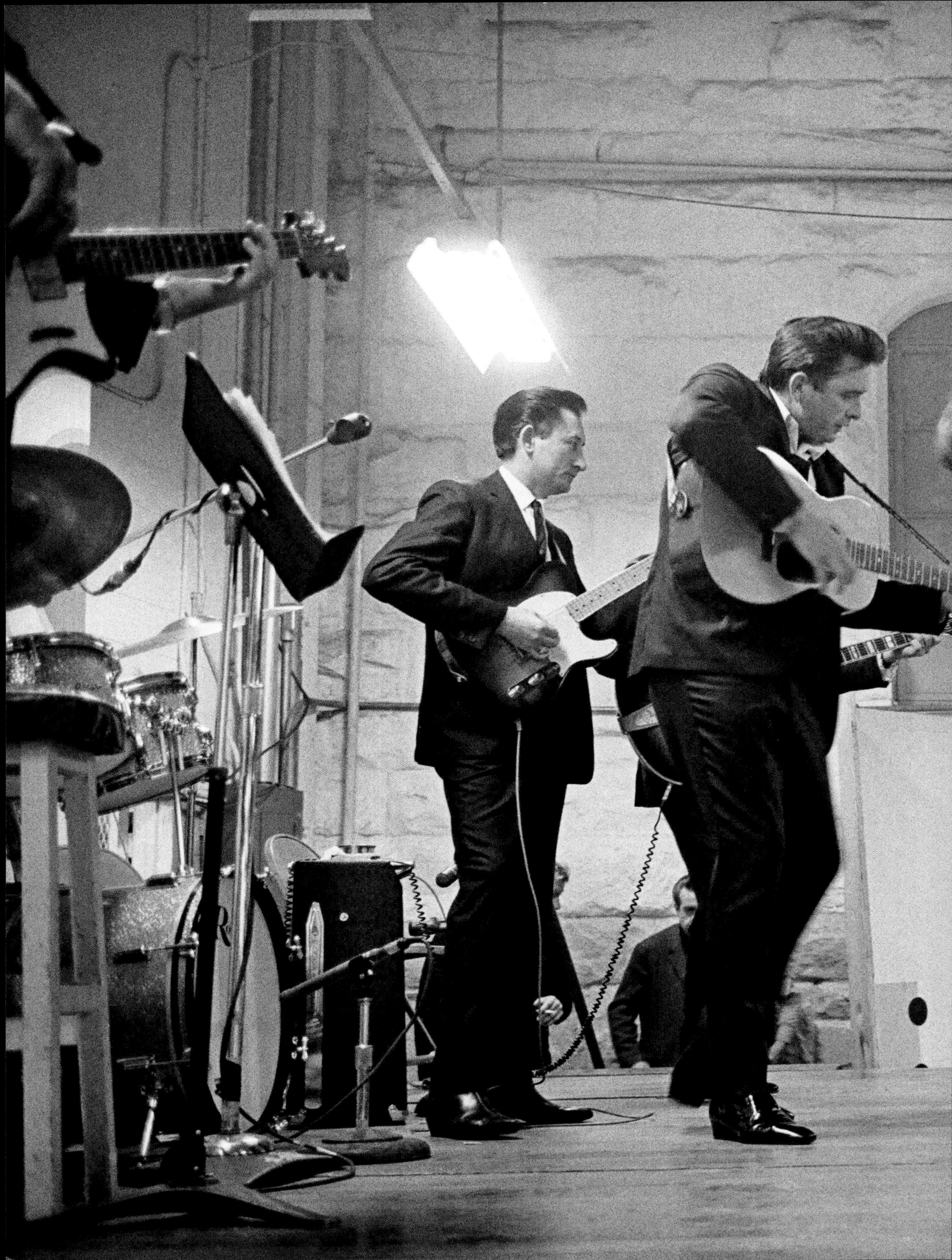

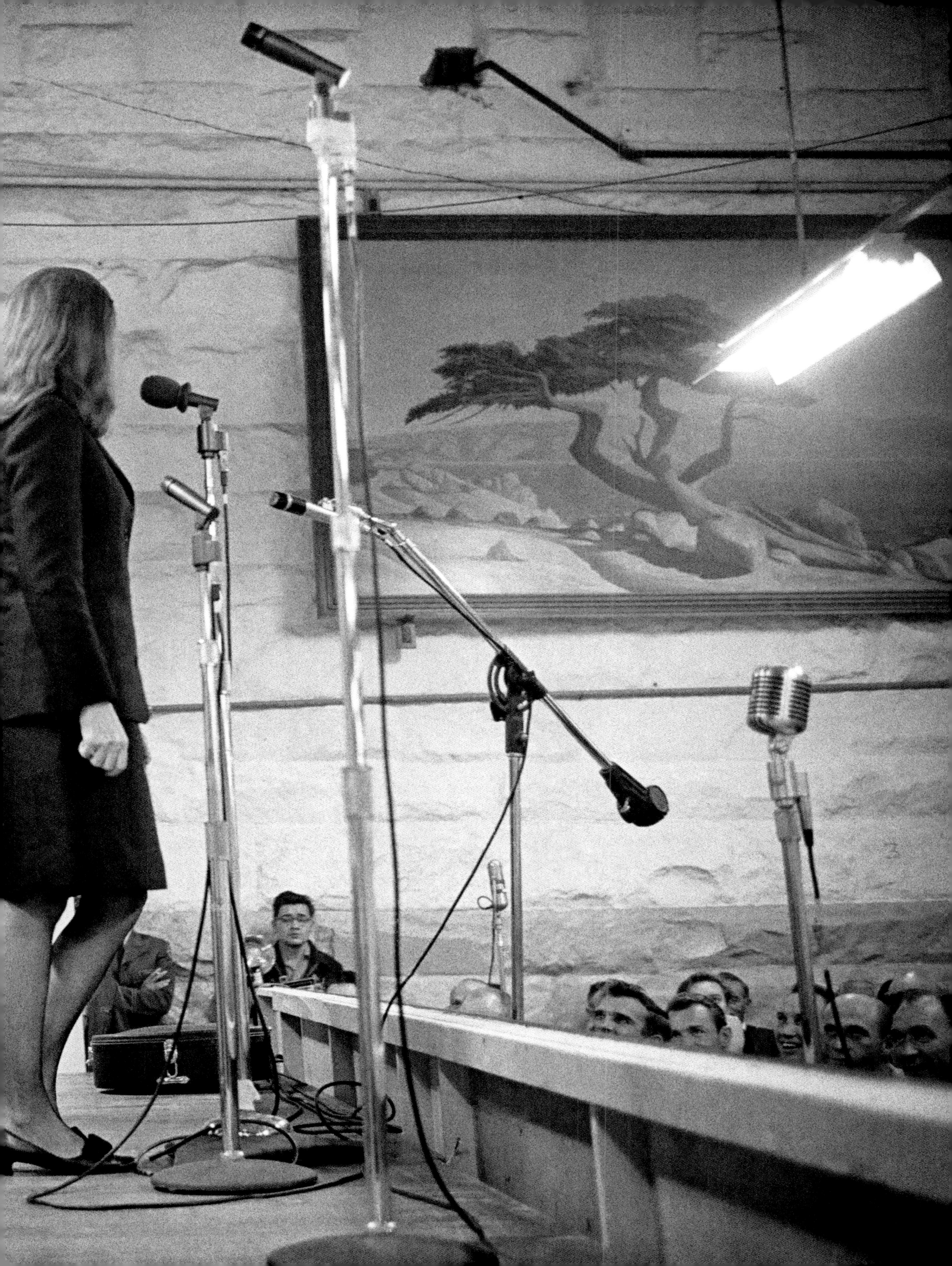

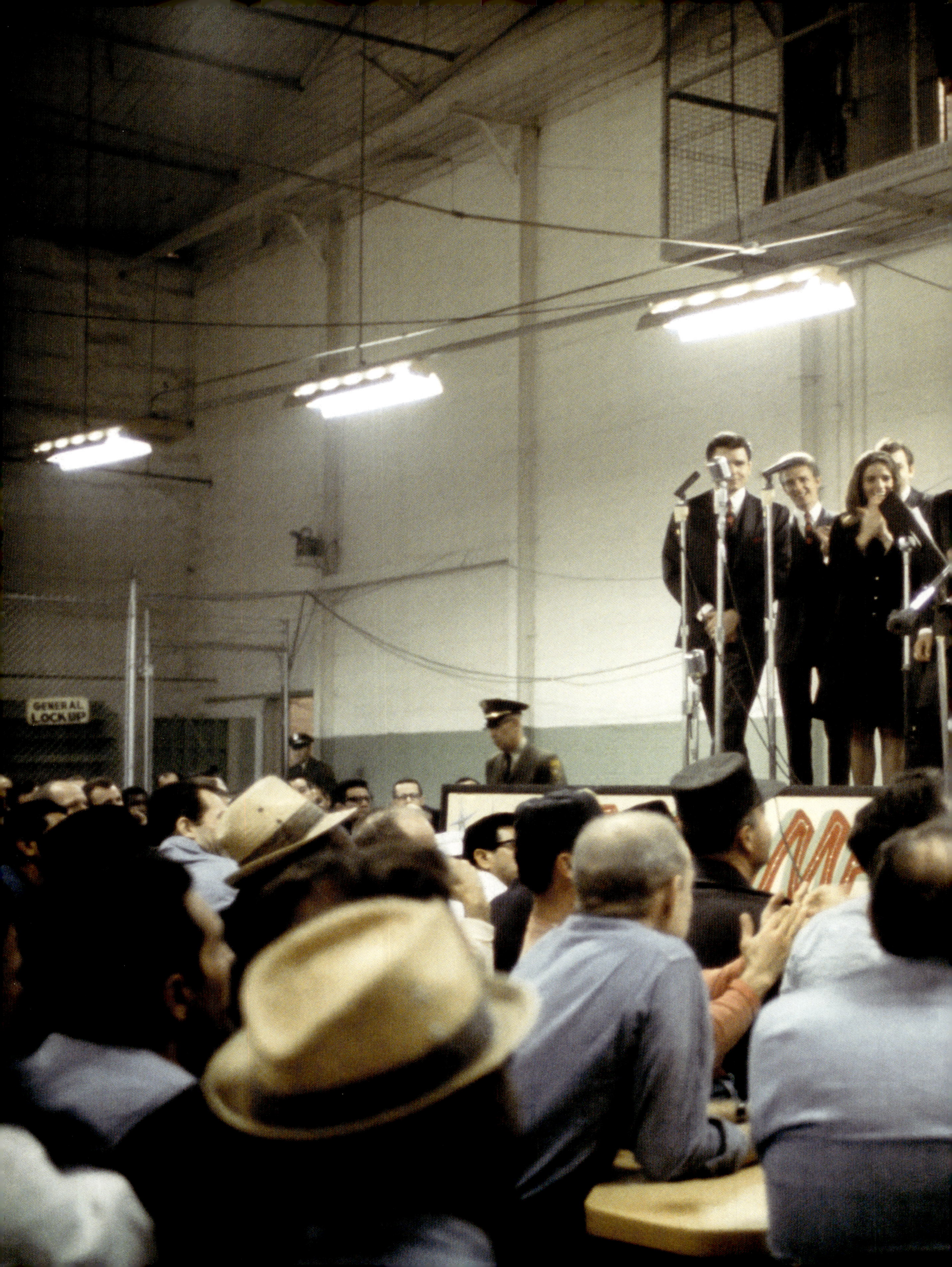

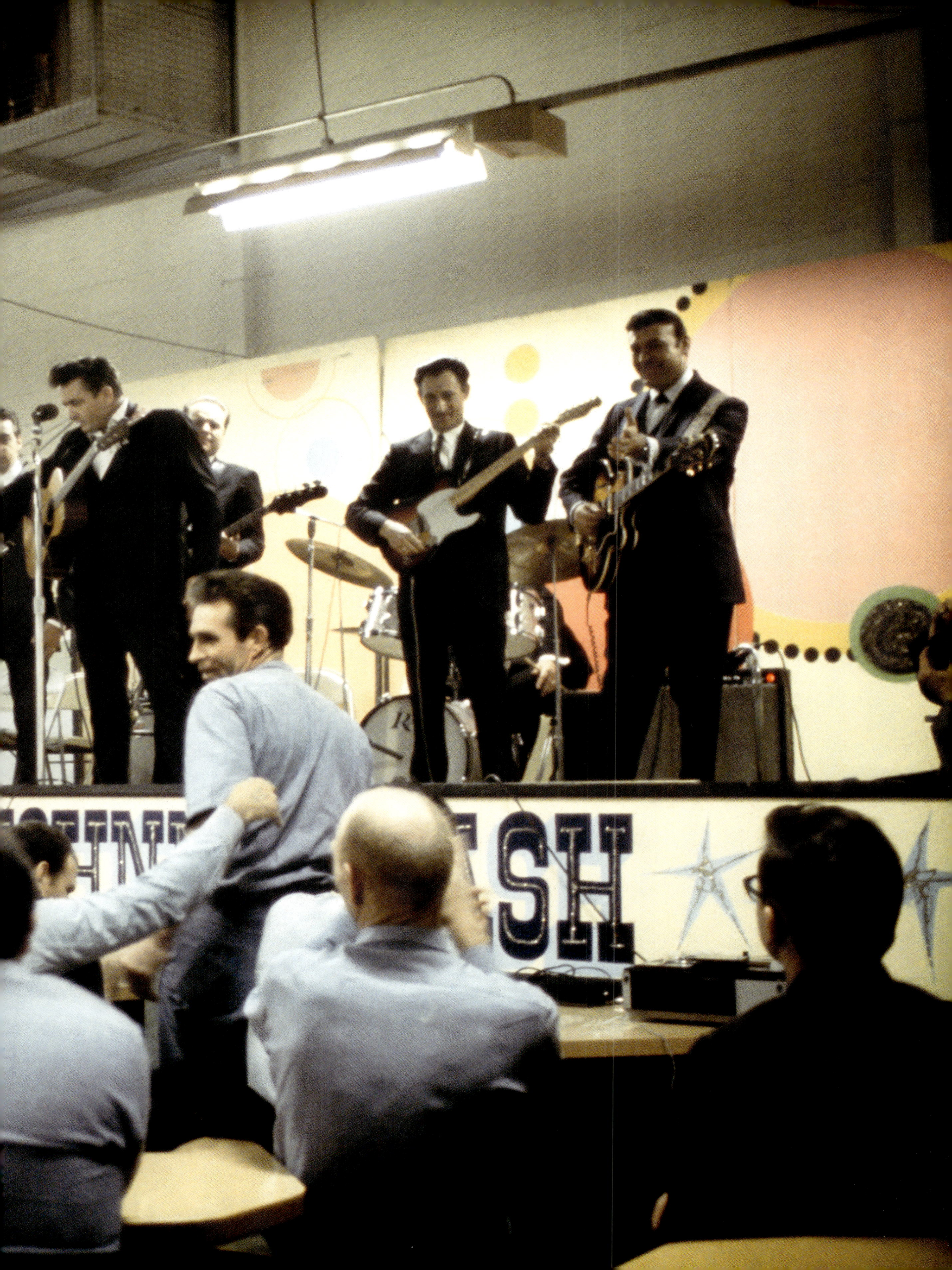
JOHNNY CASH

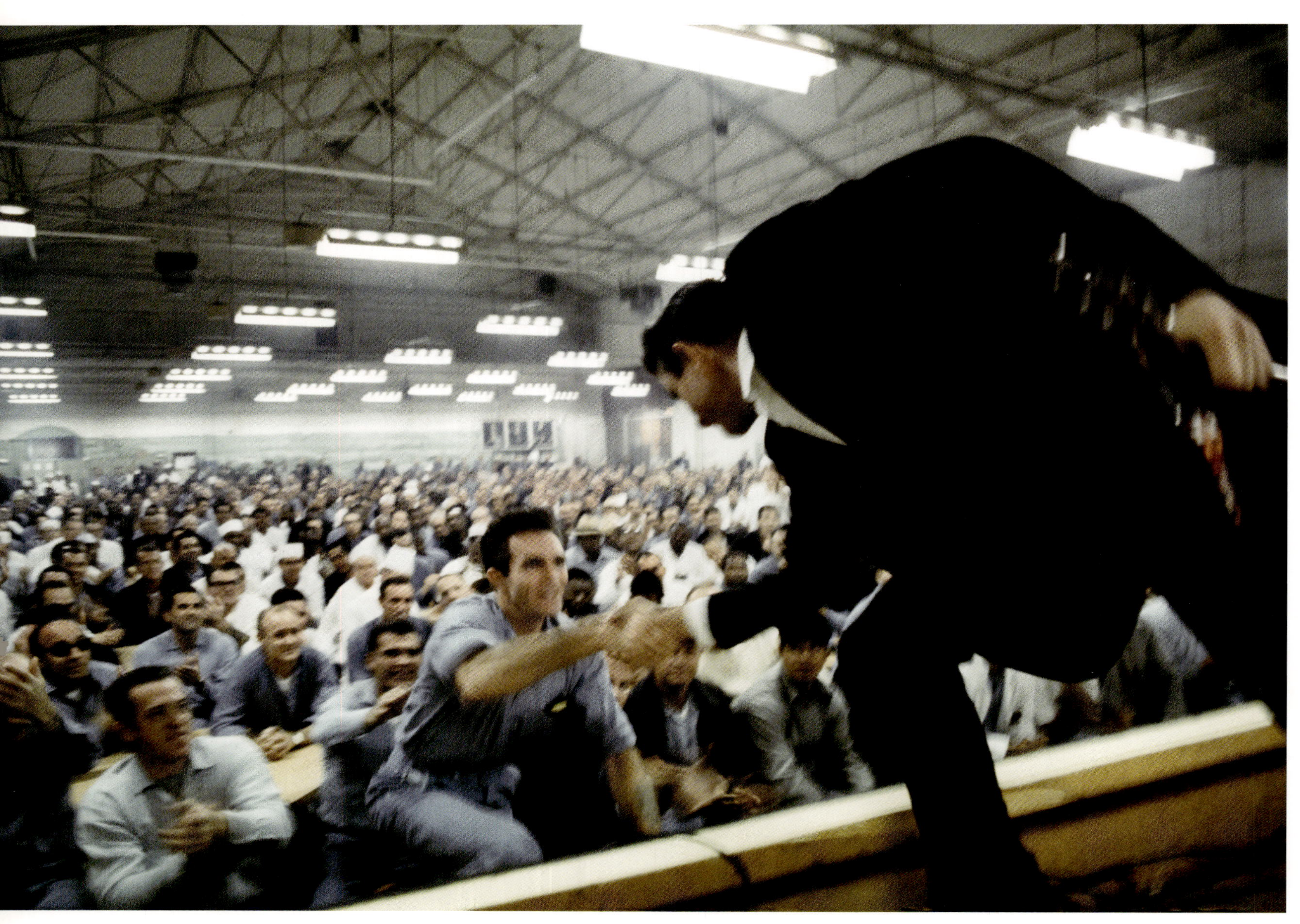

GLEN SHERLEY AND "GREYSTONE CHAPEL"

"This next song was written by a man right here in Folsom Prison," Johnny Cash announced into the microphone before performing the song that closed both his Folsom show and the resulting album. "And last night was the first time I've ever sung this song. Anyway, this song was written by our friend Glen Sherley."

Serving time for armed robbery, Glen Sherley had never met Cash and had no idea that Johnny was going to perform a song he'd written called "Greystone Chapel." Suddenly Folsom prisoner number A-59795 found himself caught up in a brief whirlwind of country music notoriety.

Glen Sherley was born in Oklahoma, but his family migrated to California in the 1940s. He was frequently in trouble with the law during his teen years, eventually serving time in San Quentin, Chico, and Soledad prisons before landing at Folsom. An amateur musician and songwriter who performed with the prison band, Sherley wrote a number of songs while incarcerated. He made a demo recording of "Greystone Chapel" (in the prison's actual Greystone Chapel), which he gave to Reverend Floyd Gressett.

In a 2005 essay for *Virginia Quarterly Review* Gene Beley recalled Gressett playing it for Cash for the first time at the El Rancho Hotel the day before the show. "You've been so busy that I haven't had a chance to tell you about it," Beley remembered Gressett telling Cash, "but I thought if you could mention tomorrow that you've heard the tape, it would please that ol' boy who wrote it." Using the tape machine Beley had brought along in his role as a reporter, Johnny listened to the song. "Cash's usual straight-faced, deep-creased cheeks began changing to a smile," Gene remembered, "with his eyes glowing, radiating enthusiasm. When the tape was finished, Cash said, 'This has got to be recorded as a single, and I want to record it tomorrow on the album during the show.' Cash began scribbling the words down in a notebook and tried singing the phrase, while beating out the rhythm with one hand on his knee, the other hand tapping a pen on the desk."

Johnny and the band learned the song during their rehearsals that night. The performance that's enshrined on the *At Folsom Prison* album was the first time Cash ever sang it in front of an audience. Prison officials made sure Sherley was seated on the front row for the surprise performance. Jim Marshall's photographs capture the face of a man who was genuinely thrilled and humbled to be recognized for his songwriting by a major country music star. "He jumped out of his chair," recalled Beley. "I thought his eyes were going to bolt out of his head. I don't think I've ever seen a happier man alive."

Following the show, Sherley was invited to the kitchen's makeshift dressing room to visit with Cash and his entourage. Johnny, who believed firmly in the power of redemption, took a special interest in Sherley's plight. He believed in Glen's potential to—like Merle Haggard before him—overcome his criminal past for a life of country music success.

Sherley would go on to write a song called "Portrait of a Woman" that became the title track for an album by country star Eddy Arnold in 1971. With Cash's help, Glen even recorded a self-titled live album in California's Vacaville Prison, where he was transferred after Folsom. Featuring session musicians from Nashville, it's believed to be the first time an album was ever recorded in a prison by an actual prisoner.

Johnny and the influential Reverend Billy Graham successfully lobbied California governor Ronald Reagan to grant Glen Sherley parole in 1971. On the day of his release Cash himself met Glen at the gates. Soon after, the pair appeared before a Senate hearing on prison reform, which had become a cause close to Cash's heart. Sherley wrote songs for the House of Cash music publishing company, joined Johnny's touring roadshow, and even married House of Cash employee Nikki Robbins. Johnny was the best man at the wedding ceremony.

Unfortunately the story of Glen Sherley's redemption is a complicated tale. "I think that because Glen had spent so much of his life in prison," bassist Marshall Grant reflected in his memoir, "he felt out of place and was very insecure on the outside." Sherley was prone to violent tendencies and, after threatening members of Cash's crew and entourage (including Grant), Johnny fired him. Substance abuse had already crept back into his life on the road and, after departing the Cash organization, his life further unraveled. With his drinking and drugging escalating dramatically, he became persona non grata in the Nashville music community, his marriage fell apart, and he eventually ended up living in his pickup truck. In 1978 Glen Sherley put a gun to his head and took his own life at the age of 42. Johnny Cash paid the funeral expenses.

"You can't hasten someone else's recovery or enlightenment," Rosanne Cash reflected in a 2008 interview with Michael Streissguth. "I think that my dad had a sense of maybe he could and it didn't turn out well all the time." Johnny was disappointed and disillusioned by the Glen Sherley experience, ultimately moving on from his focus on prisoner advocacy and prison reform. Though he returned to Folsom in 1977 he eventually stopped performing prison shows altogether. His connection with inmates—and particularly his Folsom and San Quentin shows—remain, however, an integral part of his legacy.

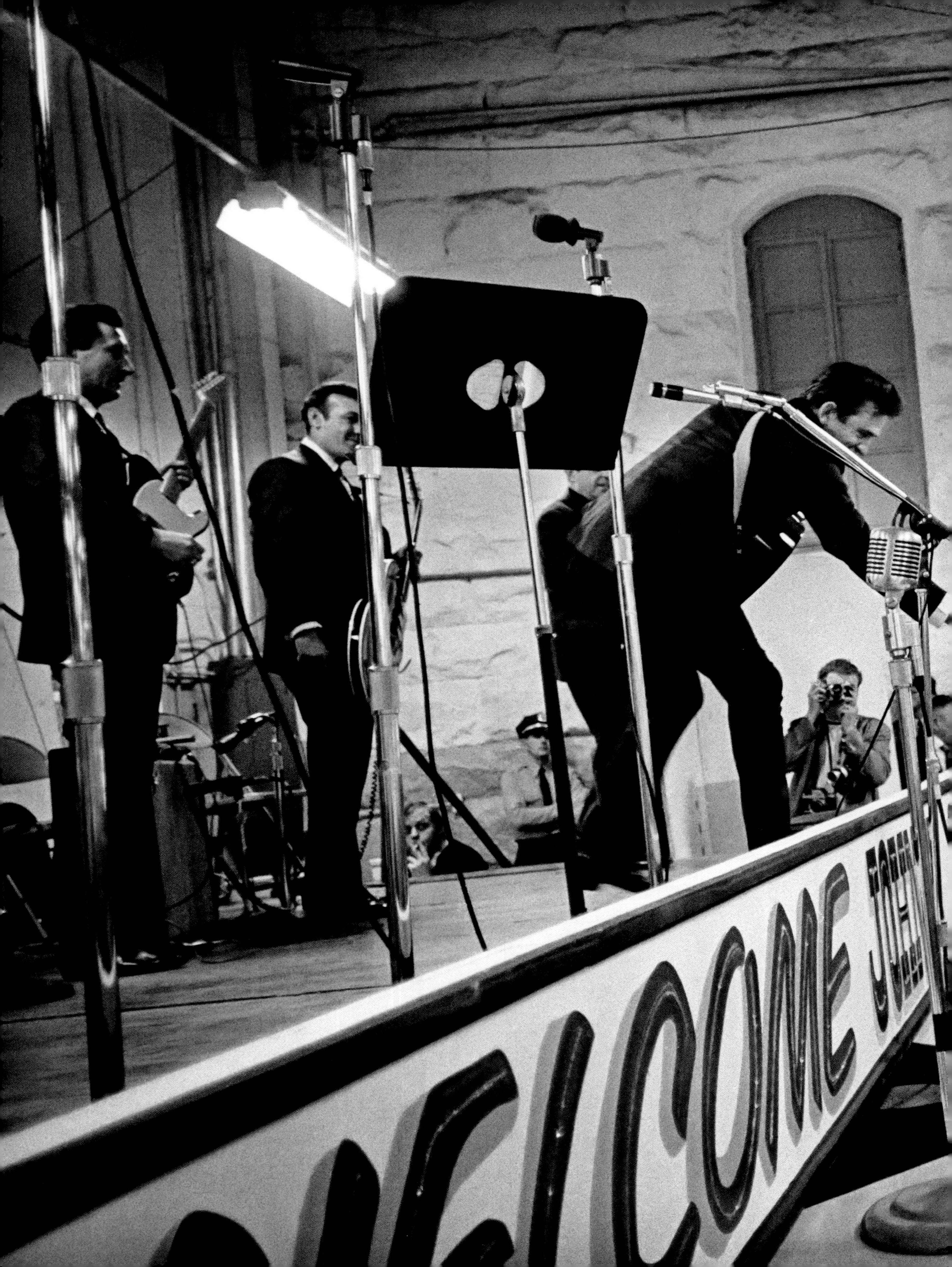
WELCOME JOHNNY

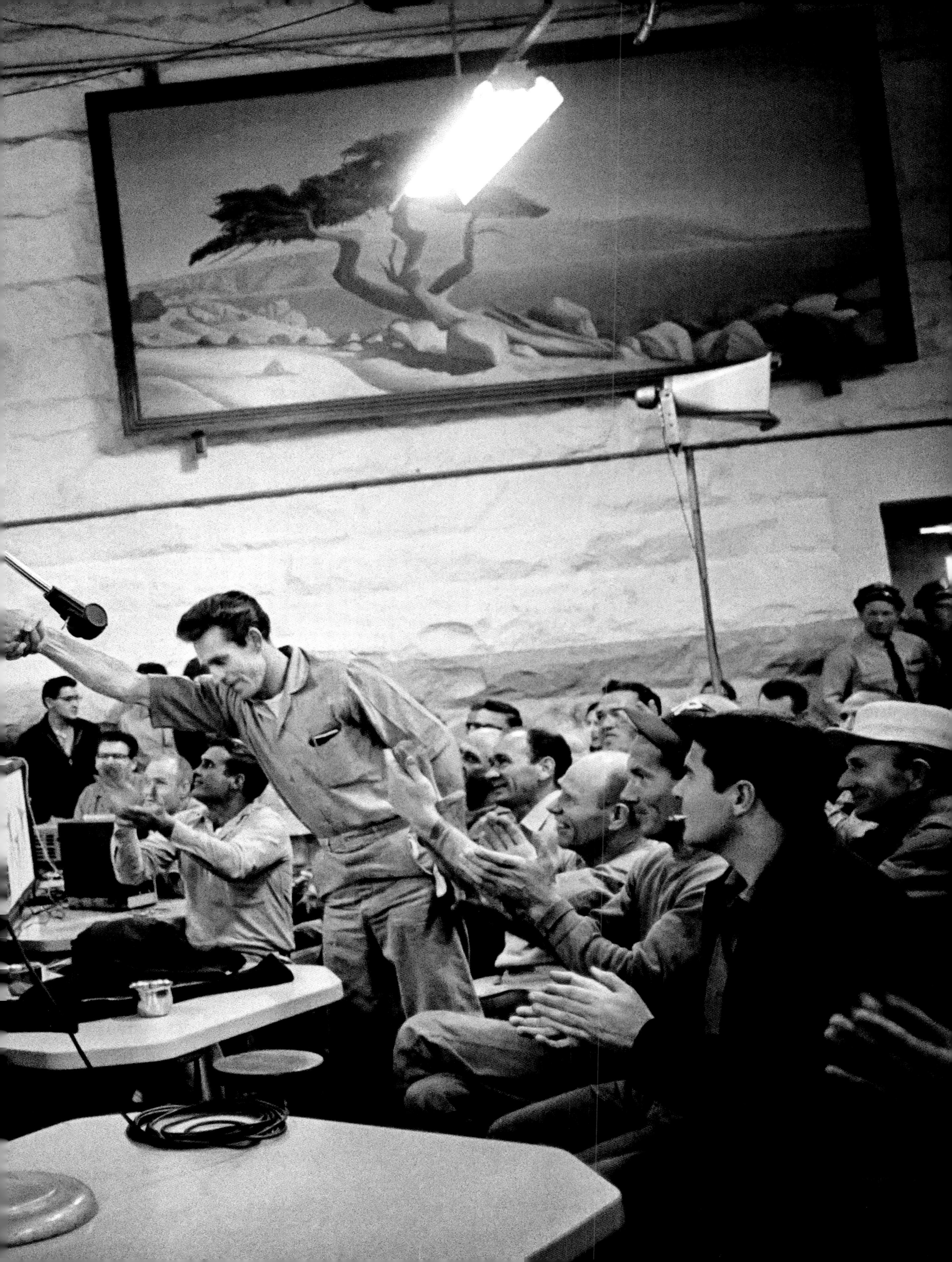

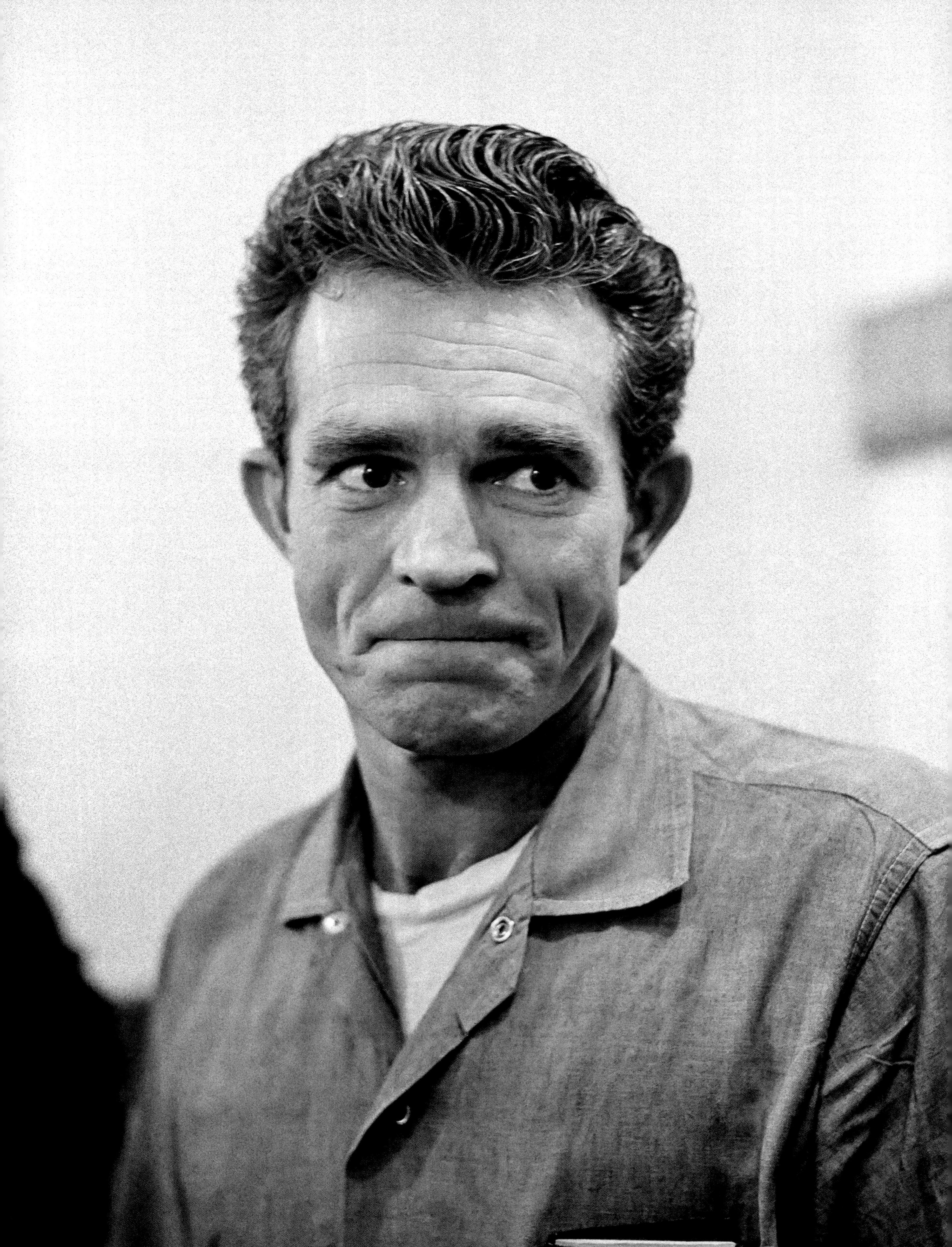

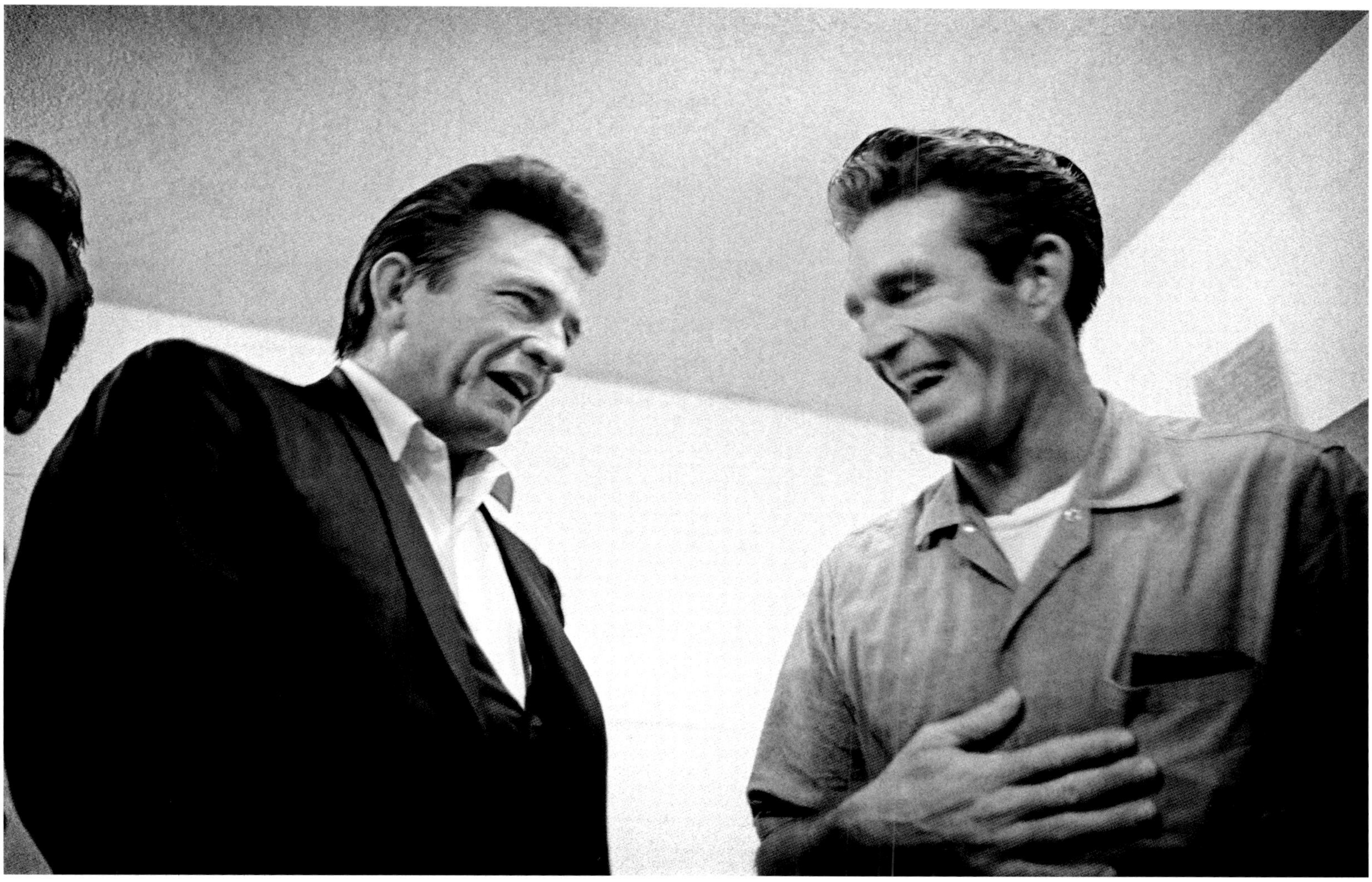

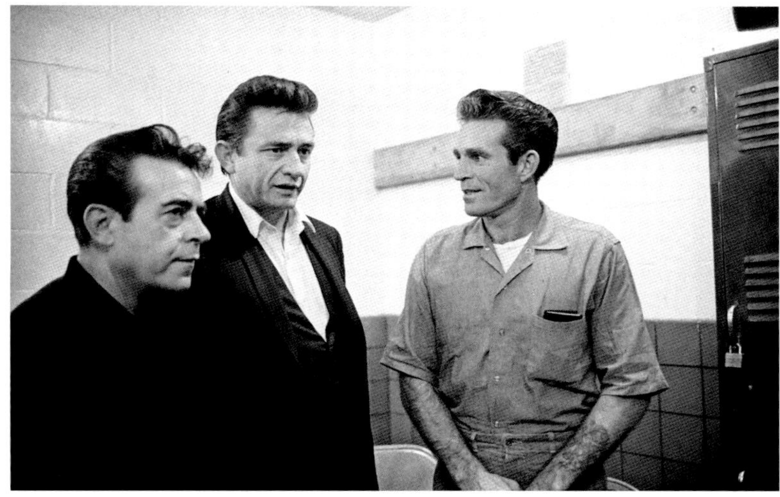

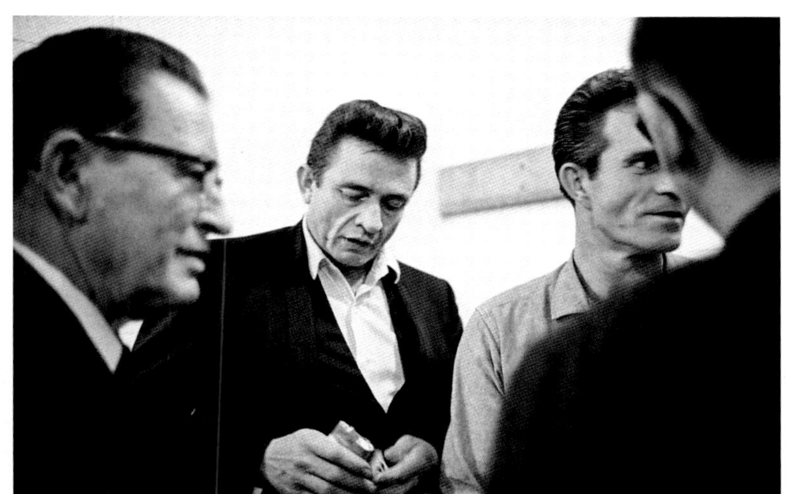

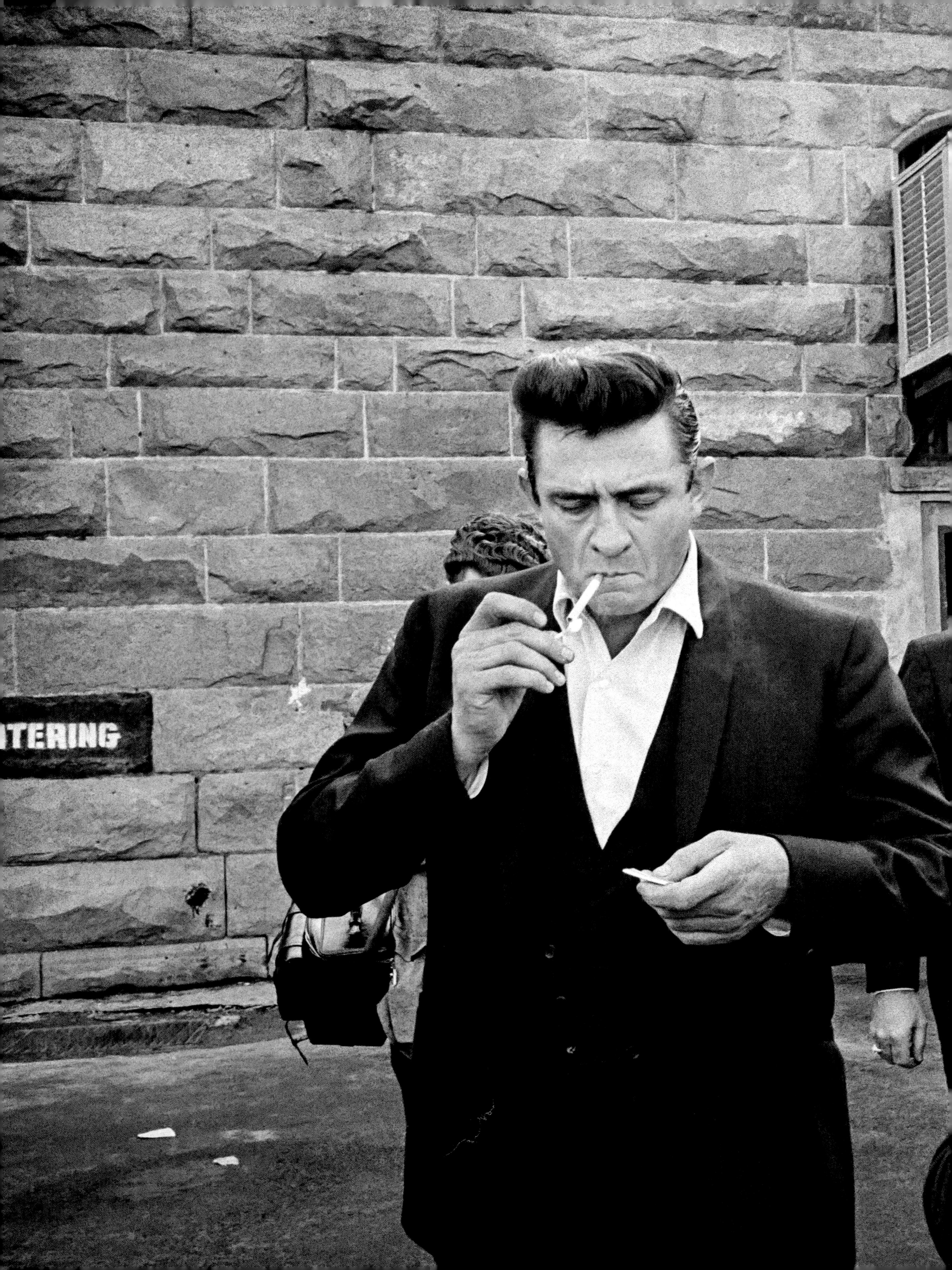
TERING

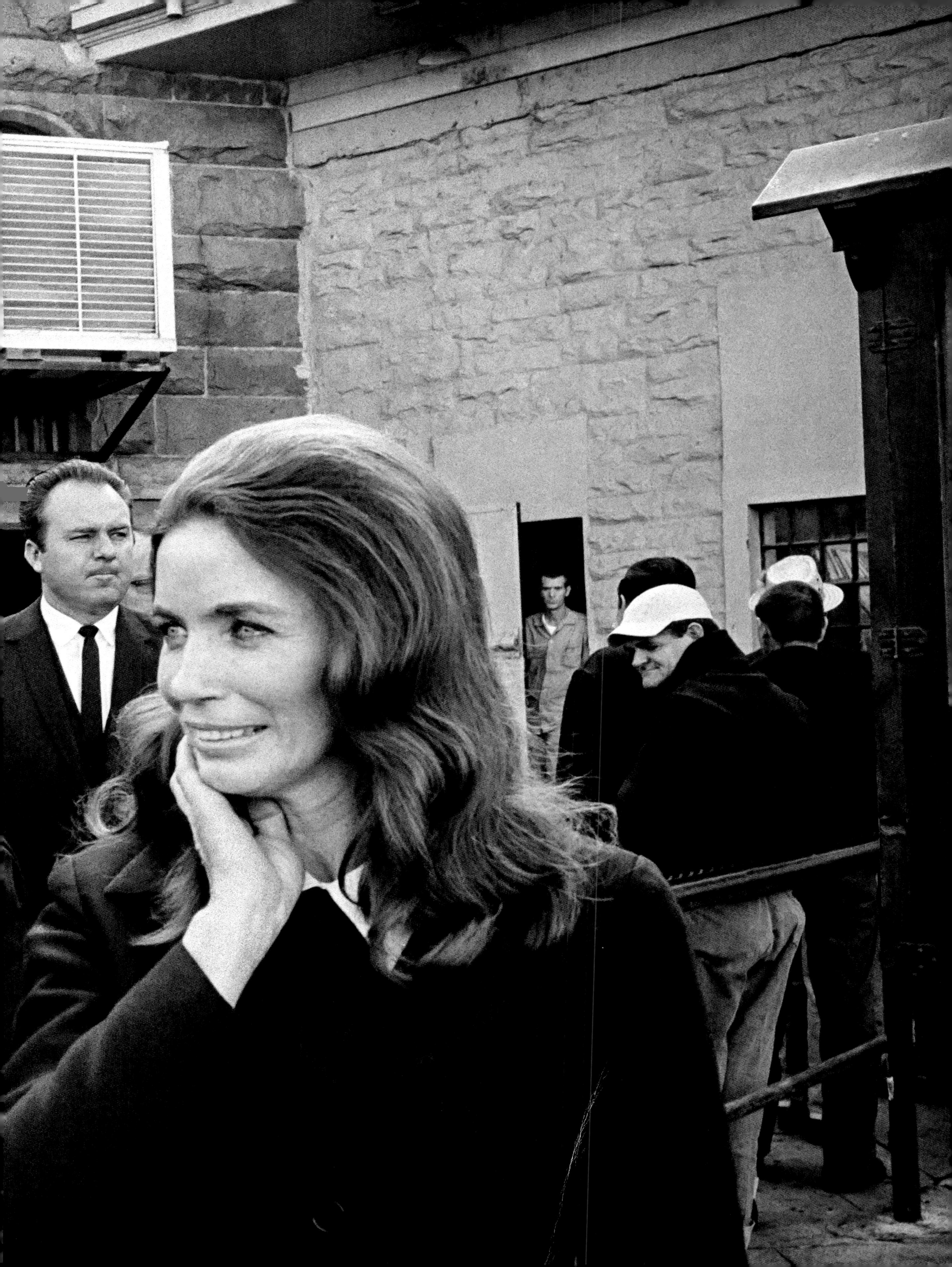

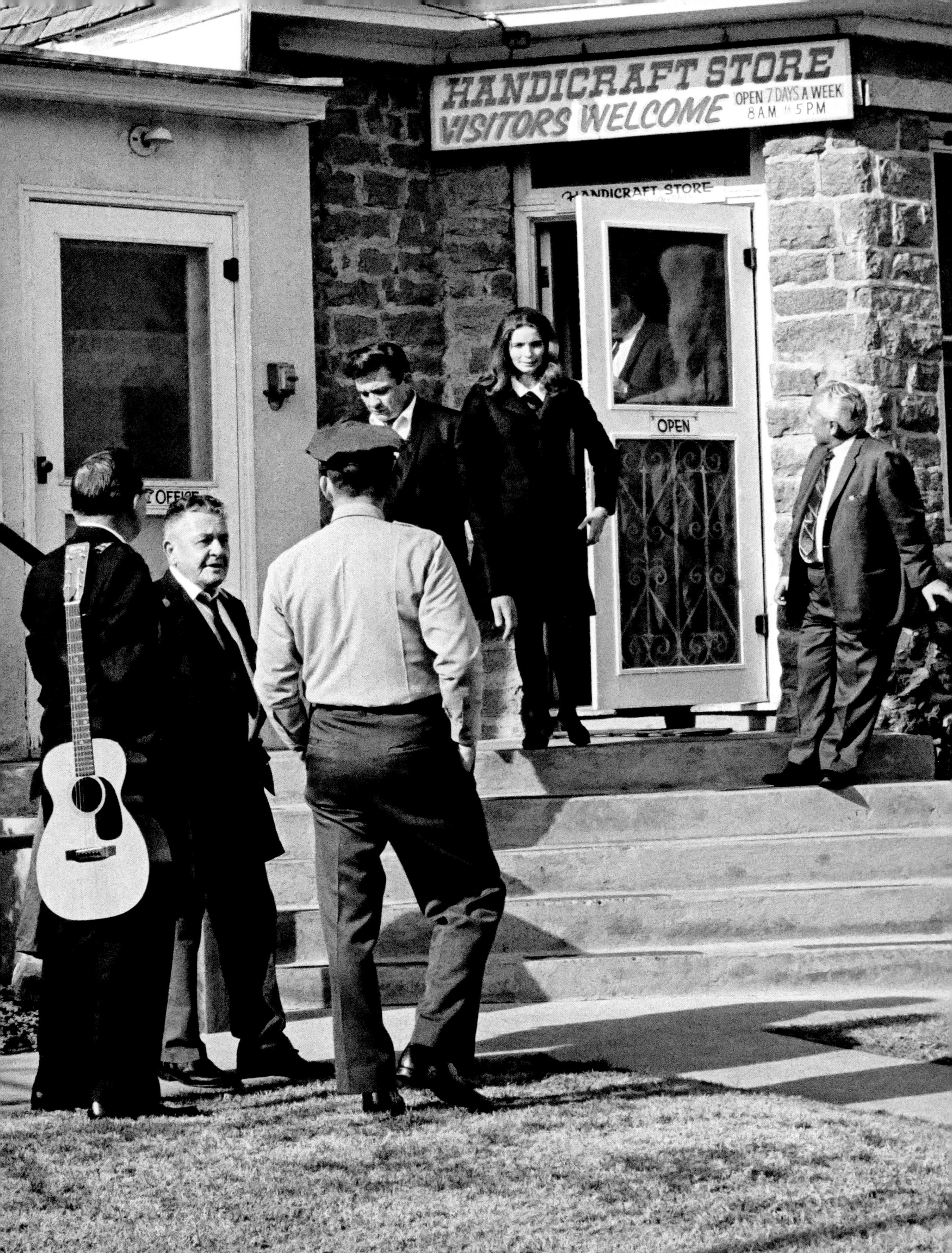

HANDICRAFT STORE
VISITORS WELCOME
OPEN 7 DAYS A WEEK
8 A.M. to 5 P.M.
HANDICRAFT STORE
OPEN
OFFICE

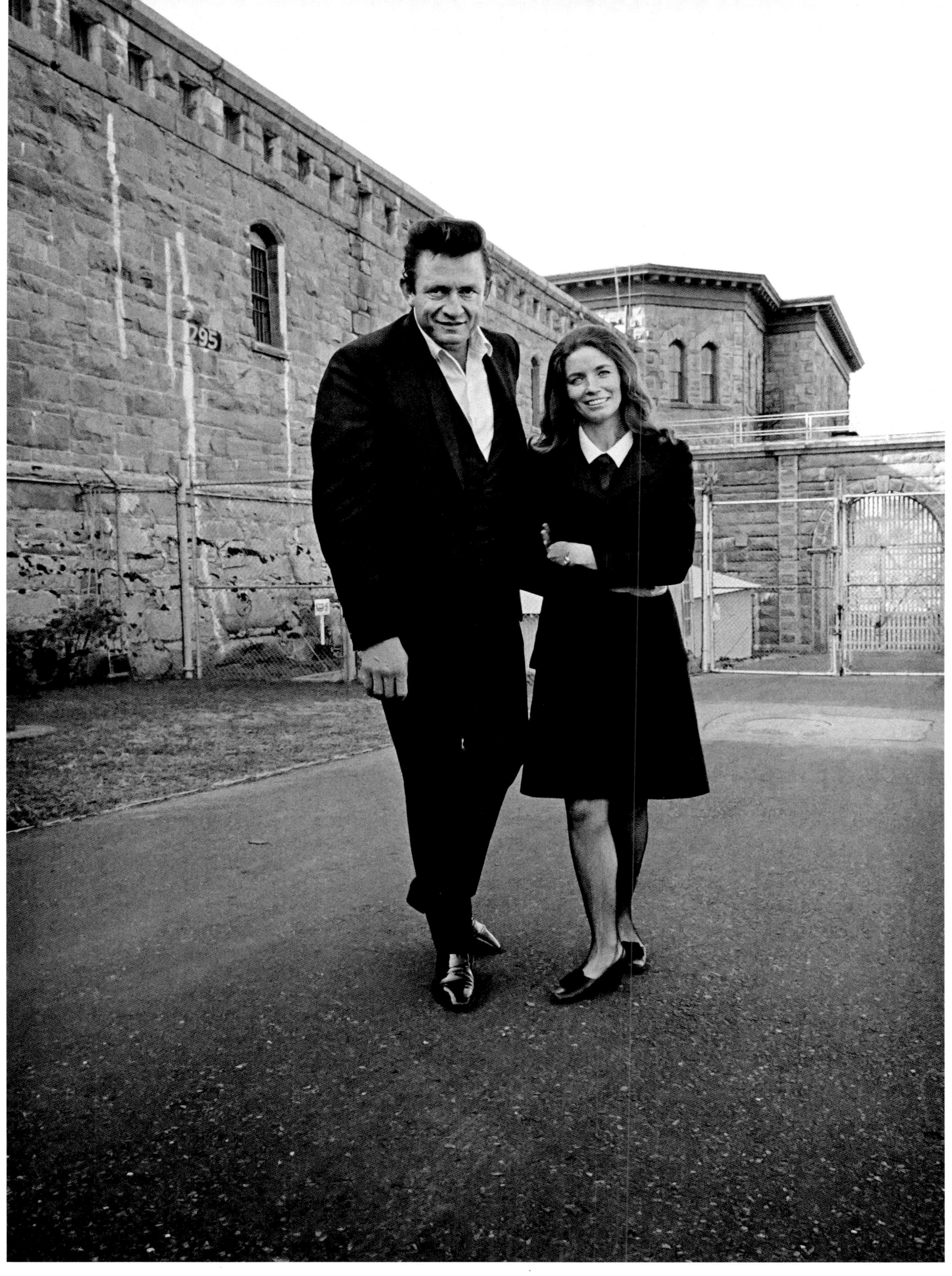

When he was finished performing Cash and his entourage visited the prison's handicraft store. The photos Jim Marshall captured of everyone following the two performances reveal the mood was beginning to lighten. Everyone knew that something magical had just happened in Dining Hall #2 and the sense of relief was palpable.

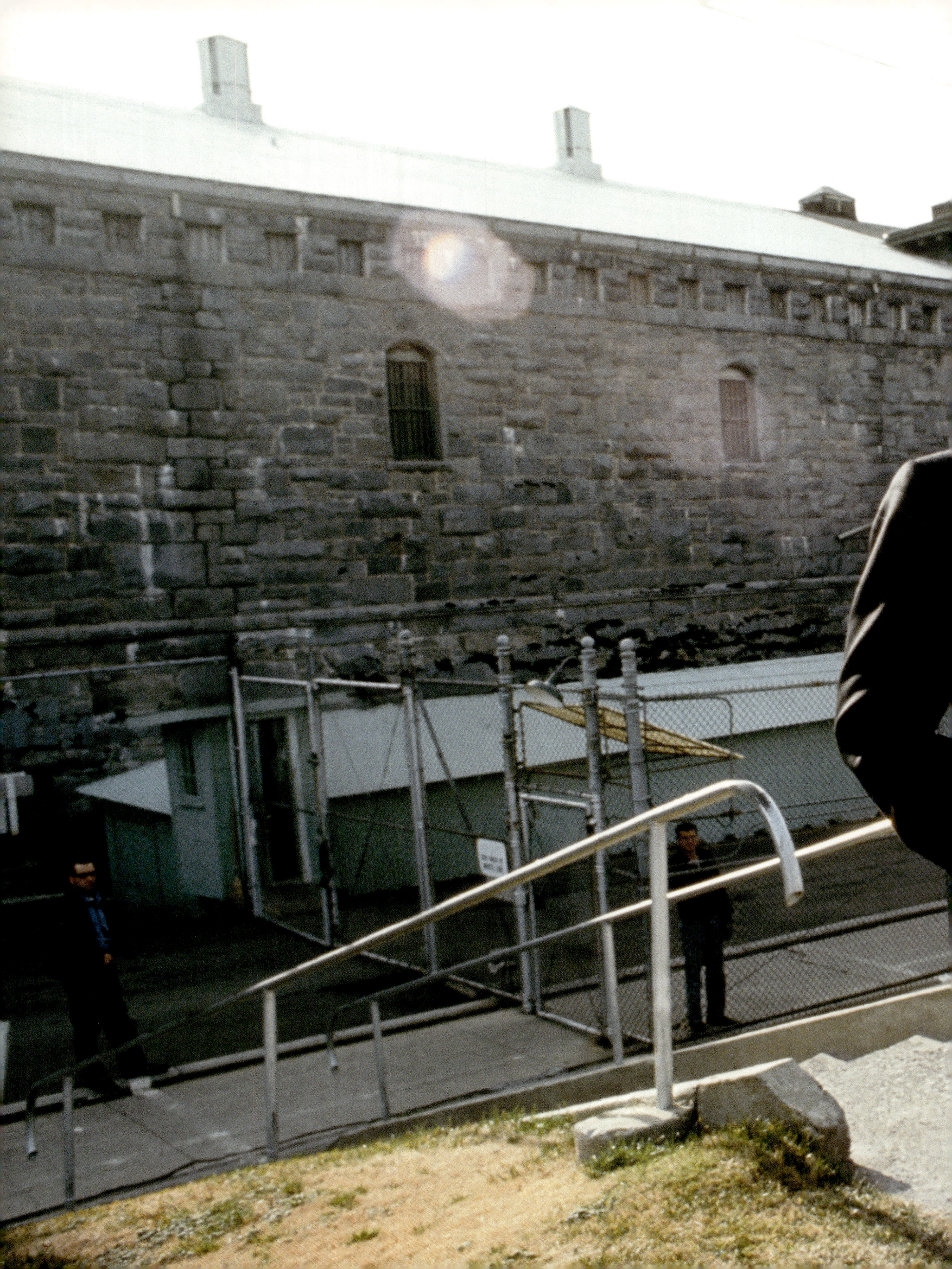

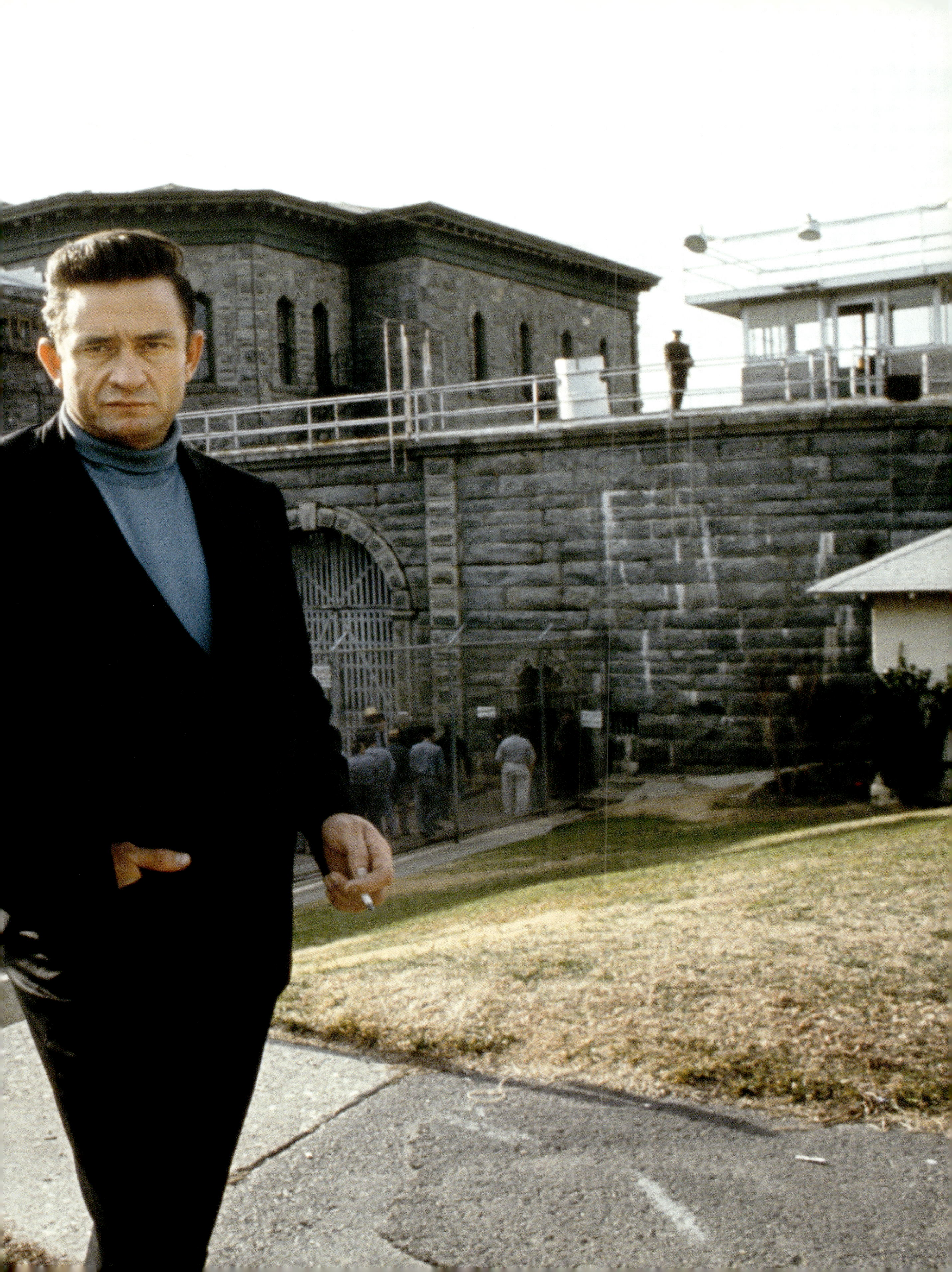

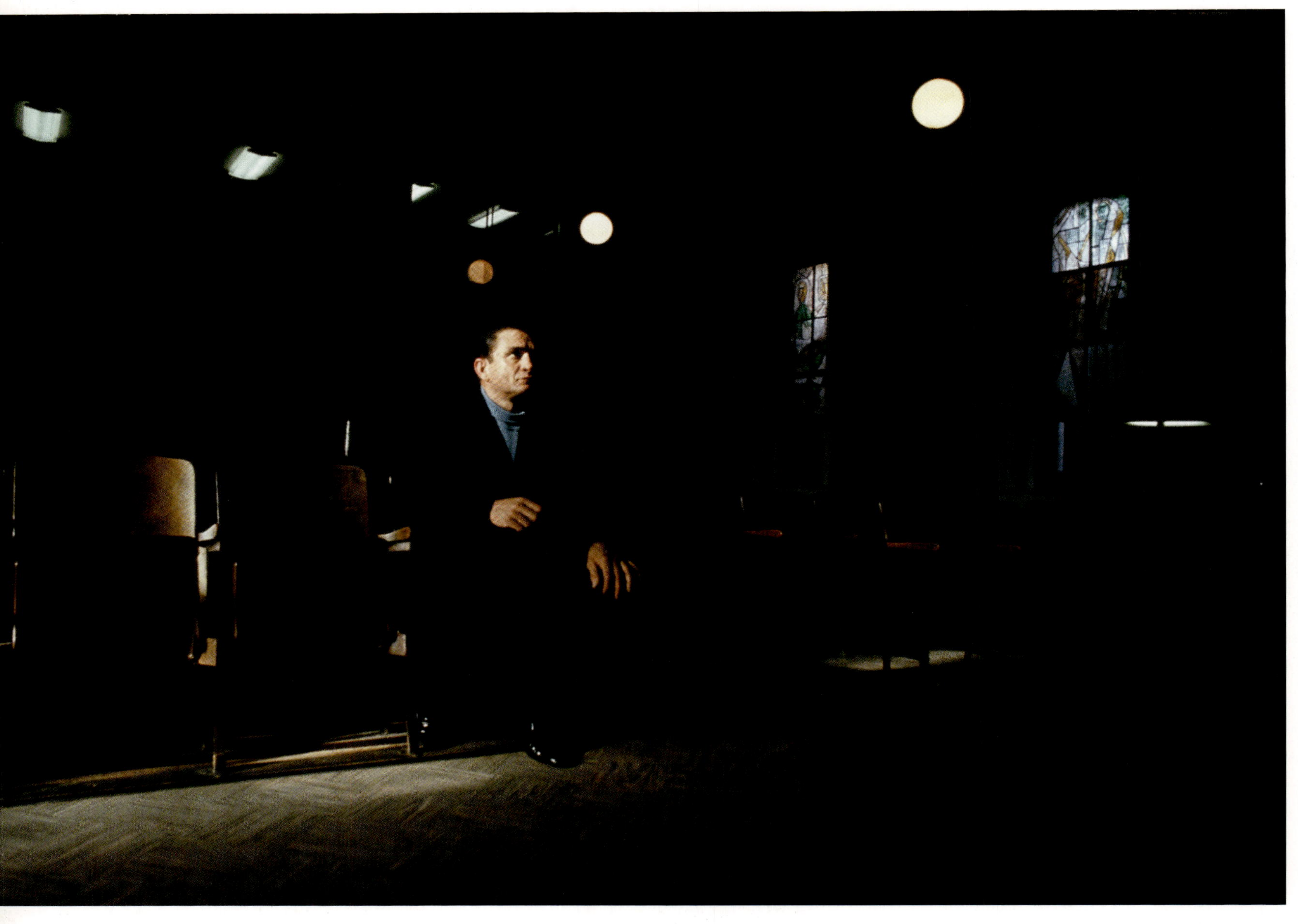

Before departing Folsom, Jim Marshall had Johnny change into a blue turtleneck so he could snap some shots for the album artwork. He captured Johnny in the prison yard and inside Greystone Chapel. He also captured some shots of Carl Perkins and the band. Though he usually preferred to shoot in black and white, these rarely-seen color images are a stunning documentation of the day's events.

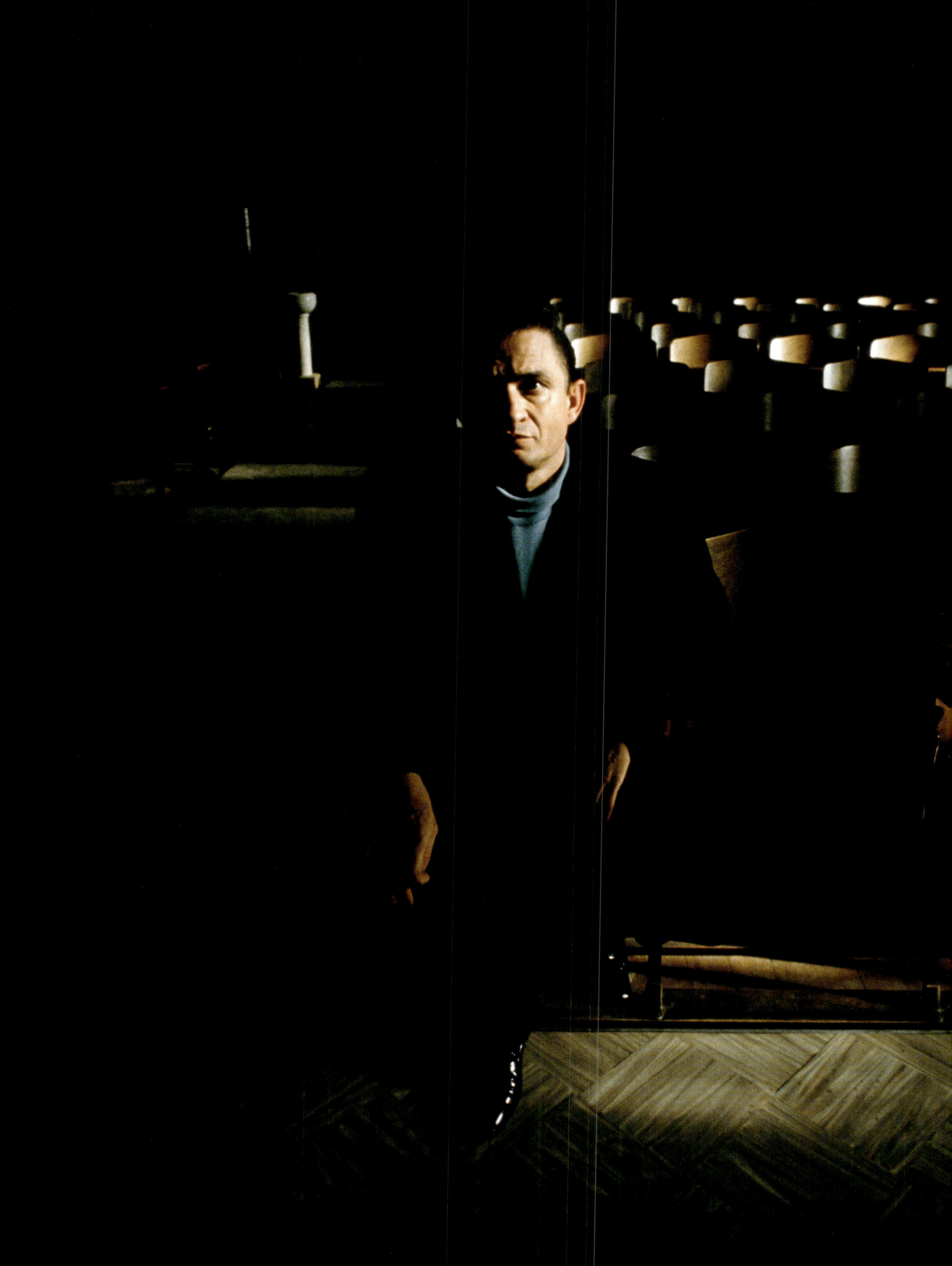

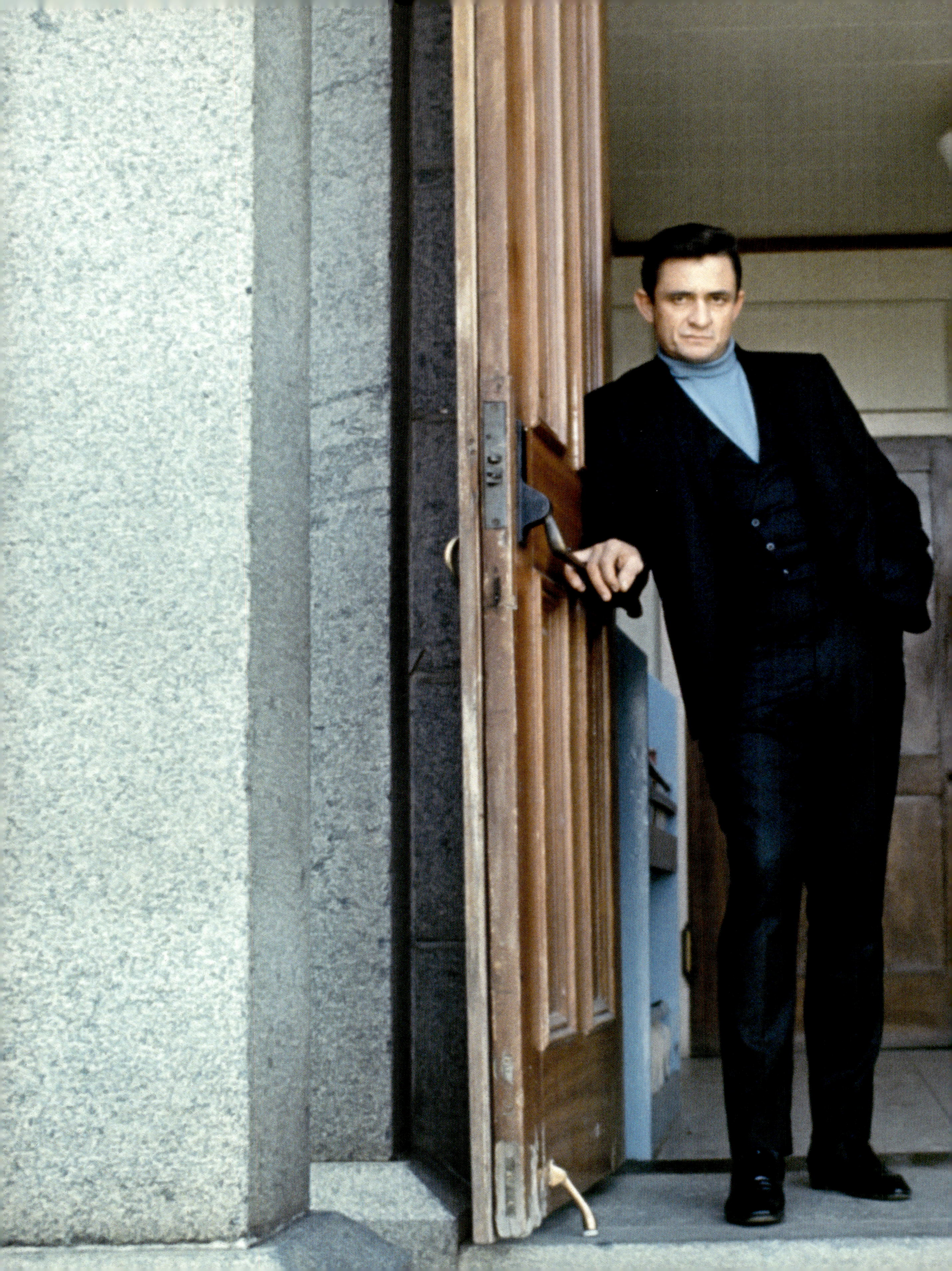

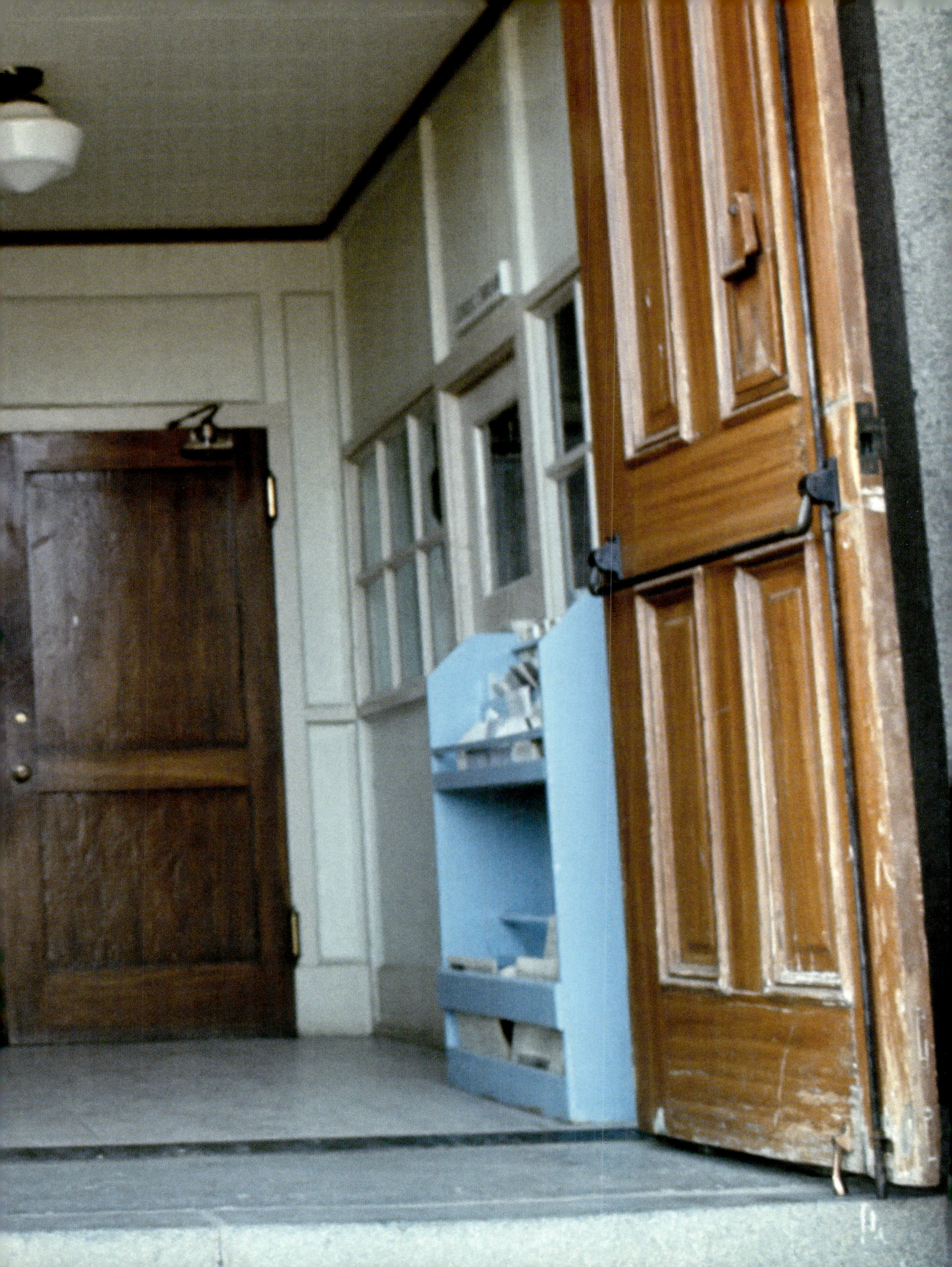

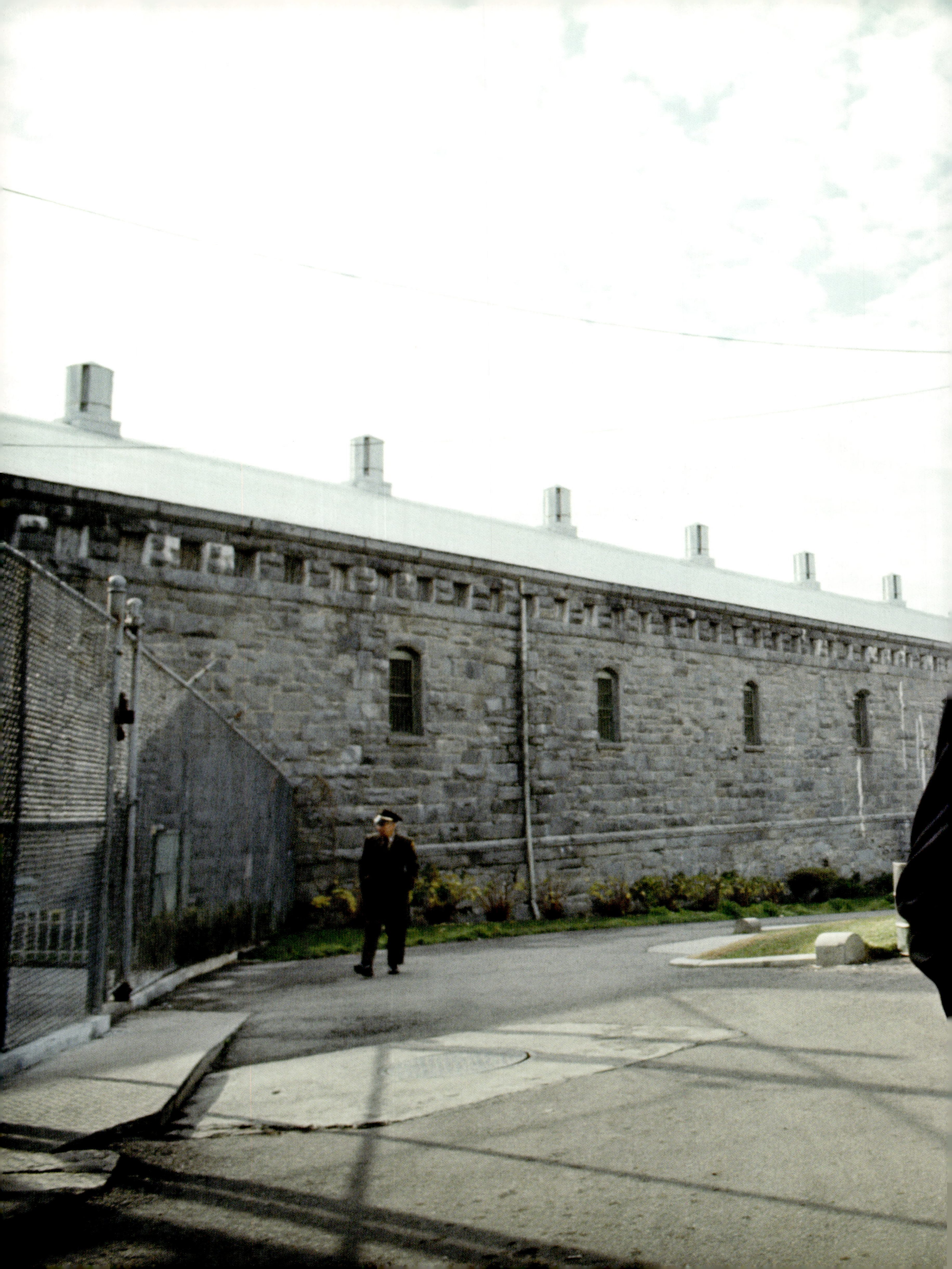

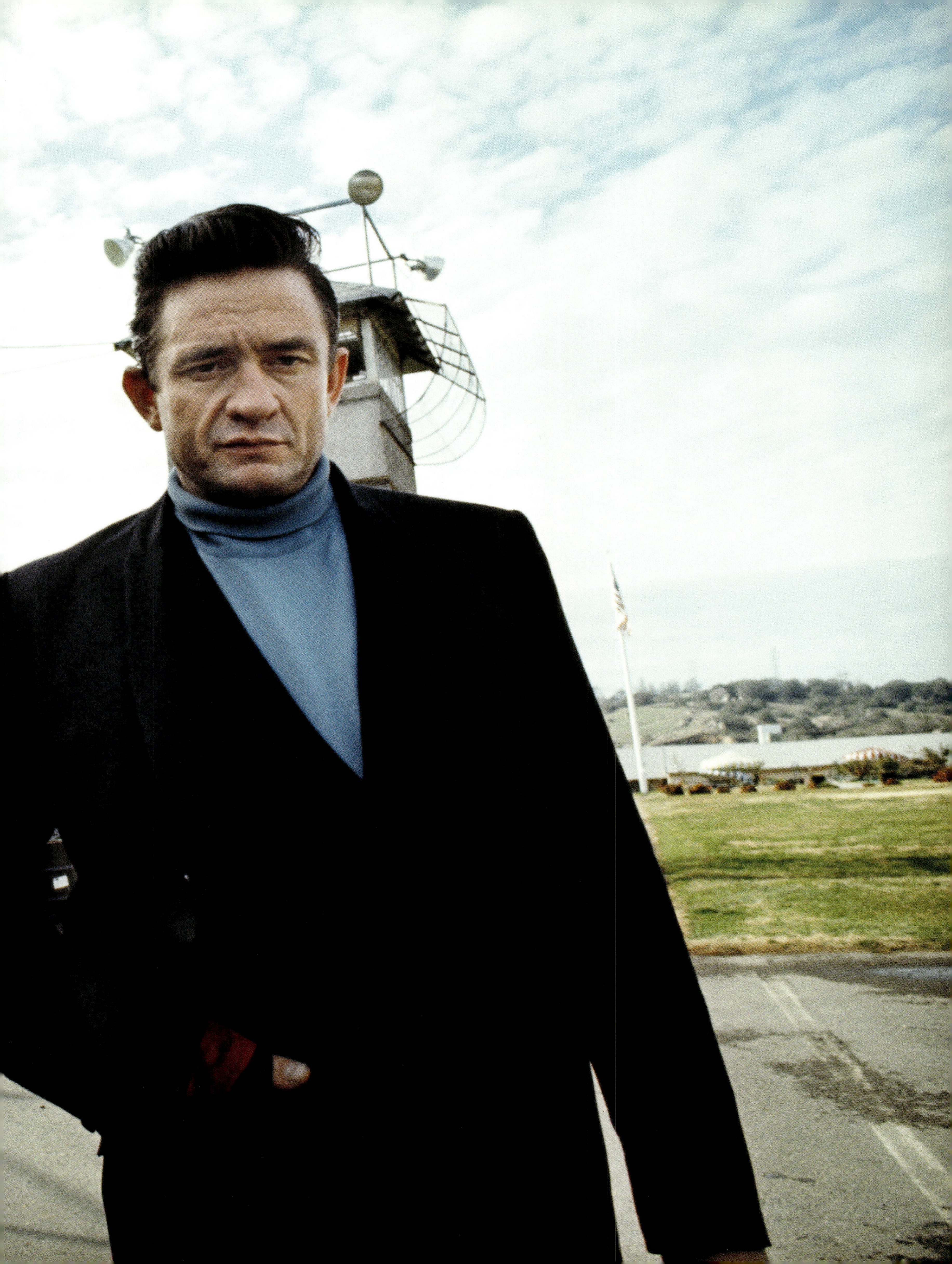

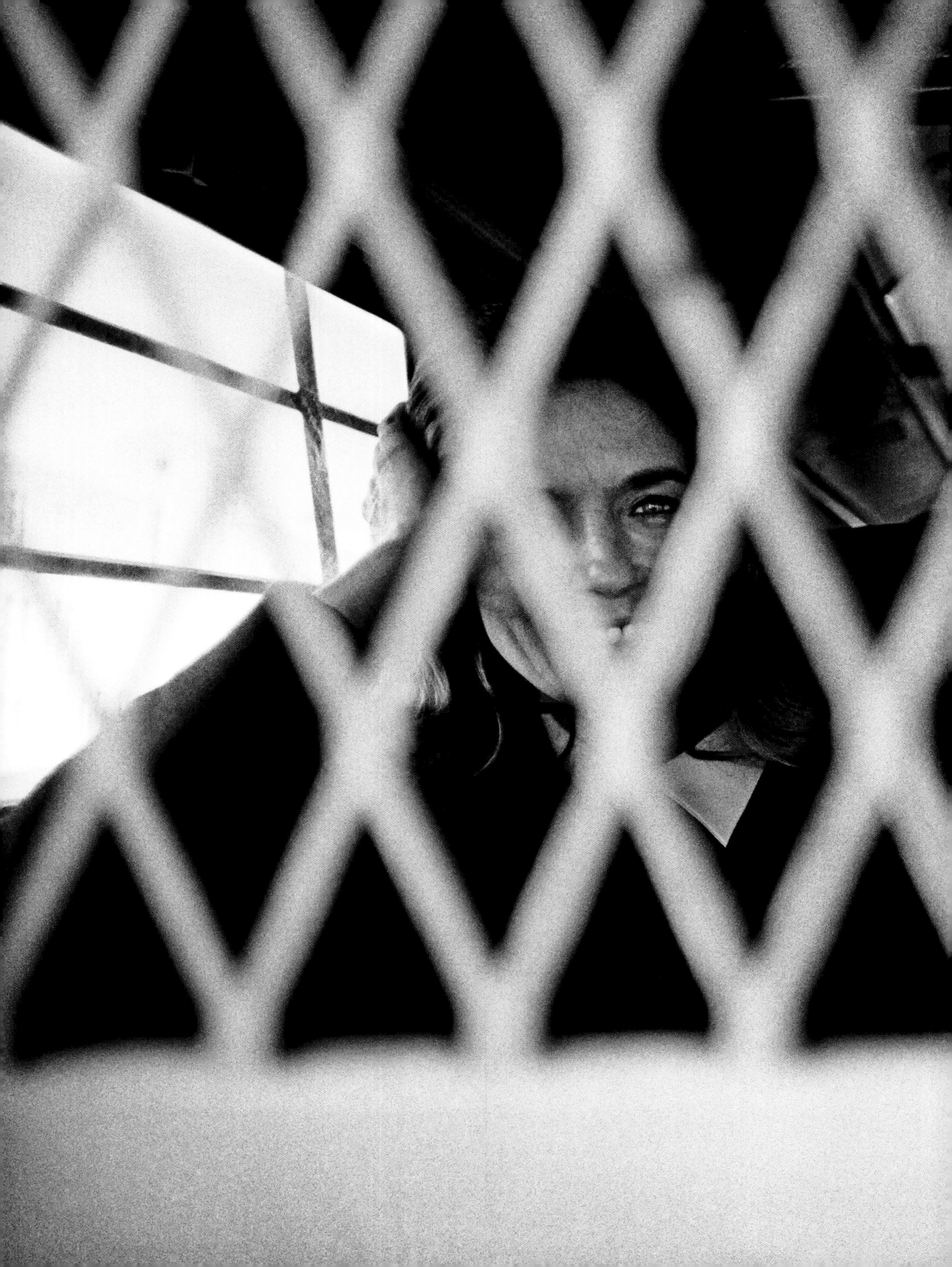

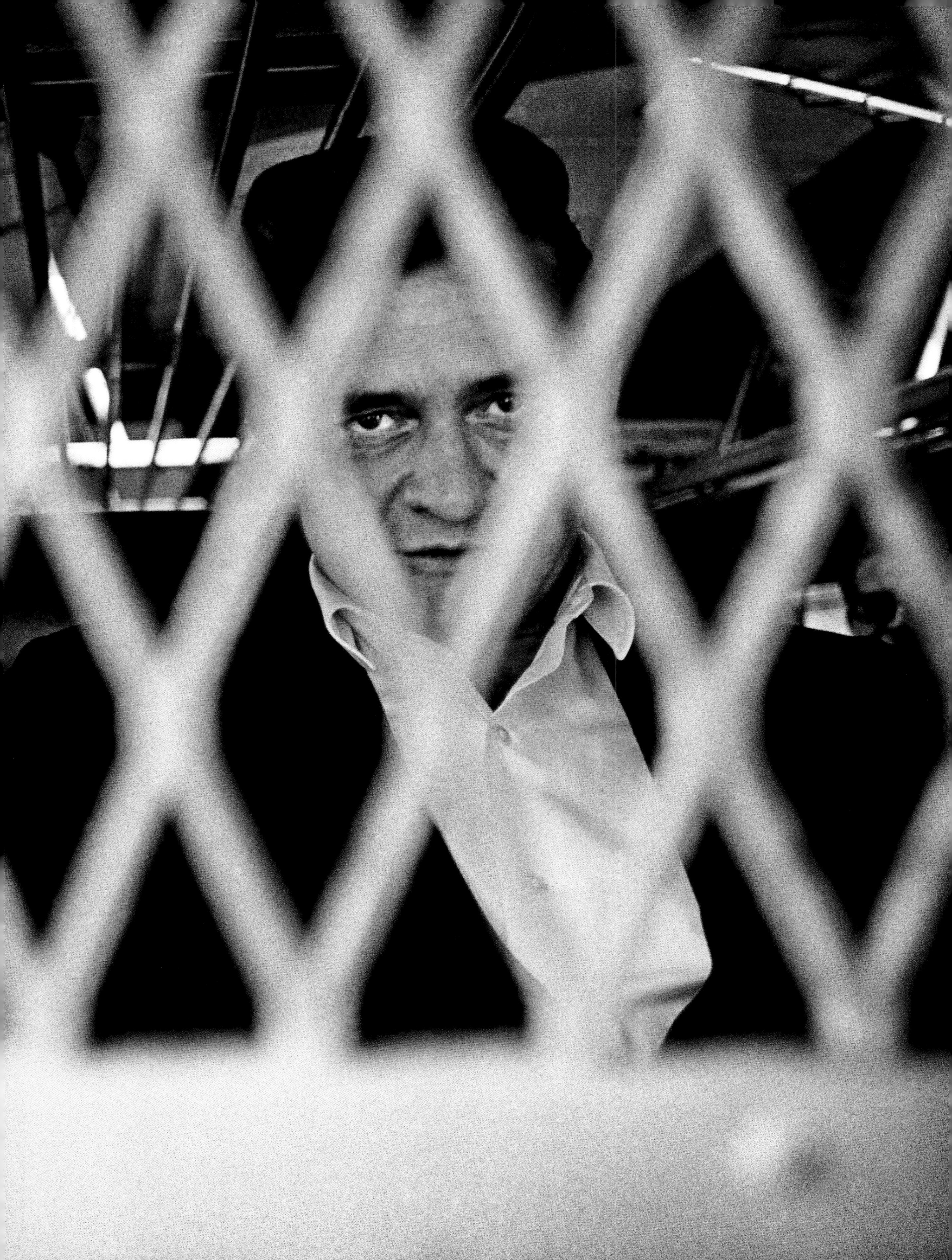

While Bob Johnston had Cash play two shows at Folsom—at 9:40 AM and 12:40 PM—all but two of the sixteen selections on the resulting album, *At Folsom Prison*, were chosen from the earlier show. The two he preserved from the second set, "Give My Love to Rose" and "I Got Stripes," had been omitted from the first performance. On the songs that were duplicated, the earlier performances were simply better. Cash put so much energy into the 9:40 show that you could hear his voice begin to wear in the second set.

The album, which Columbia released in May of 1968, perfectly captured the energy in the room. "If Johnny would've said, 'C'mon, let's crash out of here right now,' they'd have done it," Jim Marshall recalled in the 2008 documentary Johnny Cash at Folsom Prison. "They'd have followed him. He had that aura of being one of them."

At Folsom Prison entered both the pop and country album chart in June, eventually topping the country chart for four weeks and climbing as high as #13 on the pop rankings. The single, "Folsom Prison Blues," also reached #1 for four weeks on the country chart and cracked the pop Top 40. It was exactly the triumph Cash needed. "John was notorious for trying things that nobody else would even think of attempting," Marshall Grant recounted in his book, "but after the Folsom Prison album, he started taking things a little more seriously than he had in several years. He started looking for better songs and doing better recording sessions. Everything seemed to be getting a little better, and while John wasn't completely straight, he was maintaining control, and that was good enough for us at the time."

"That's where things really got started for me again," Johnny admitted in a 1973 *Rolling Stone* interview. His career was back on track, his creative juices were flowing once again, the renewed attention ultimately earned him an ABC-TV variety show, and the woman he loved was by his side for good. Johnny and June married less than two months after the Folsom appearance. The following year he won two more Grammy awards: Best Male Country Vocal Performance for "Folsom Prison Blues" and Best Album Notes for *Johnny Cash at Folsom Prison*. Over time the album has only grown in stature and historical importance. It's in the Library of Congress' National Recording Registry and is listed among *Rolling Stone*'s "500 Greatest Albums of All Time."

"Folsom probably solidified the image of my dad as a rebel who was outside the realm of polite society," Rosanne Cash explained to Michael Streissguth in 2008. "He had done it before by getting arrested and by the drug use and trashing hotel rooms and all of the behavior that went along with rebellion. Then he kind of transformed it into art. And that's when it really worked. It wasn't hurting anybody, and it was good."

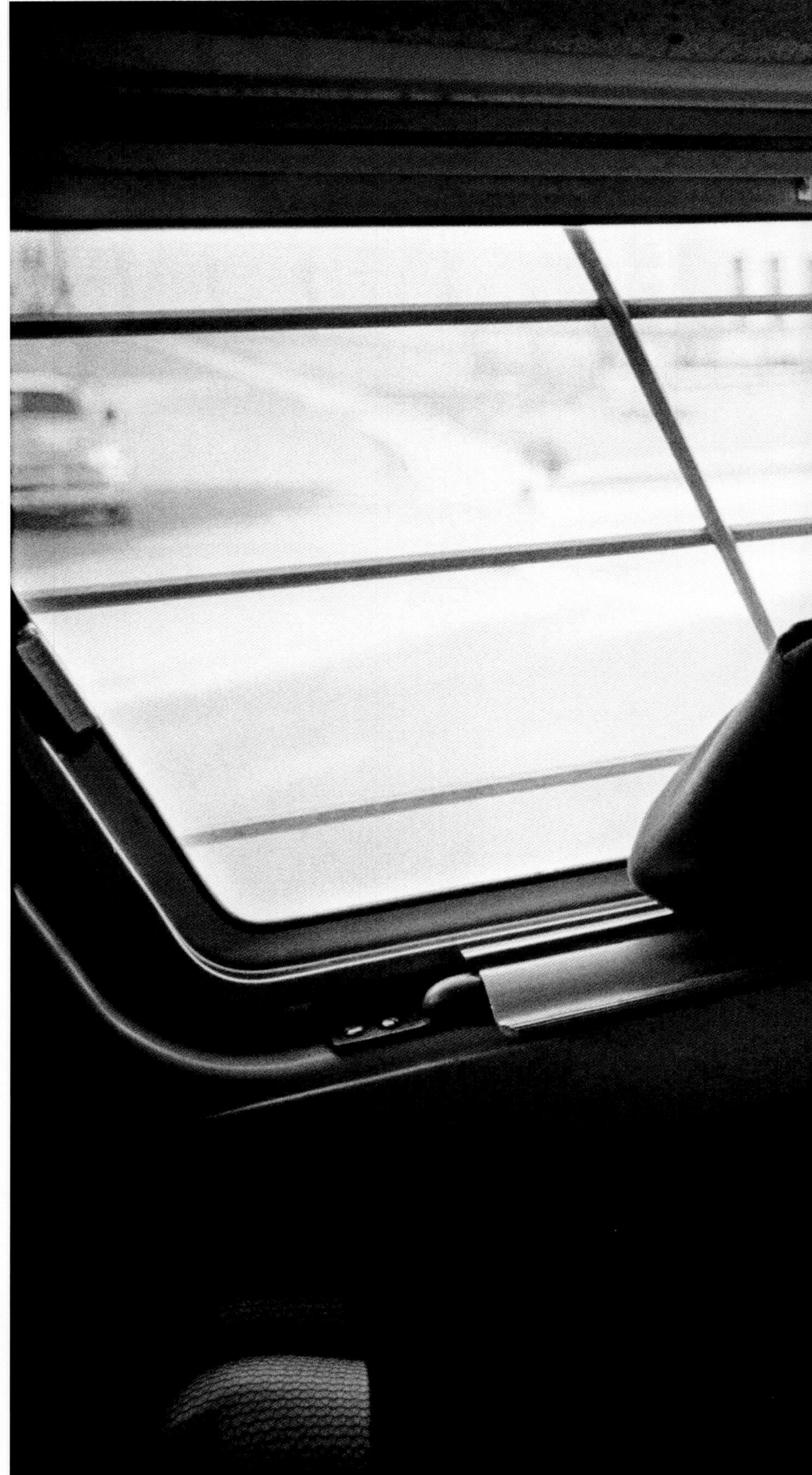

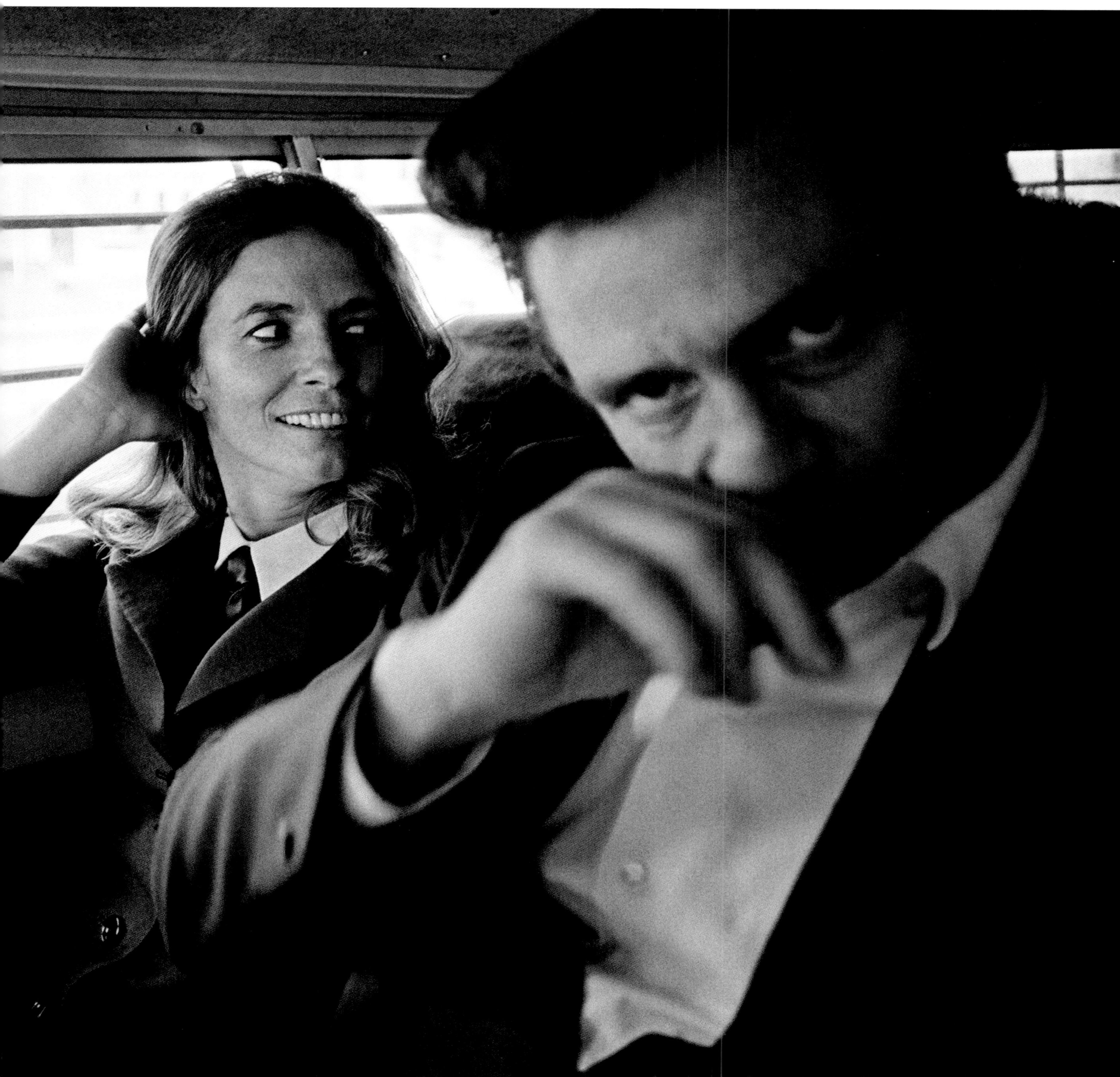

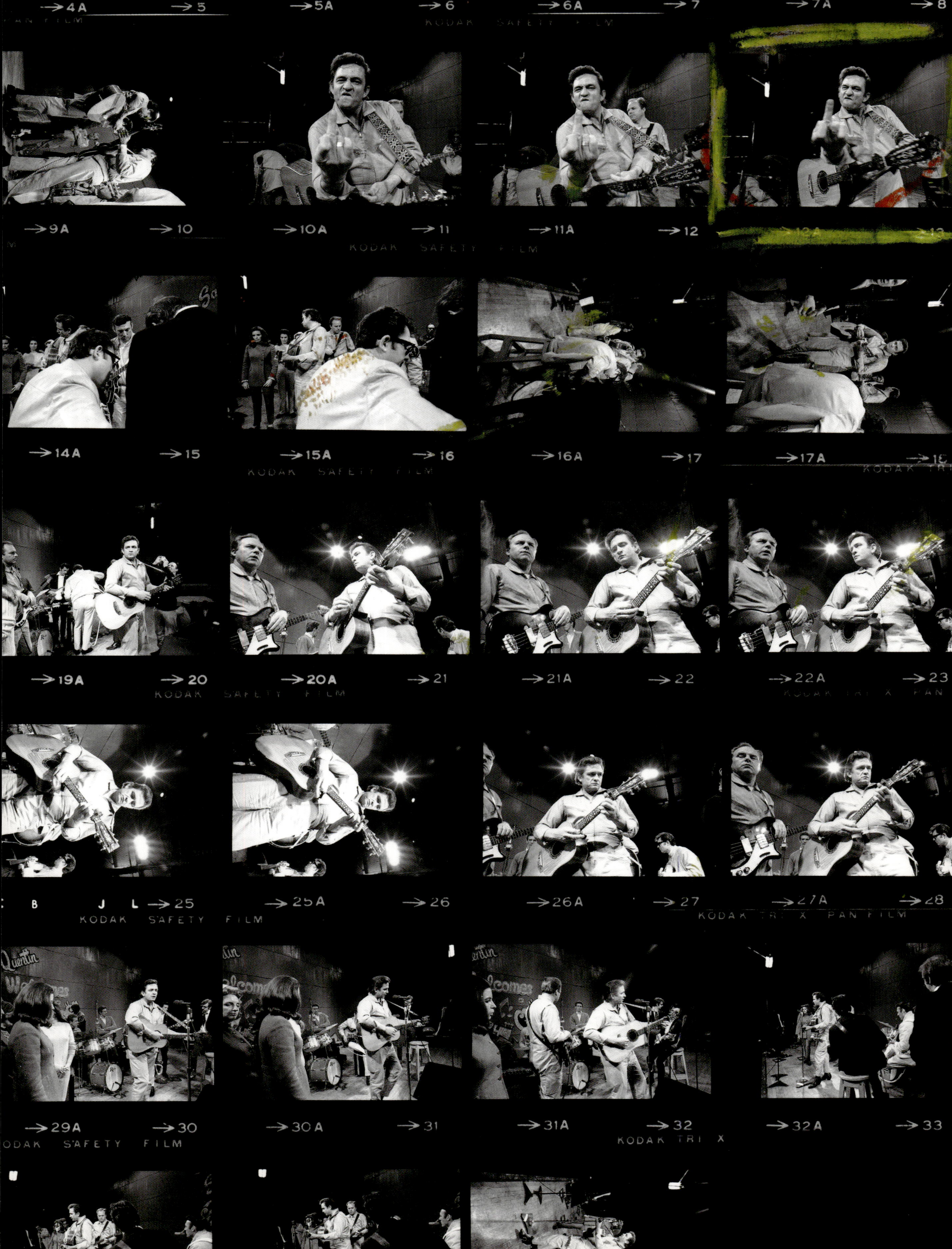

AT SAN QUENTIN

FRIDAY, FEBRUARY 24, 1969

"I think the prisoners really appreciated that Cash was there for them, and I really believe that John really believed that he was doing something right. He wanted to make a difference in these guys' lives. I really believe that a lot."
Jim Marshall

"John had these men in suspense, they were mesmerized, hypnotized and spellbound and so were we. 'San Quentin' was their song and Johnny Cash was theirs, and they decided not to riot that day. He held them by a thread, and we were saved by that thread."
June Carter Cash

"In the 13 months between the Folsom and San Quentin concerts, a lot had changed for Johnny Cash," Sylvie Simmons wrote in the liner notes for the album's deluxe Legacy Edition. "He would find God, kick his amphetamine habit, and finally get June Carter to agree to marry him (doubtless something to do with finding God and kicking amphetamines)." Not only was his personal life in order, but Johnny Cash was riding a pop culture wave. He was beloved by virtually every record-buying demographic and decided he wanted to repeat the experience of recording a prison album. One would think the novelty might have worn off with the public, but *At San Quentin* was even more commercially successful than its predecessor.

As with the Folsom shows, Bob Johnston produced and Cash insisted that Jim Marshall serve as the official photographer. They were also joined by a Granada Television film crew from the UK that captured the event for a documentary produced and directed by Michael Darlow.

Though Cash had gotten back on track over the course of the previous year, he went into the San Quentin show missing a key member of his band. One of the original Tennessee Two, Luther Perkins, had been performing with Cash since the very beginning. In August of 1968 he died in a house fire after falling asleep smoking a cigarette. While Cash still had Carl Perkins, who was not related to Luther, he had undeniably lost a key component of his sound.

In September Johnny played a concert in Fayetteville, Arkansas. Carl Perkins' flight was delayed and he was unable to make the show. Guitarist Bob Wootton, who was in the audience, asked if he could sit in. Cash, with no other options, decided to give him a shot. Wootton turned out to be a Luther Perkins disciple who could replicate his hero's parts flawlessly. Cash was dumbfounded and, within days, asked Bob to join the Tennessee Three.

With Bob Wootton in Luther's spot, the Johnny Cash show lineup that performed at San Quentin was similar to the lineup at Folsom. Carl Perkins was there. So were The Statler Brothers and June Carter,

who was now June Carter Cash. Unlike Folsom, June's singing family came along. Mother Maybelle Carter and the Carter Sisters—Helen, June, and Anita—were the next incarnation of the Original Carter Family who were integral to defining country music as a genre and were revered by Johnny.

Though June had been at Folsom, San Quentin was harder and tougher. It housed the state's death row and had a palpable sense of danger. "If you're a woman visiting a prison, you have crazy ideas," June reflected more than 30 years later. "San Quentin is a maximum security prison. Some men are here for armed robbery, rape, pedophilia, arson, murder. And there were a few innocent men. It felt like a dream. 'Oh Lord,' I cried. For I could still see all the men jumping on my bones, and my sisters' bones, too. They were beautiful girls."

As with the Folsom concert Cash took extra time to practice with the band before the show. This time it was on the same stage where they would play later that evening. Jim Marshall captured candid moments from the rehearsal that are as compelling as the actual performance: Johnny walking everyone through the setlist while wearing a prison jumpsuit; Helen Carter covering her head with a scarf to obscure the curlers in her hair that she wore to prepare for the upcoming evening show; the musicians sitting around casually, but concentrating intently. The immediacy of the images suggests that Marshall and his camera were virtually part of the band.

Unlike Folsom, the San Quentin concert was a single show. That night's concert began with Carl Perkins' "Blue Suede Shoes," followed by The Statler Brothers performing "Flowers on the Wall." Mother Maybelle and the girls took the stage for a couple of songs before Cash came out and performed seven selections, including a medley of "The Long Black Veil" and "Give My Love to Rose." The rest of the show featured all the performers interspersed, taking turns in various configurations.

Midway through the show Cash relaxed with a series of songs that

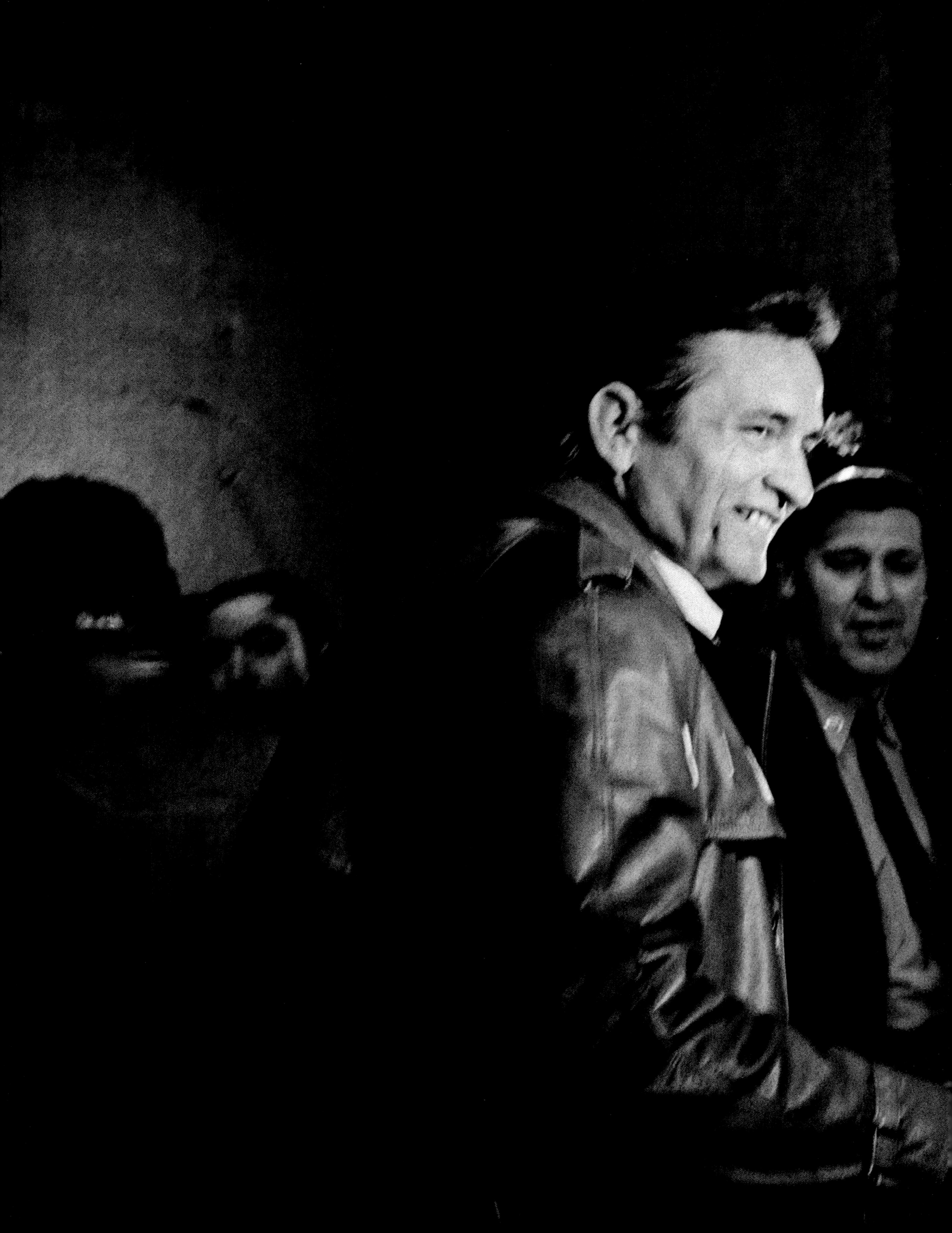

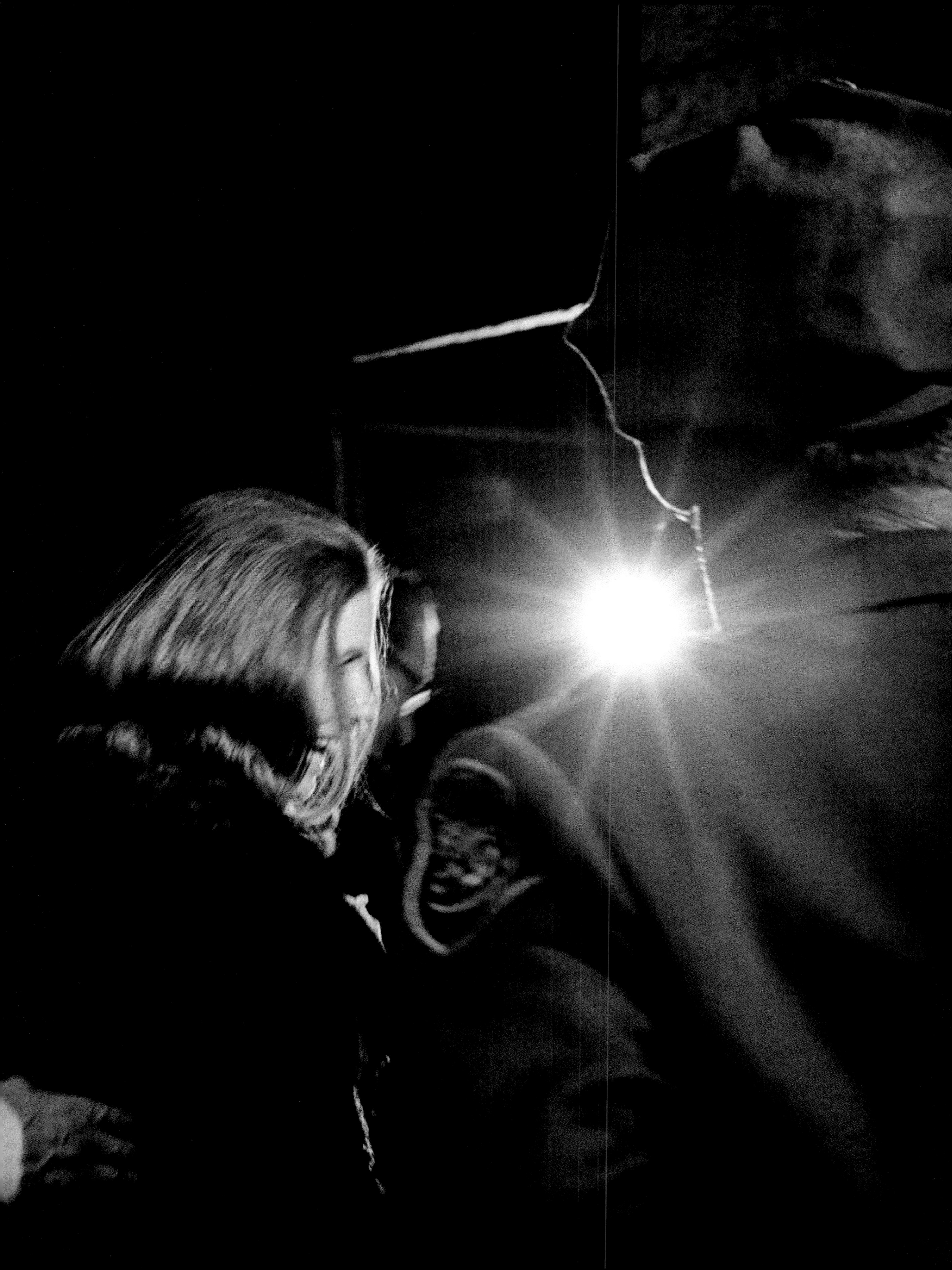

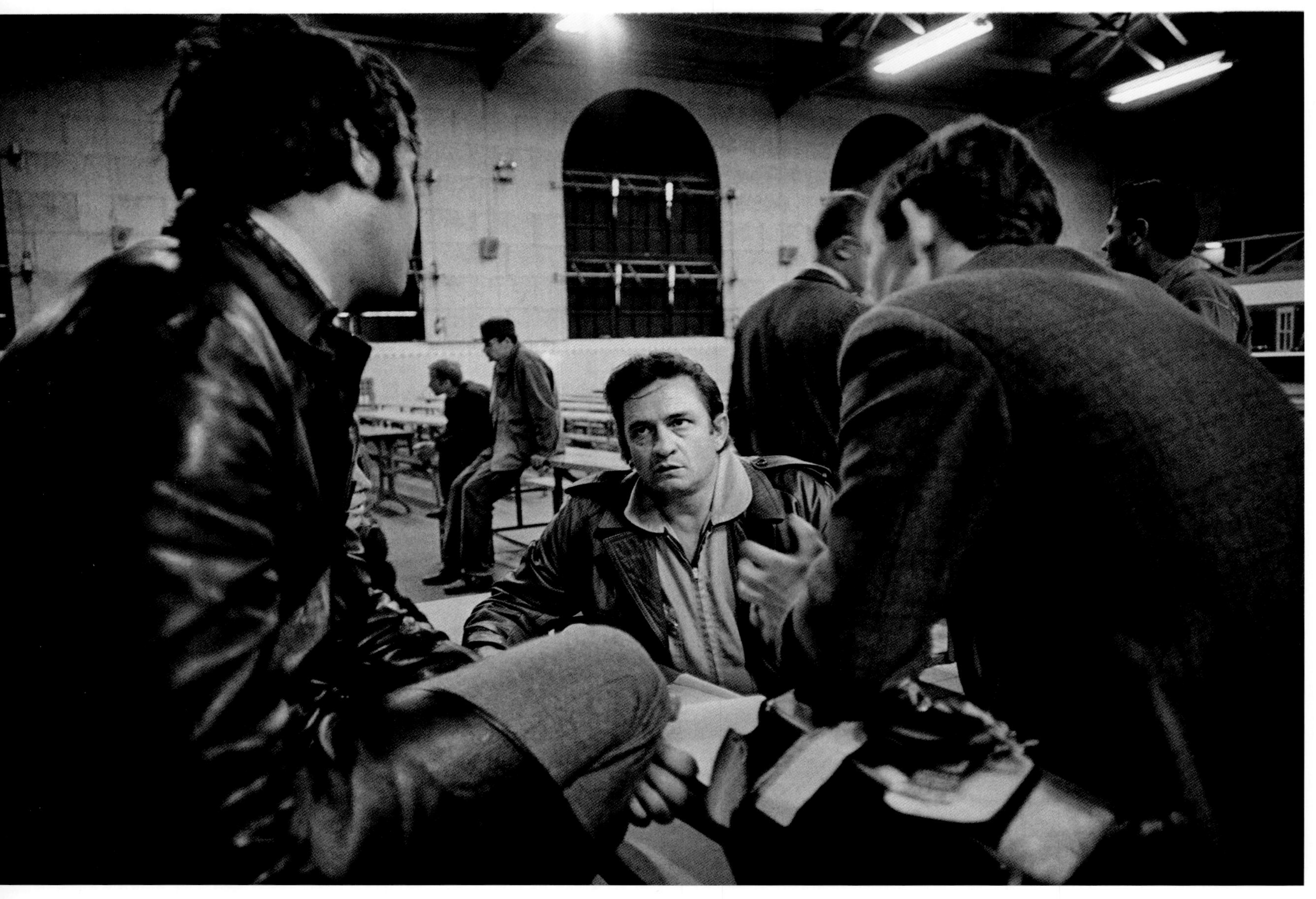

were simply too new to be fully polished. One of them that wasn't included on the original album release was "I Don't Know Where I'm Bound," which echoed Cash's Glen Sherley moment from the previous year. "There's a young man here at San Quentin tonight that wrote a song that I just saw written down on paper for the first time yesterday," he told the audience. "I liked the lyrics so much I started singing my own tune to it. ... Let's just try a little bit of it right here." The song originated with inmate Terry Cuddy, who had somehow gotten the sheet music to Cash the previous day.

Johnny followed it up with two brand new originals, "Starkville City Jail" and "San Quentin." He had written both songs within a day or two of the show. The latter included the line, "San Quentin may you rot and burn in hell." The prisoners loved it so much they called for an encore. Bob Johnston included both versions on the final album. "When he did it again, they were all up on the table," Johnston recalled in a radio interview. "I was looking around and I thought, 'Where's the most guards?' And they were over there by the door so I went over there by them because if anything happened, I wanted to be one of the first out!"

As far as off-the-cuff moments from the San Quentin show, however, none tops "A Boy Named Sue." Songwriter Shel Silverstein had given the song to Johnny, who had the lyrics in a notebook in his briefcase. He asked someone to retrieve it from backstage midway through the show. The band had no idea what he was doing and simply improvised the instrumental backing as Cash led the way. "It was the first time any of us had ever heard it," Marshall Grant recounted. "It was so funny, we laughed all the way through it and weren't very focused on what we were playing—and then we remembered they were recording the show! We kept right on going, and the song went over so well that the inmates jumped to their feet and hollered and screamed and laughed and cut up. And so did we."

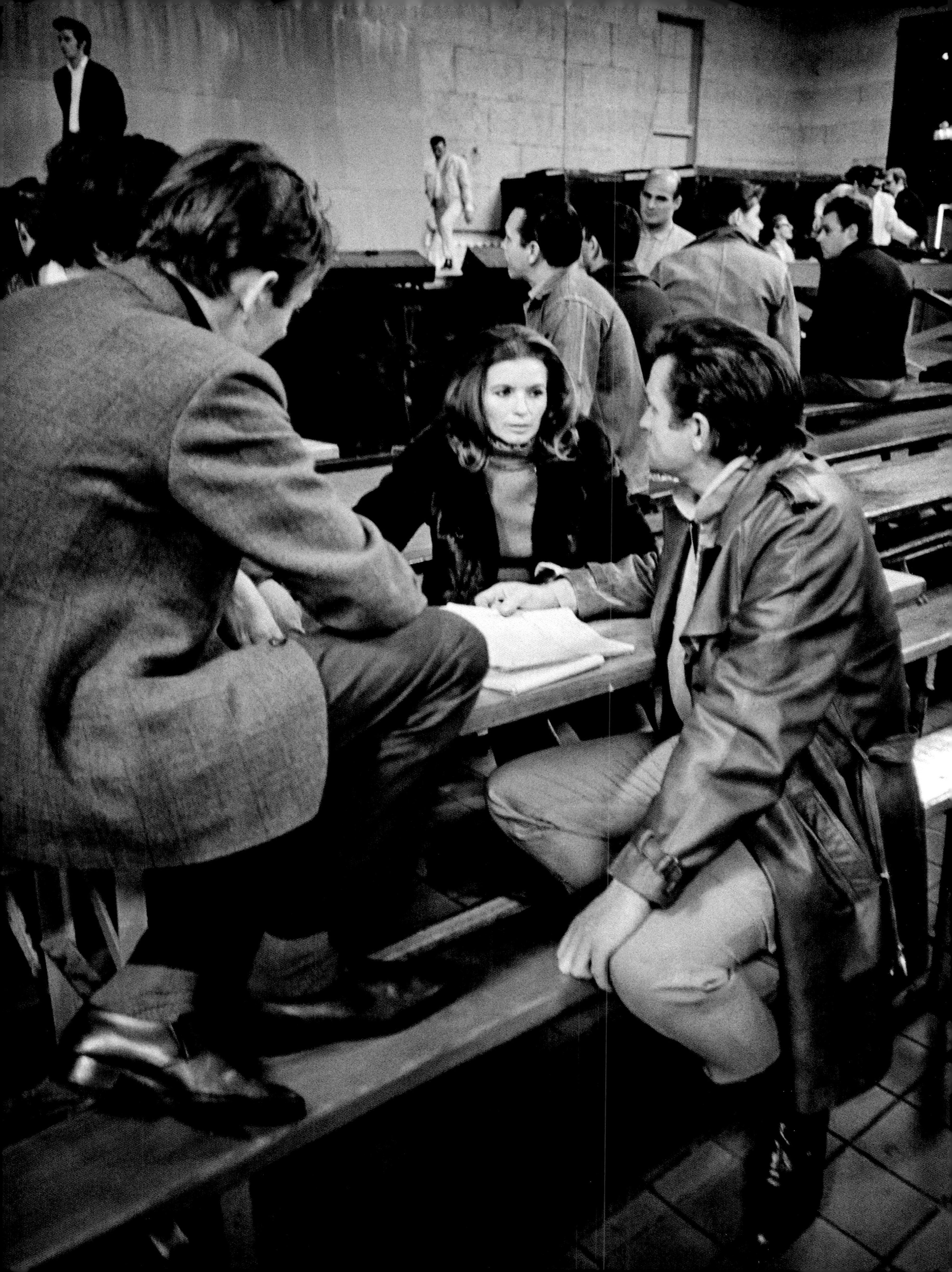

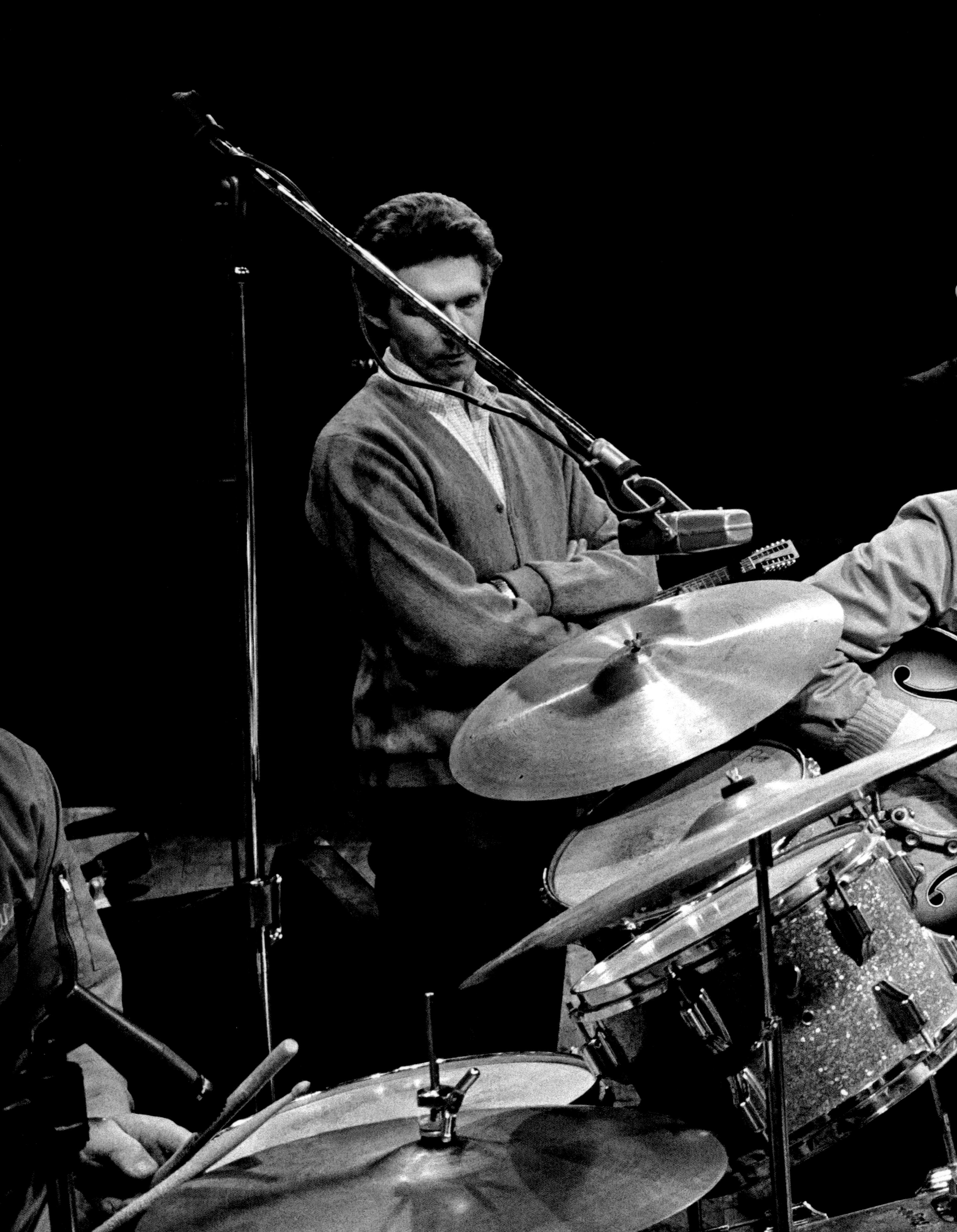

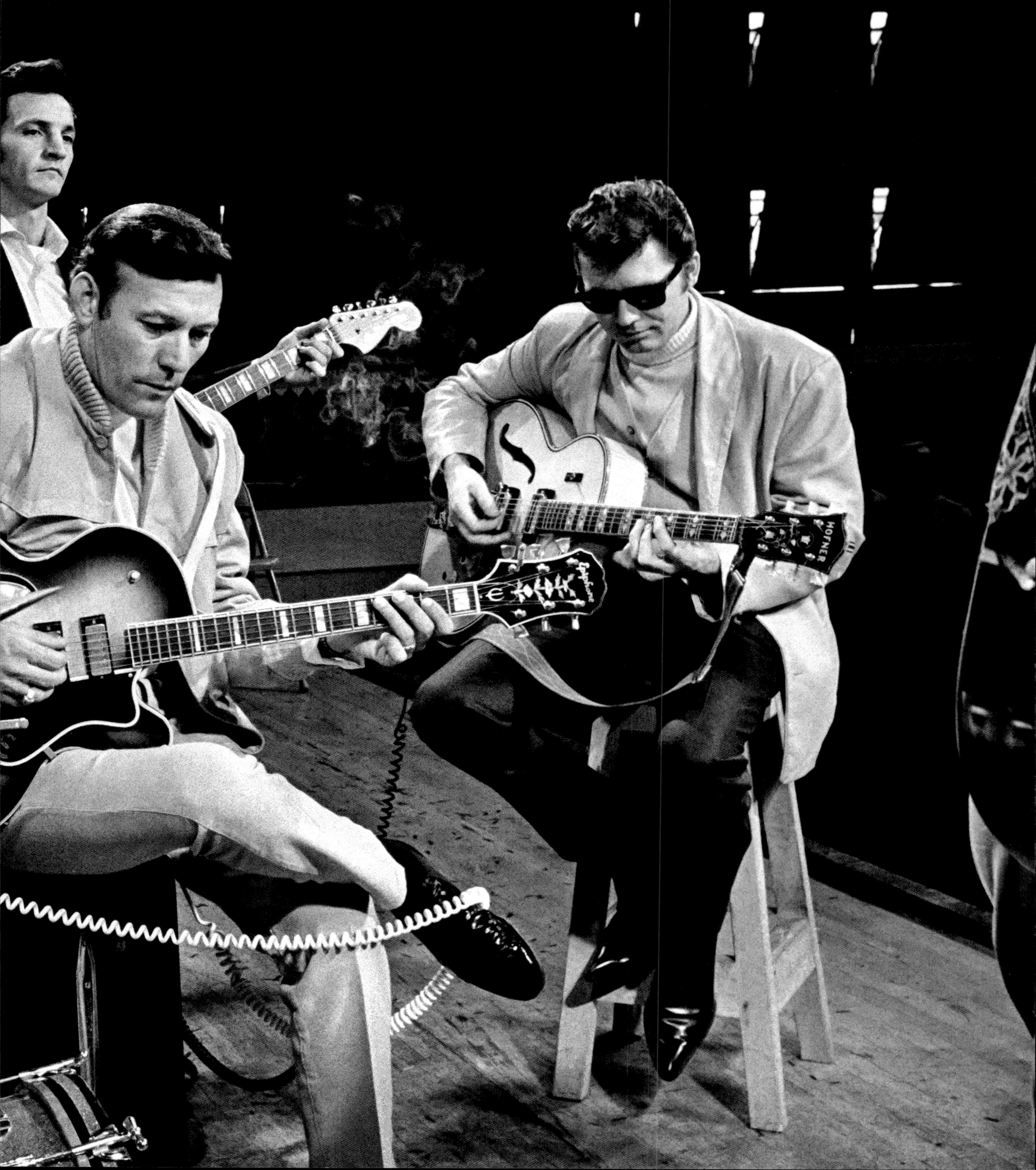

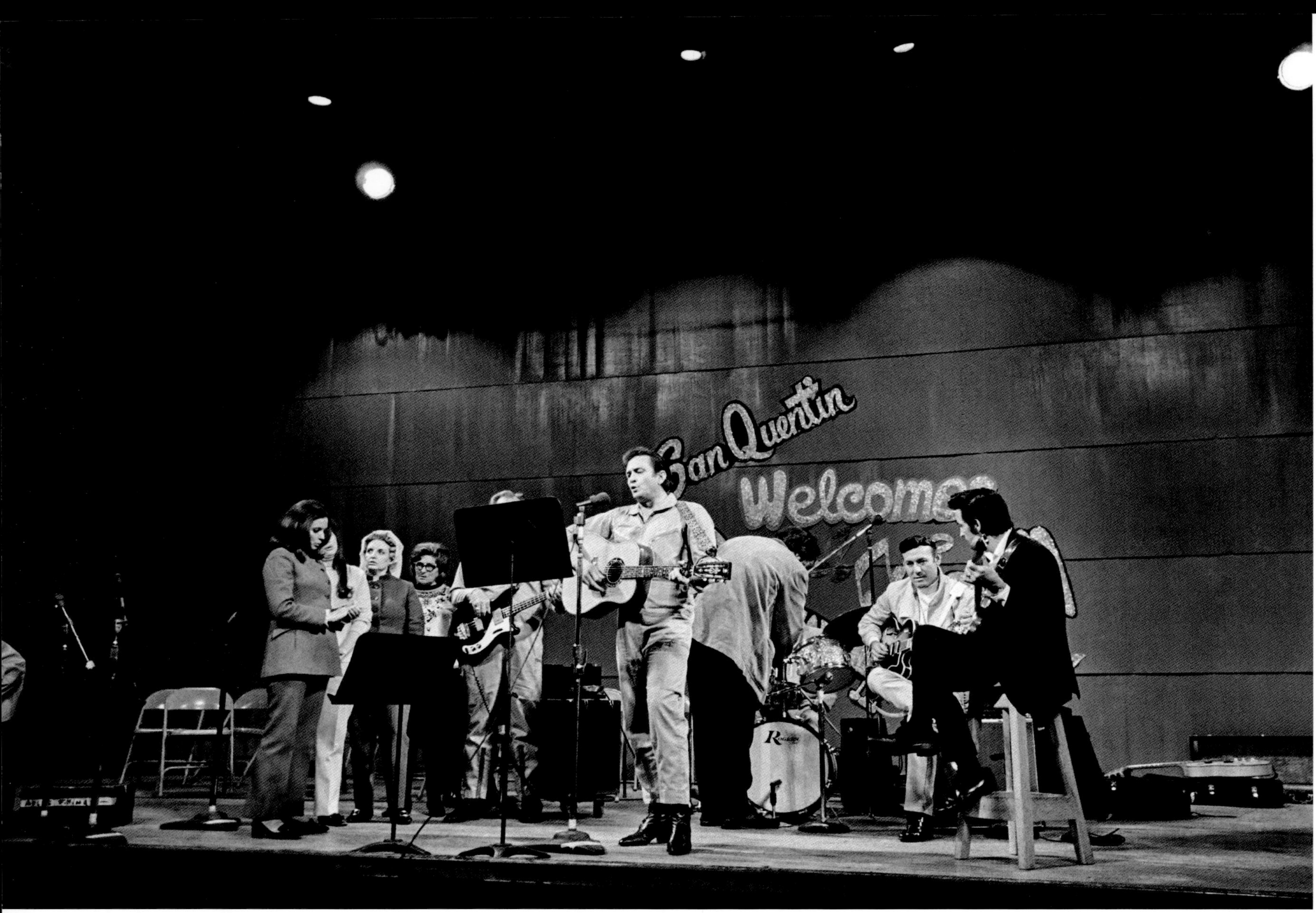

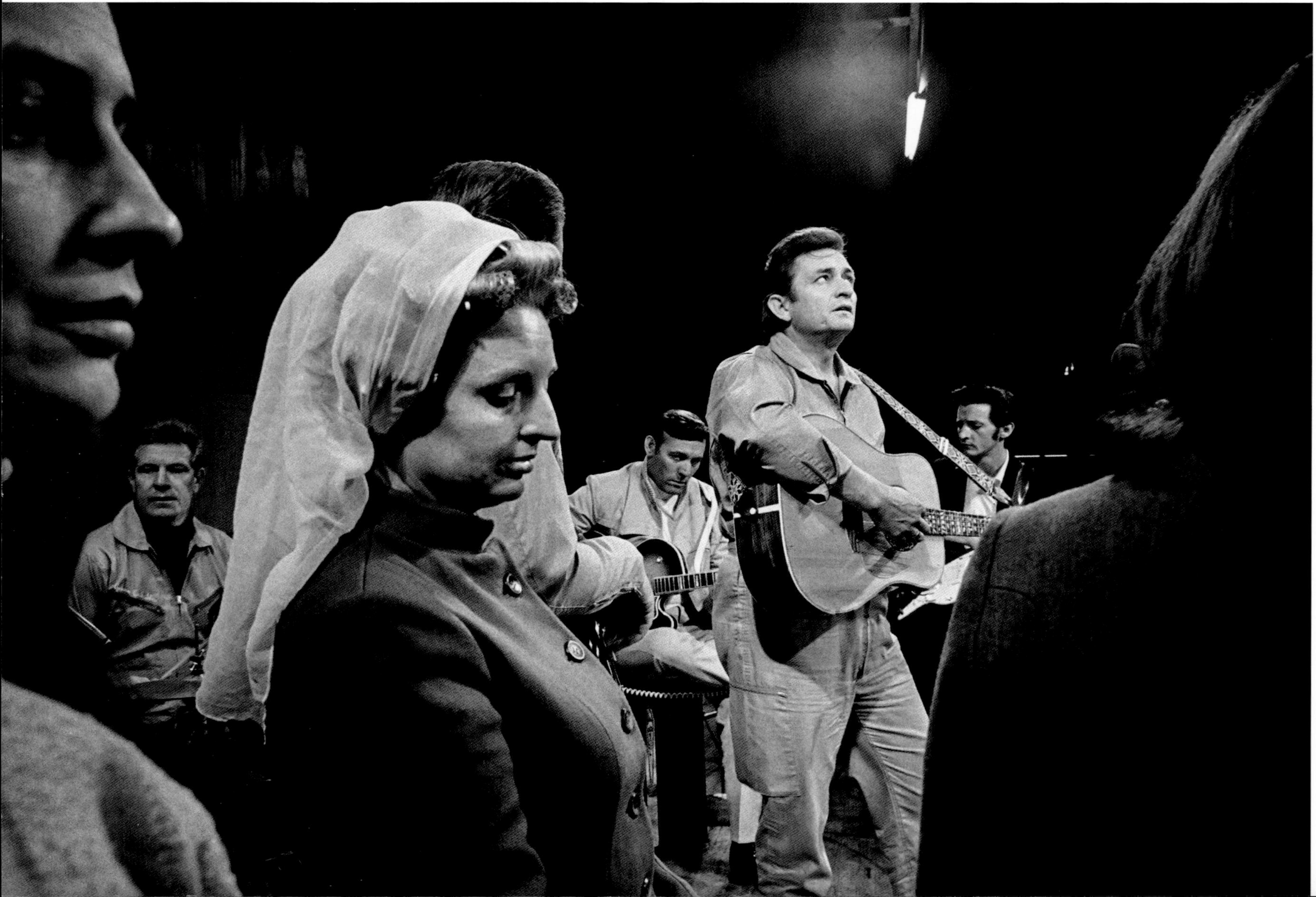

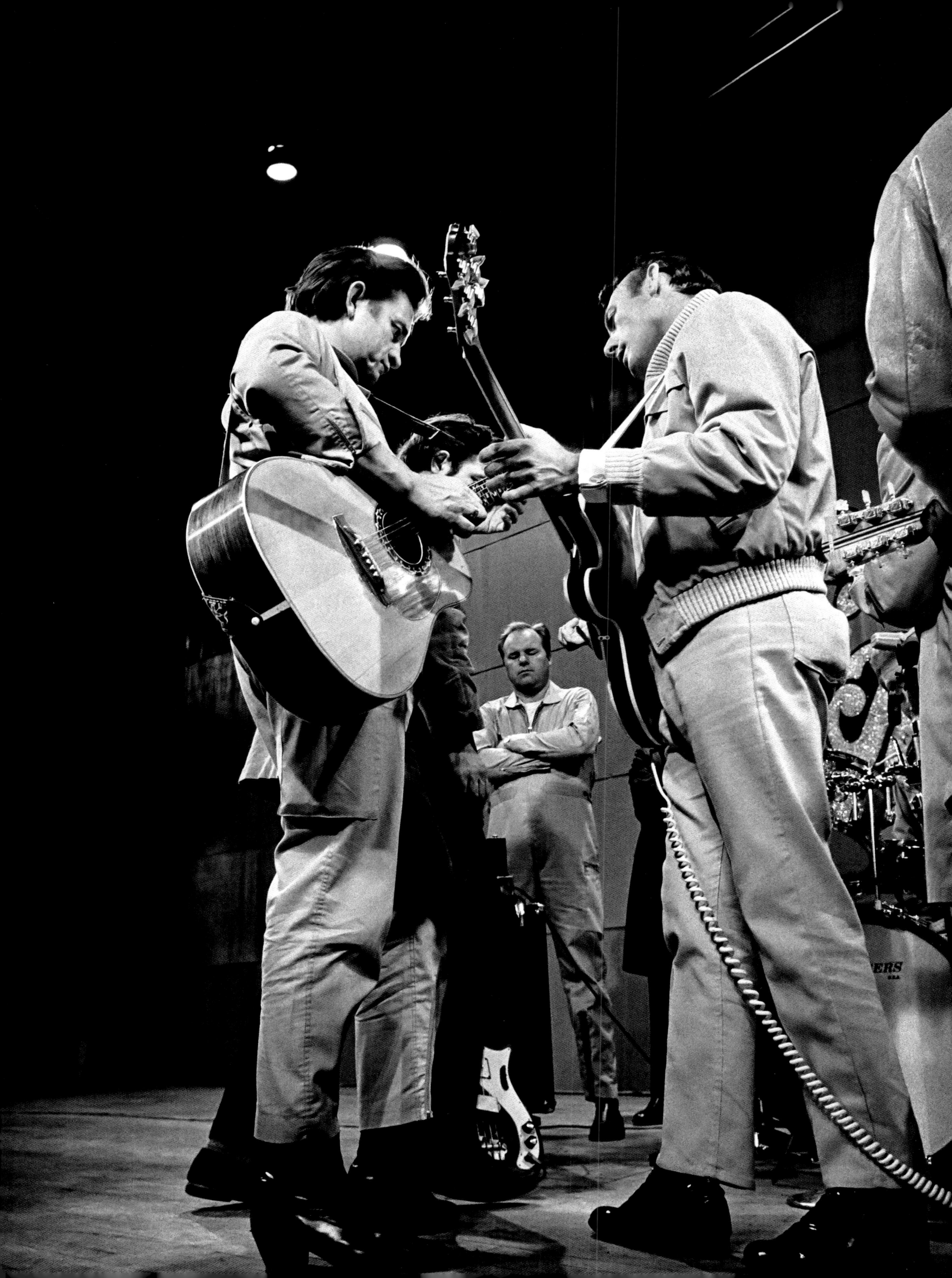

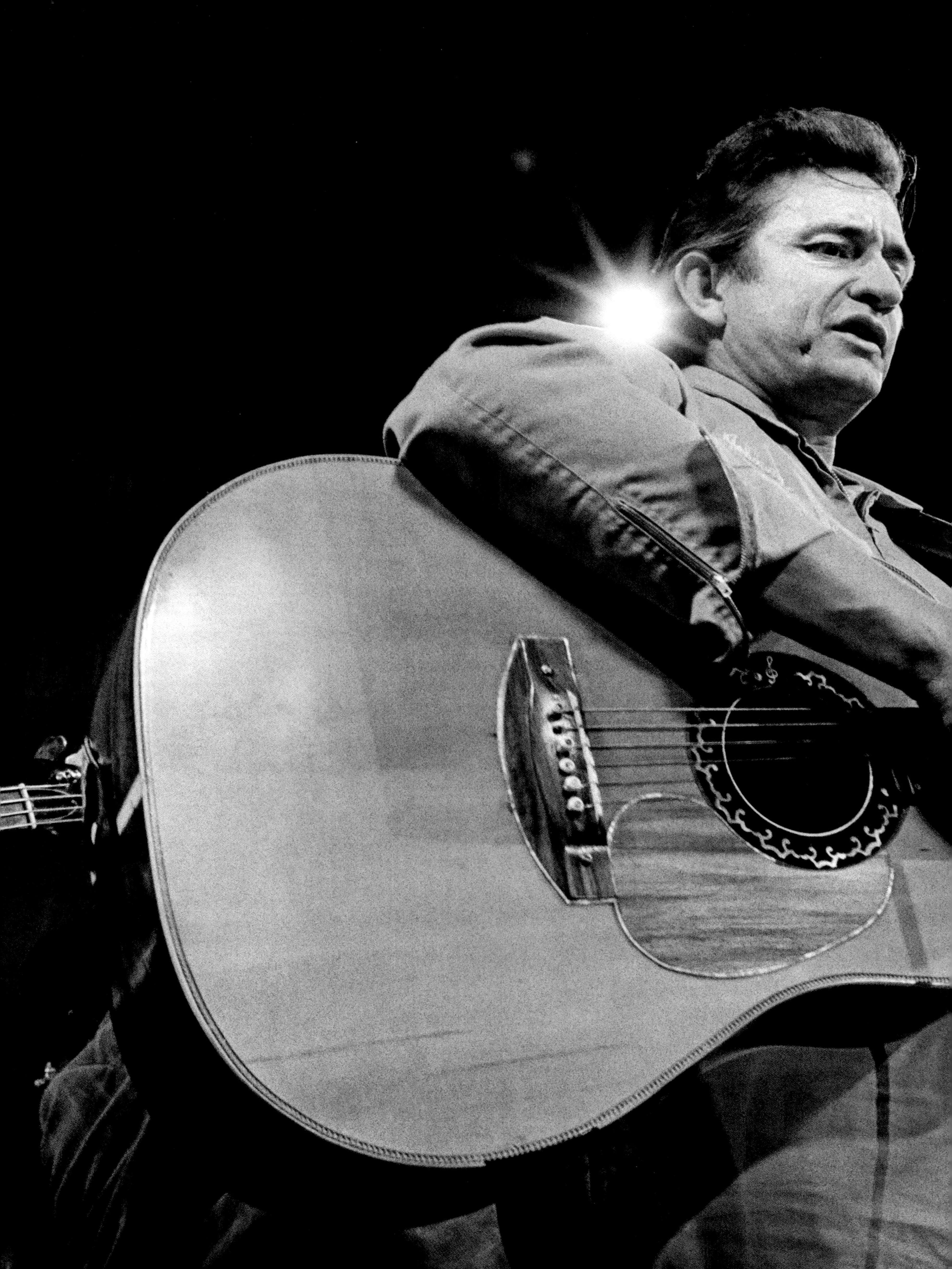

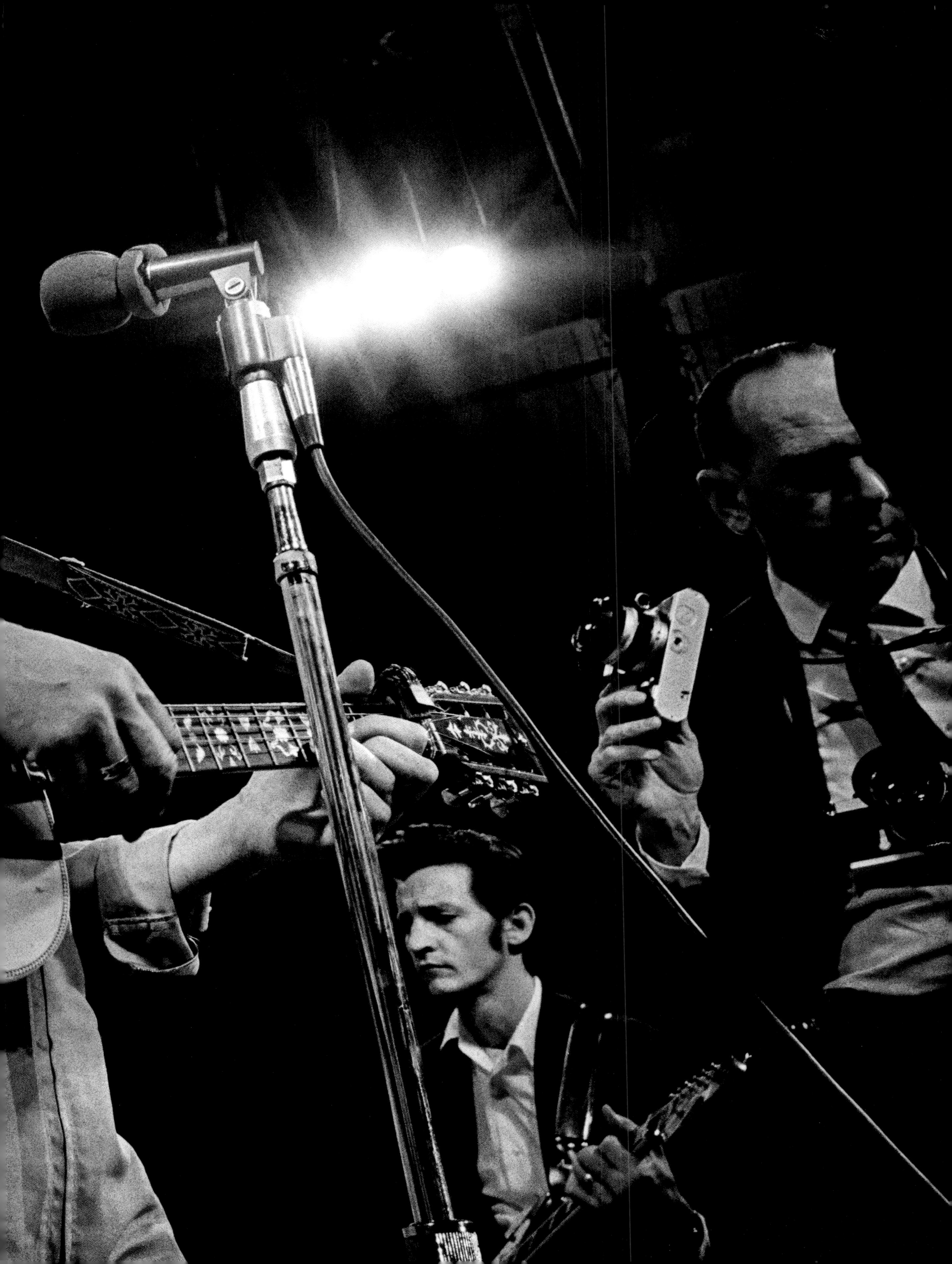

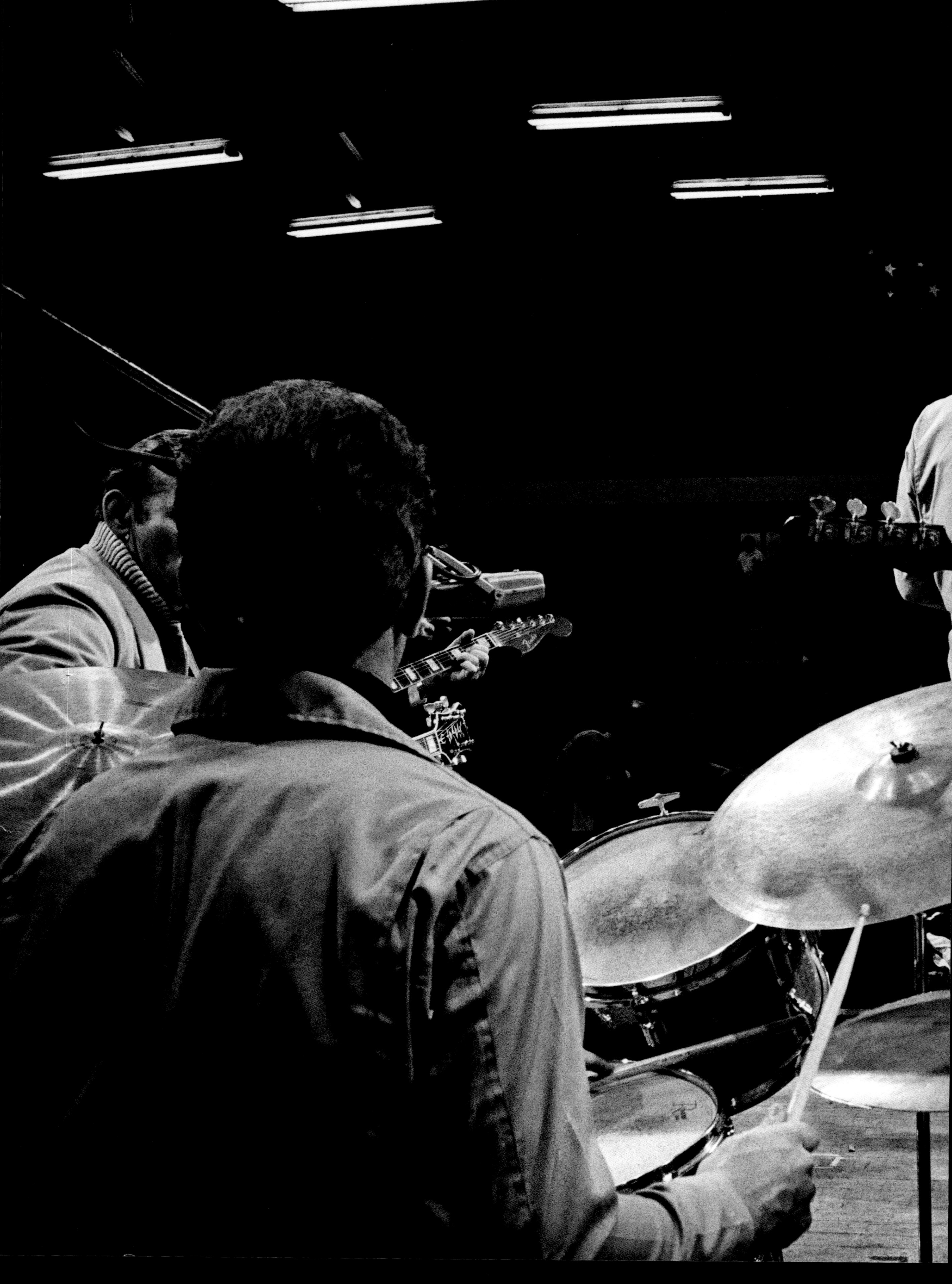

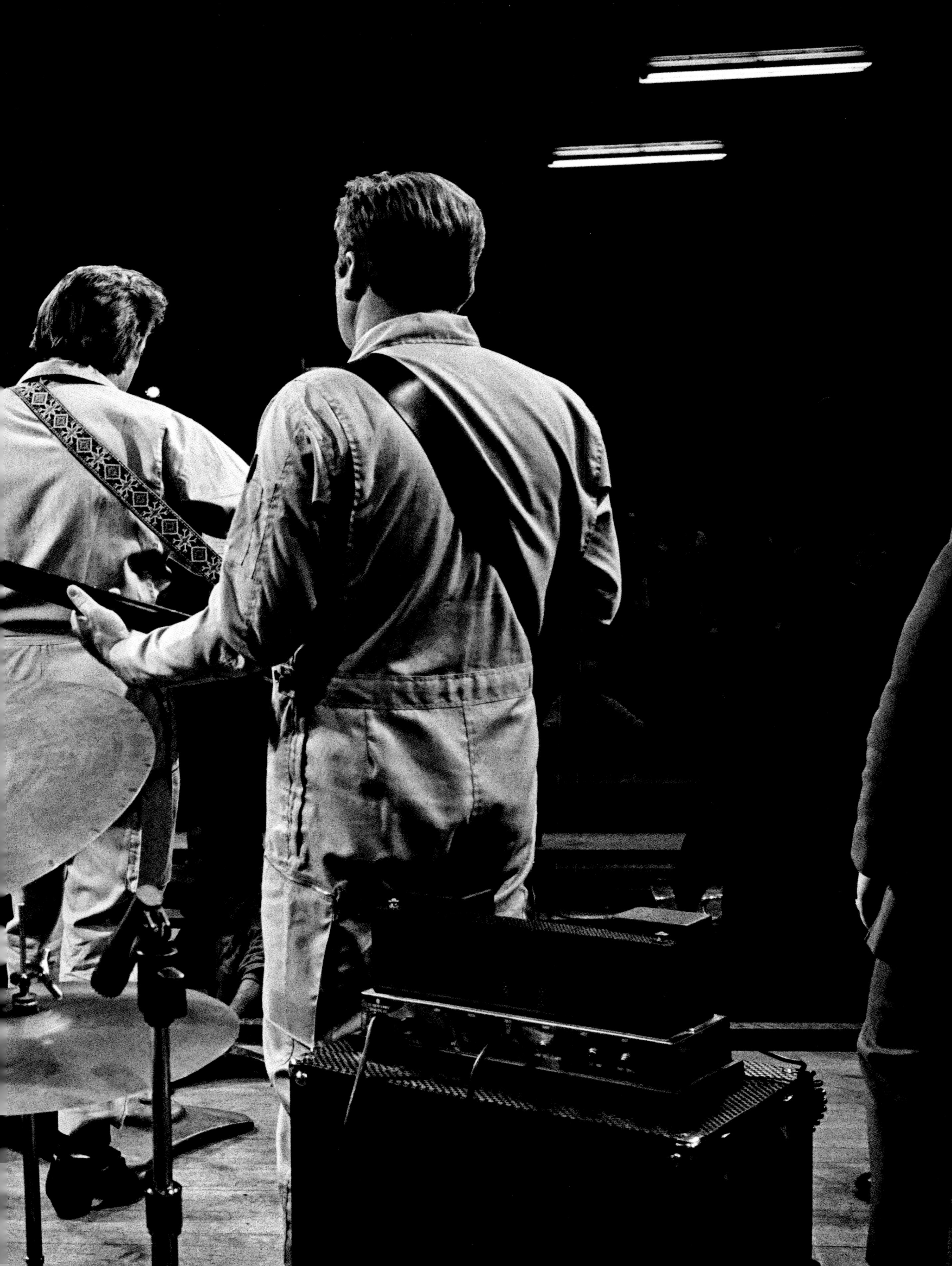

"THE FINGER"

Perhaps the most iconic photo Jim Marshall ever snapped—if not the most iconic photo ever taken of a musician—is Johnny Cash defiantly flipping the bird at San Quentin. The image was certainly too edgy for Columbia Records to include on a country artist's album jacket in 1969, so the photo was rarely seen for many years.

While Cash was a country icon in the 1970s, his popularity eventually waned. Columbia Records dropped him from the roster in the mid-1980s. He moved to the Mercury label, but got little attention. He didn't score any hits and eventually lost that deal in the early 1990s. The country music establishment was no longer interested in Johnny Cash.

In a move that made little obvious sense on the surface, Rick Rubin—best known for his work with Run-D.M.C., The Beastie Boys and Slayer—became Cash's producer for the 1994 album *American Recordings*. Released on Rubin's label of the same name, it reinvigorated Cash's career, introduced him to a new generation of rock fans, and earned a Grammy Award for Best Contemporary Folk Album. The follow up release, *Unchained*, was even more successful, winning a Grammy for Best Country Album in 1998, despite having been largely ignored by the country industry.

That's when "the finger" photo re-emerged. It had been included in a 1997 book called *Not Fade Away: The Rock & Roll Photography of Jim Marshall*. Rick Rubin fell in love with it and took out a full-page ad in *Billboard*, following the Grammy win for country album. The entire page was filled with the image and included a small message in the upper left corner that read, "American Recordings and Johnny Cash would like to acknowledge the Nashville music establishment and country radio for your support." Nearly 30 years after it was taken the photo became a sensation, appearing on countless posters, T-shirts, and dorm room walls.

But why was Johnny Cash flipping the bird at the camera in the first place? And why are there actually three similar images of the moment? Was he angry at Jim Marshall for taking his picture? Was he upset about the sound or some other technical difficulty? Had someone just made him mad? Cash himself offered an explanation in 2000, indicating he was frustrated with the documentary film crew. "It seemed that everybody that worked for Granada TV was on stage in front of me," Cash recounted. "At some point, I walked around my microphone and yelled, 'Clear the stage! I can't see my audience!' Nobody moved. So I gave them 'the bird.' Hence that picture."

The images themselves offer a different scenario. Cash was wearing the prison jumpsuit, indicating that the photo was taken during the rehearsal and not during the actual show. Jim Marshall also had a different memory of the moment, as he explained in a 2006 interview. "The finger was done at sound check," he remembered. "I said 'John, let's do one for the warden,' and he flipped the bird." Examining the photos in succession suggests the evolution of the moment. First Cash looked into the lens forming a defiant "F" that he later told Marty Stuart was actually "fried chicken." Jim loved it and fired off a couple of shots. Then he grabbed another camera as Cash intensified the facial expression and added the middle finger.

The first two takes of the finger shot show some Granada TV crew members in the background. They're bent over examining something on the stage and seem to take no notice of what's going on. Marshall Grant appears to be noodling on his bass guitar and isn't even looking at Cash. Mother Maybelle Carter, Johnny's mother-in-law, looks on expressionless. In the first photo she's wearing her glasses. In the second she's removing them. In the third she's taken the glasses off and is looking the other way. It appears she noticed Jim's camera was pointed her direction and she didn't want to be photographed while wearing them. The point, of course, is that nobody seems concerned. In fact, nobody seems to be paying much attention at all, which strongly suggests that Cash had not, in fact, lost his temper.

While Jim's explanation is certainly more plausible, he enjoyed the legend that built up around the image and didn't want to take anything away from the Cash mystique. "It might have been directed at the television crew who was filming there," he once noted, "or I might have suggested doing a special shot for the warden, but for whatever reason, this has become a very famous, iconic picture." Regardless of the precise impetus, it was the spirit of the image that was most important to Marshall. "It shows John's individuality," he explained on his website years later, "but the gesture was definitely done in jest. John's got a great sense of humor and this was not a serious shot."

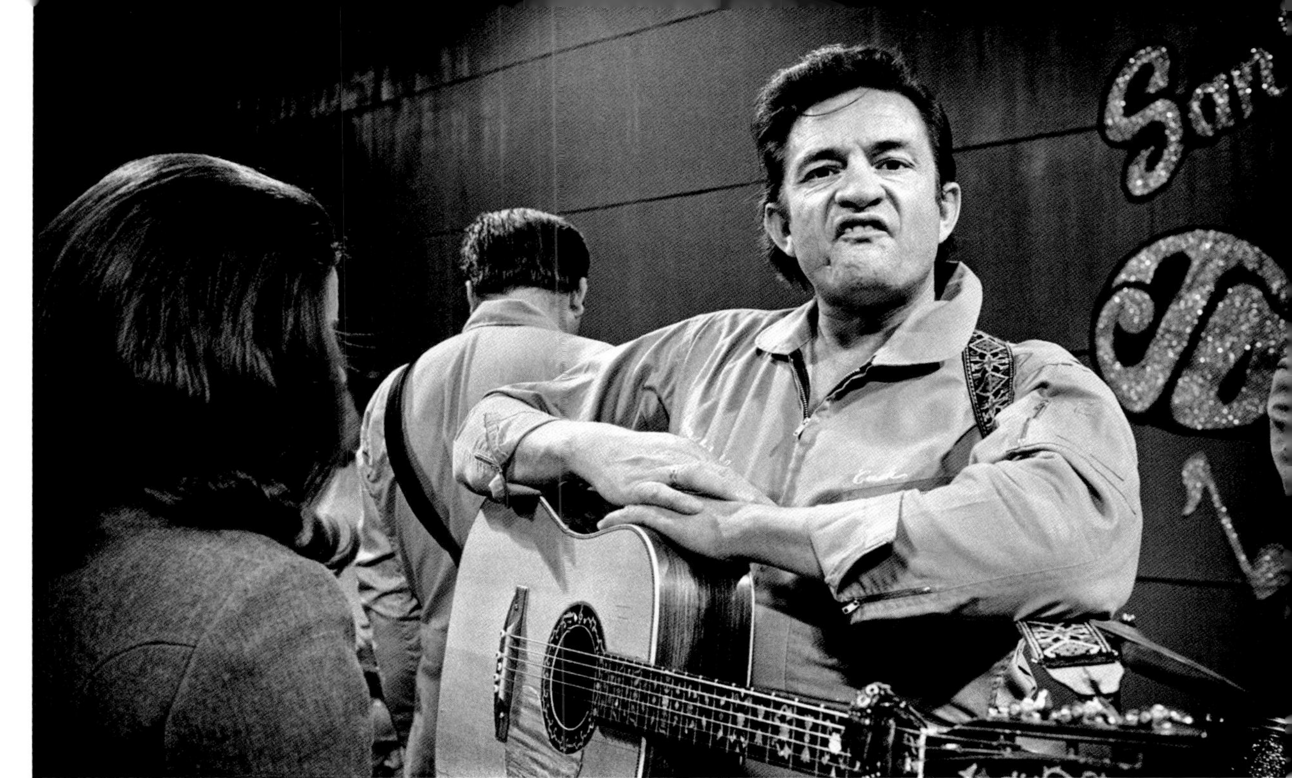

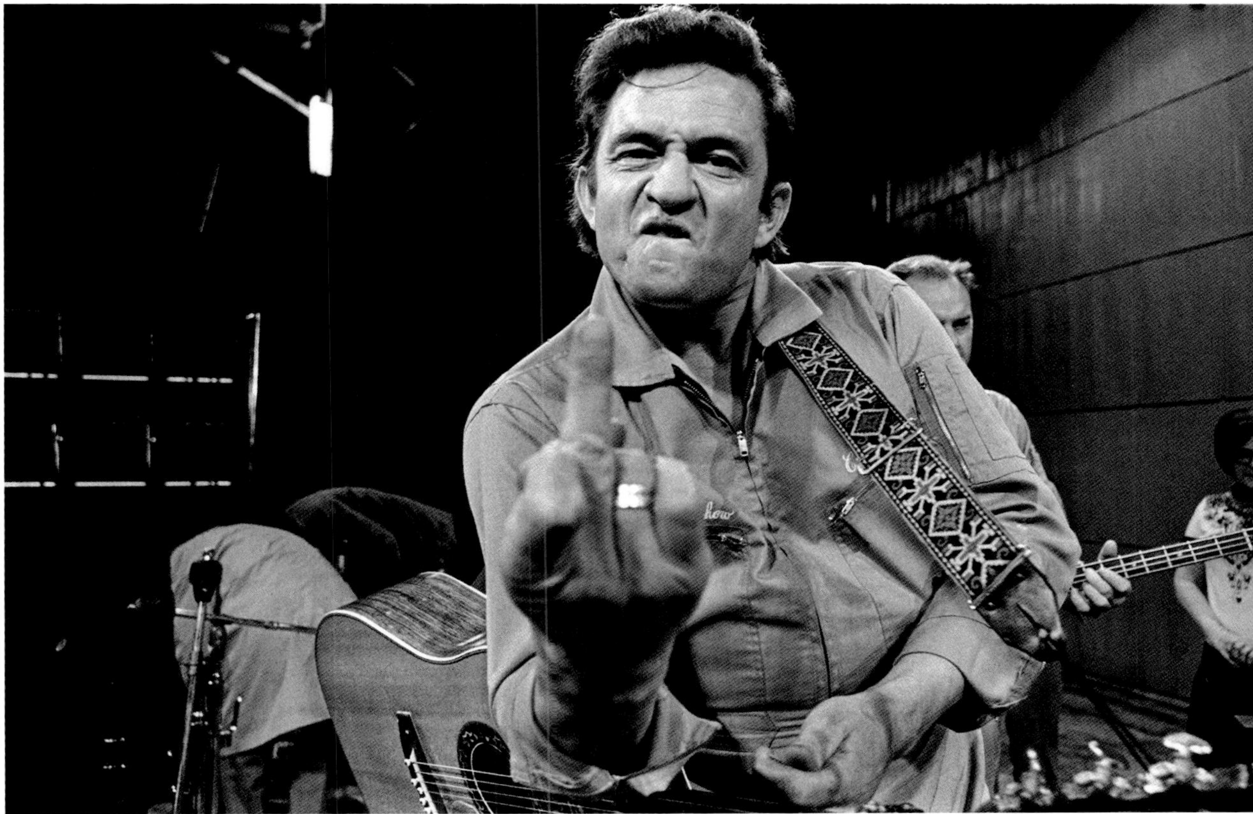

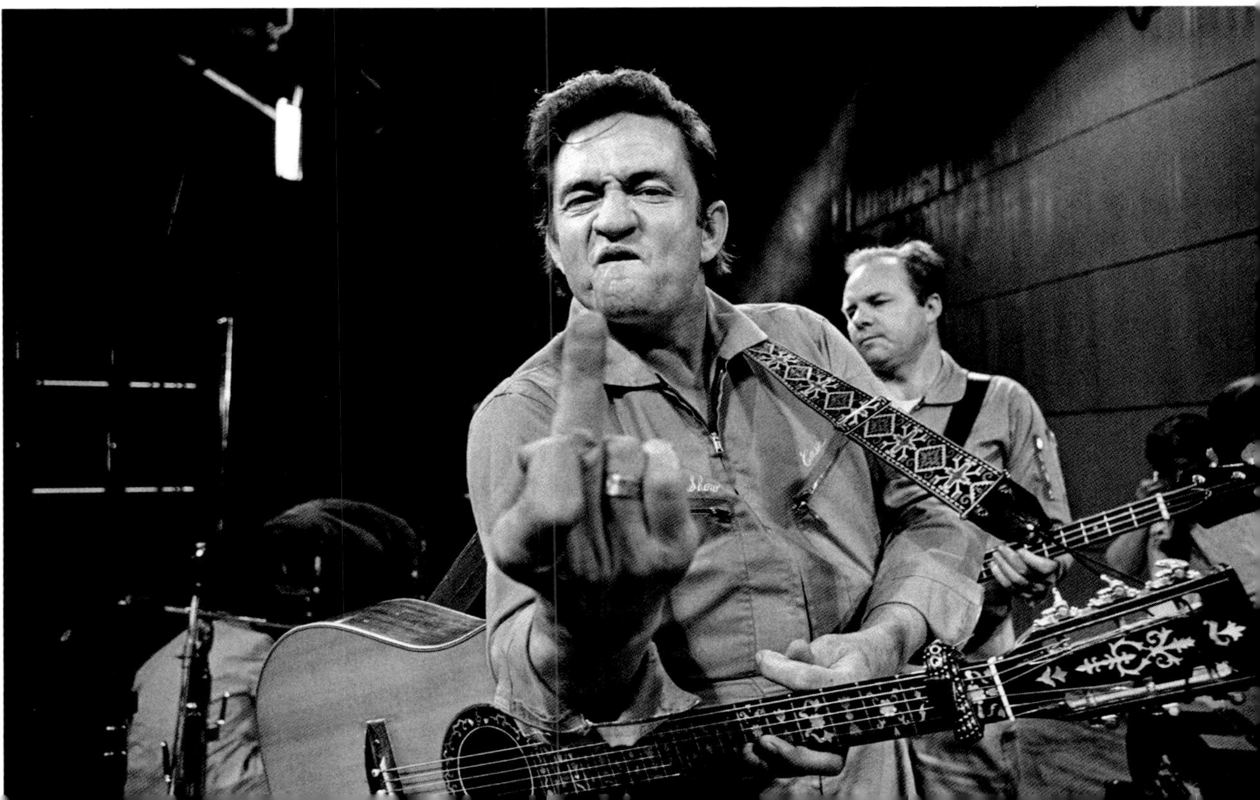

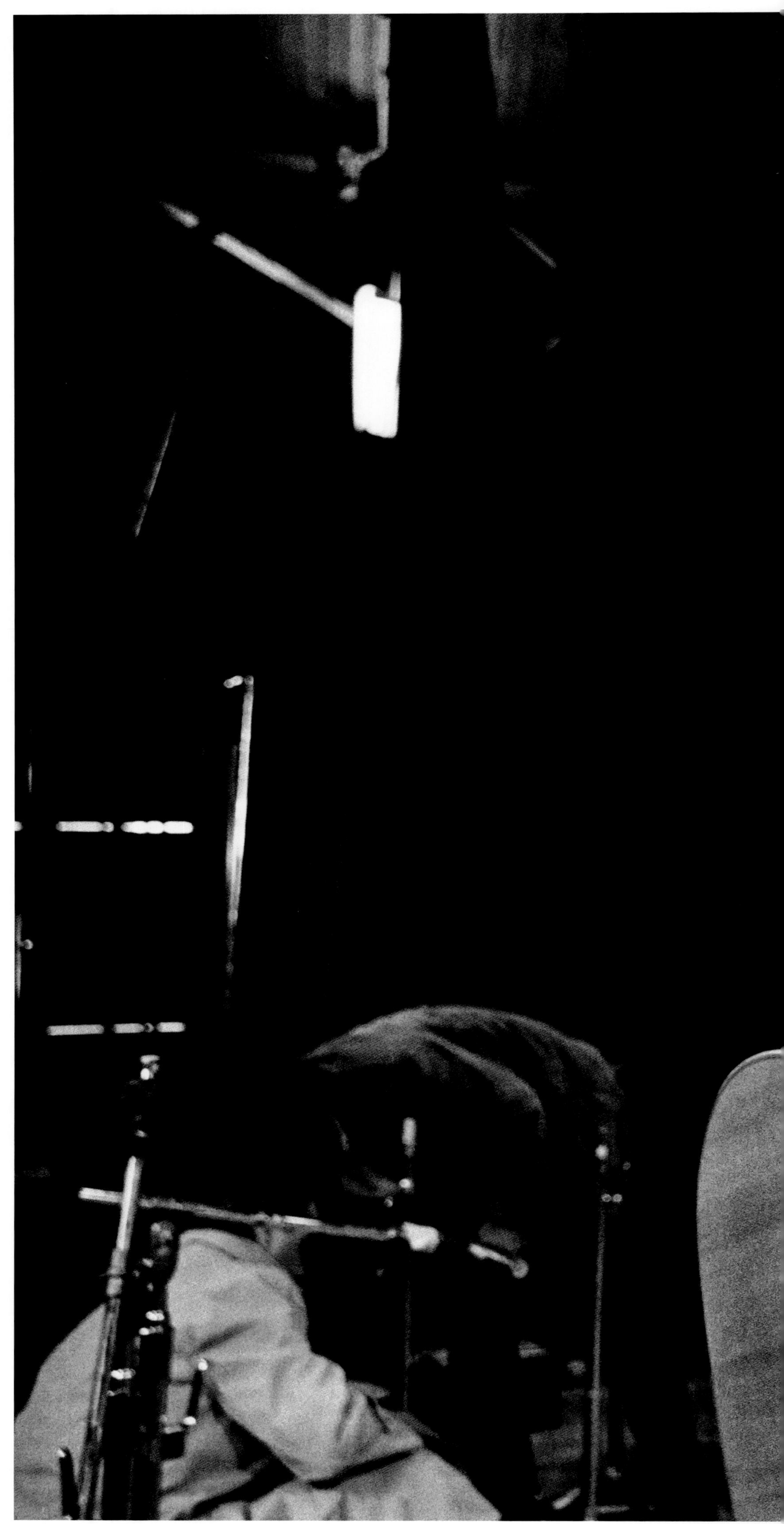

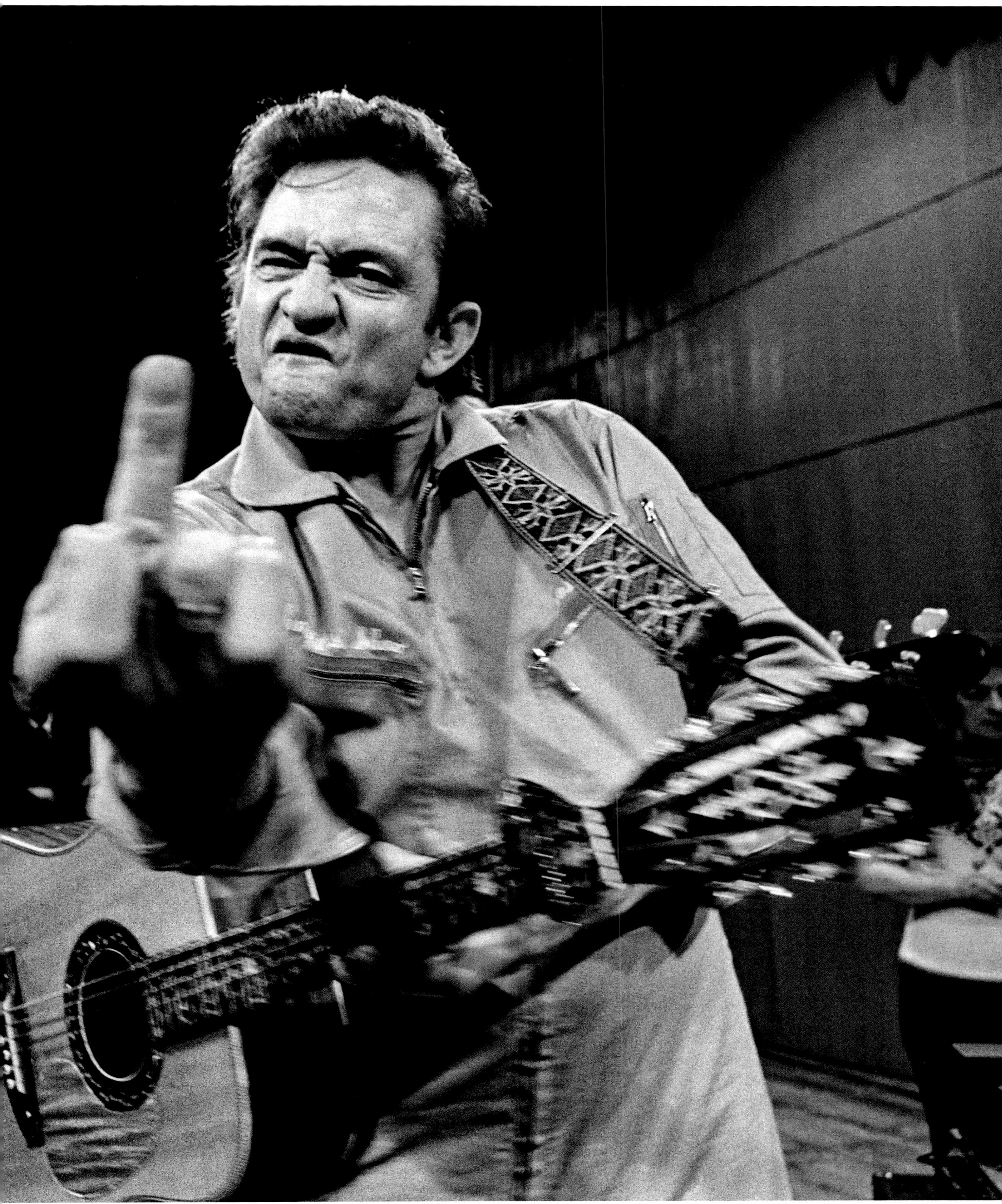

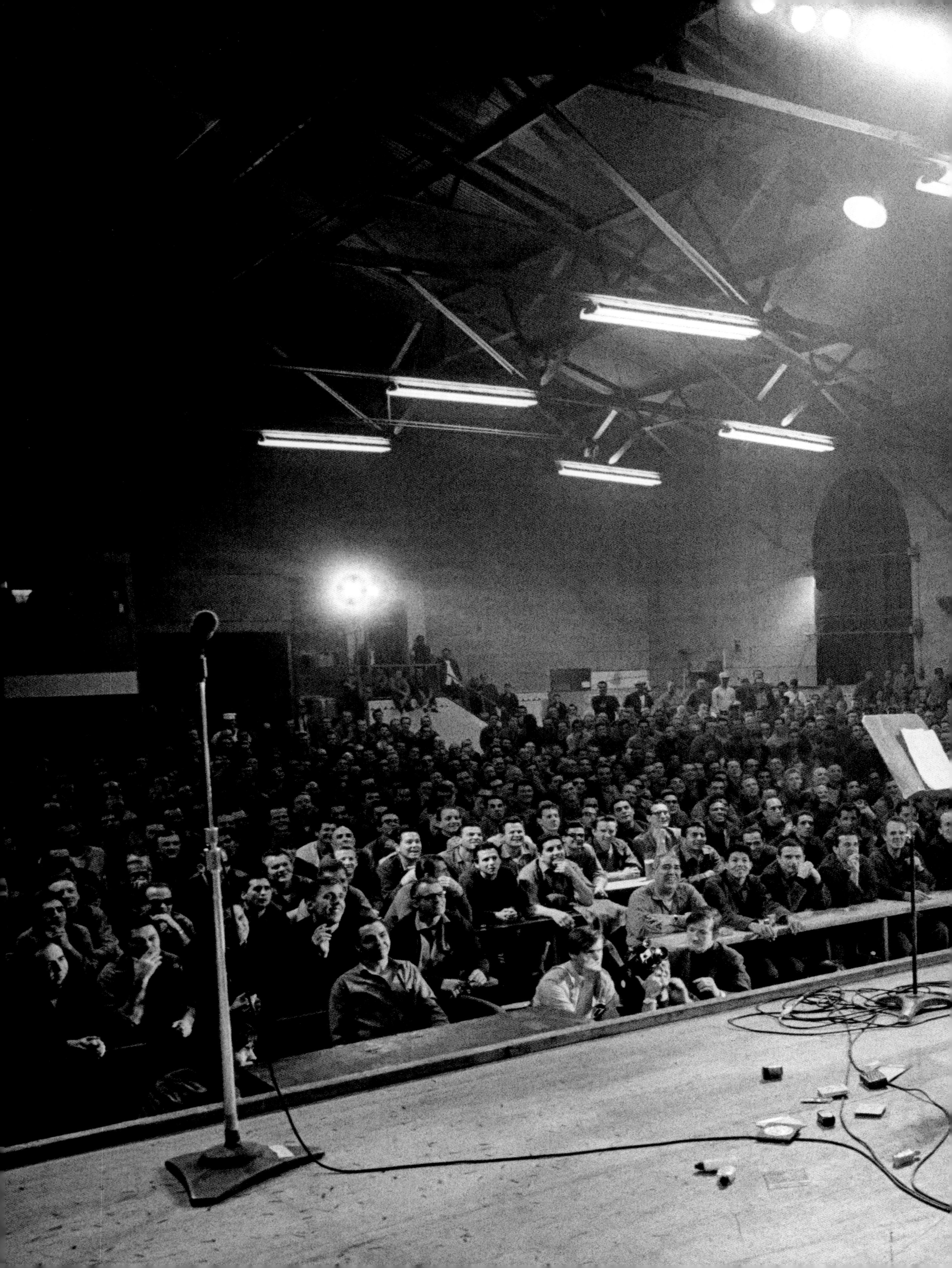

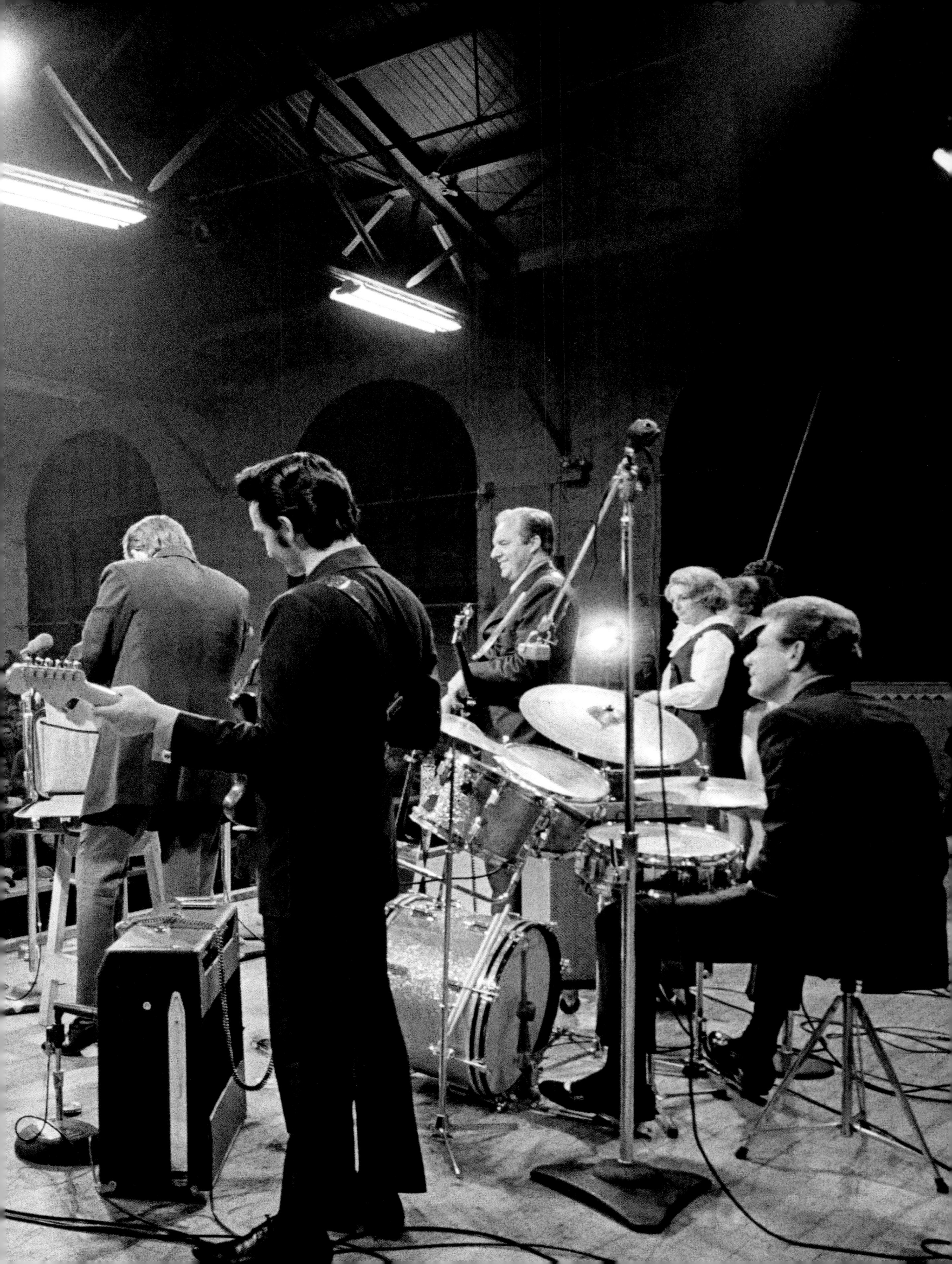

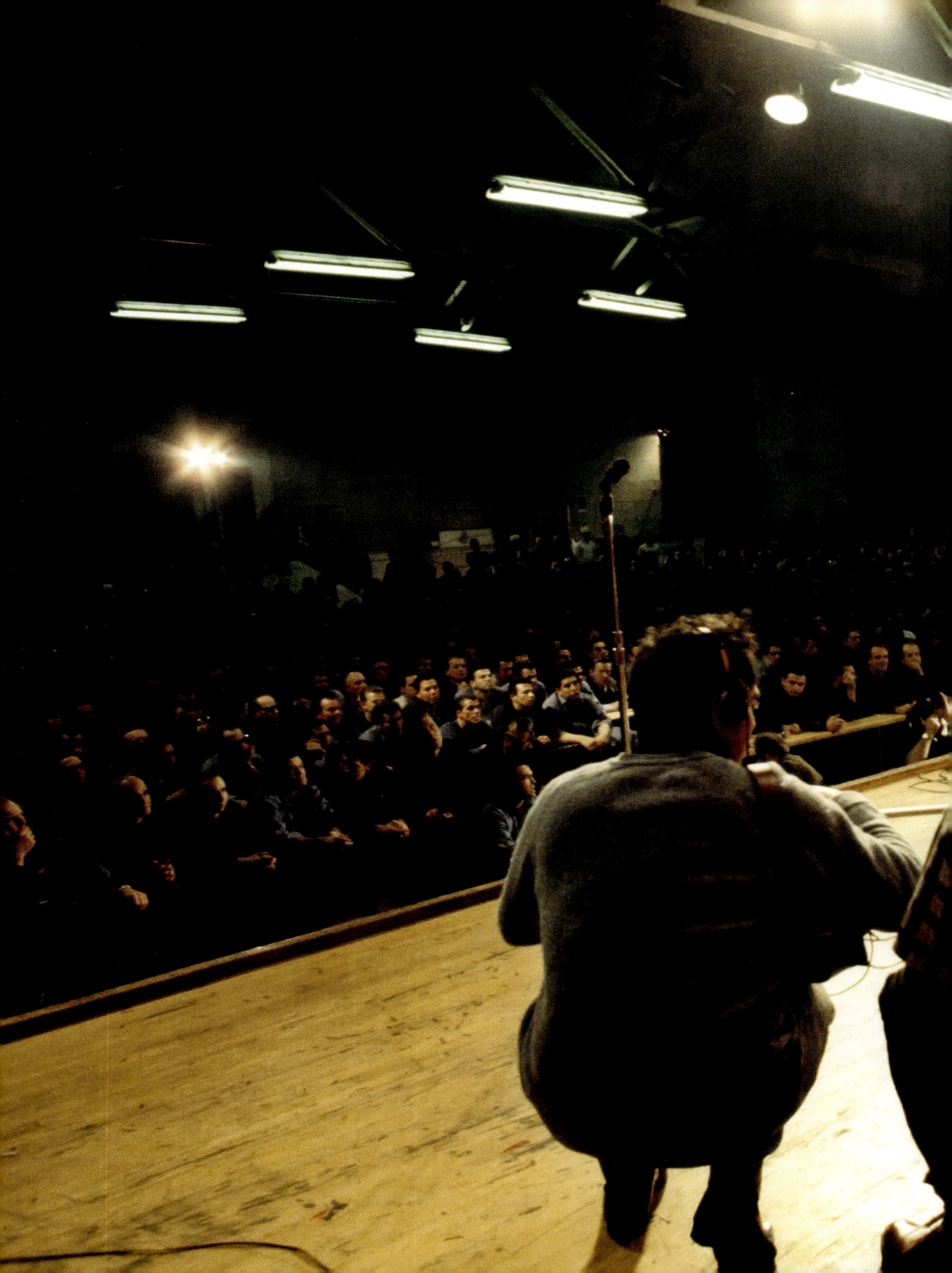

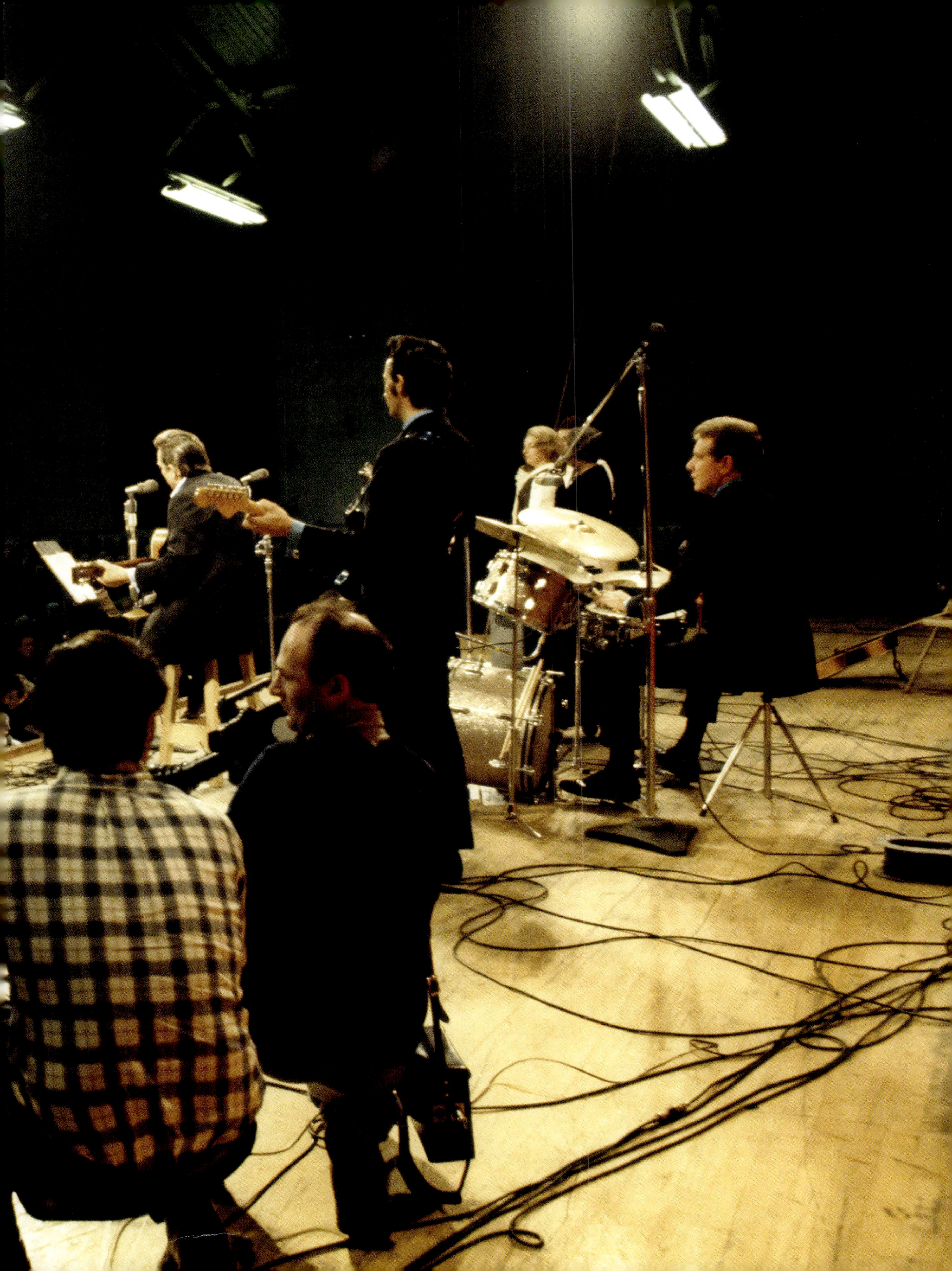

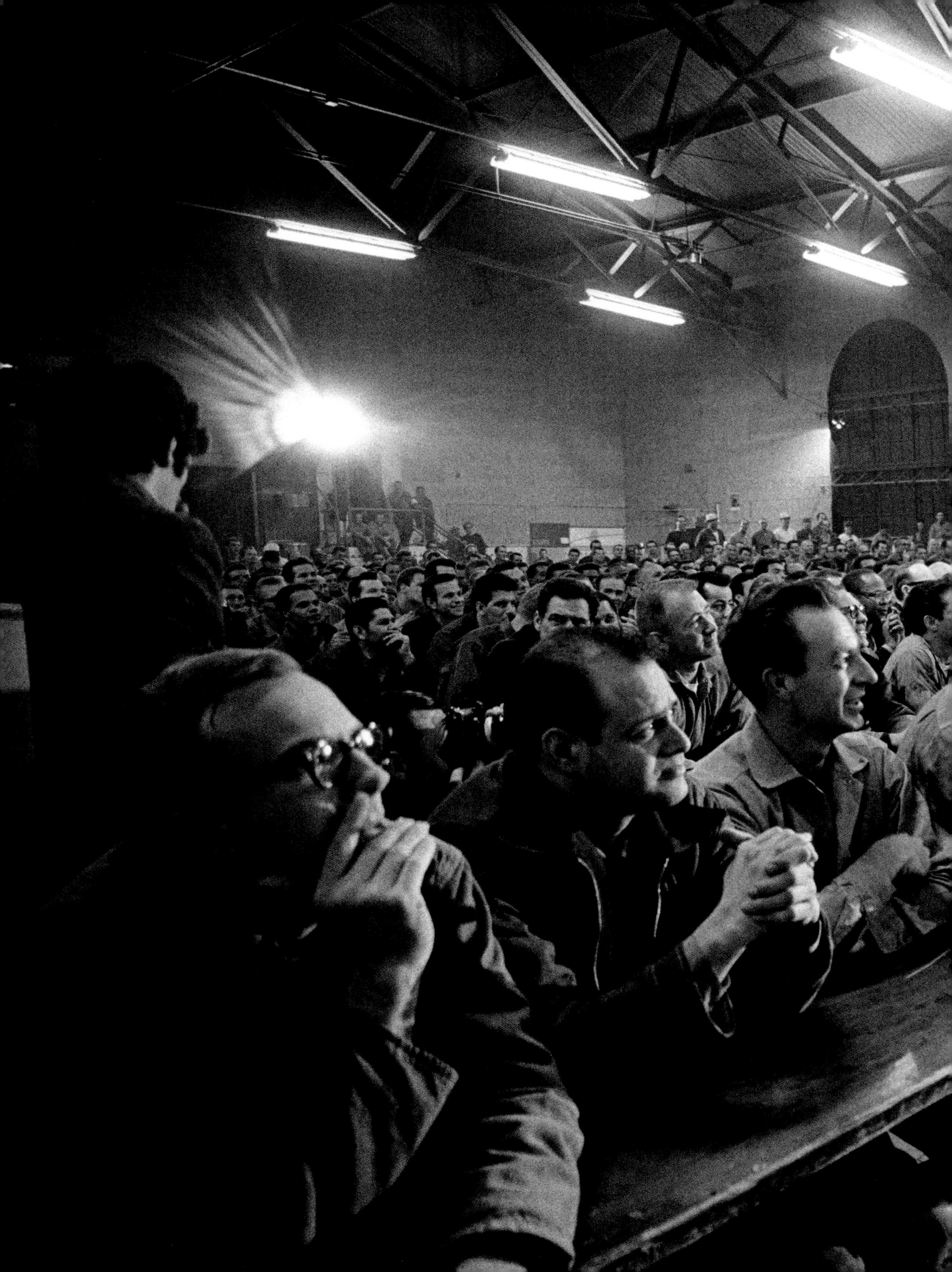

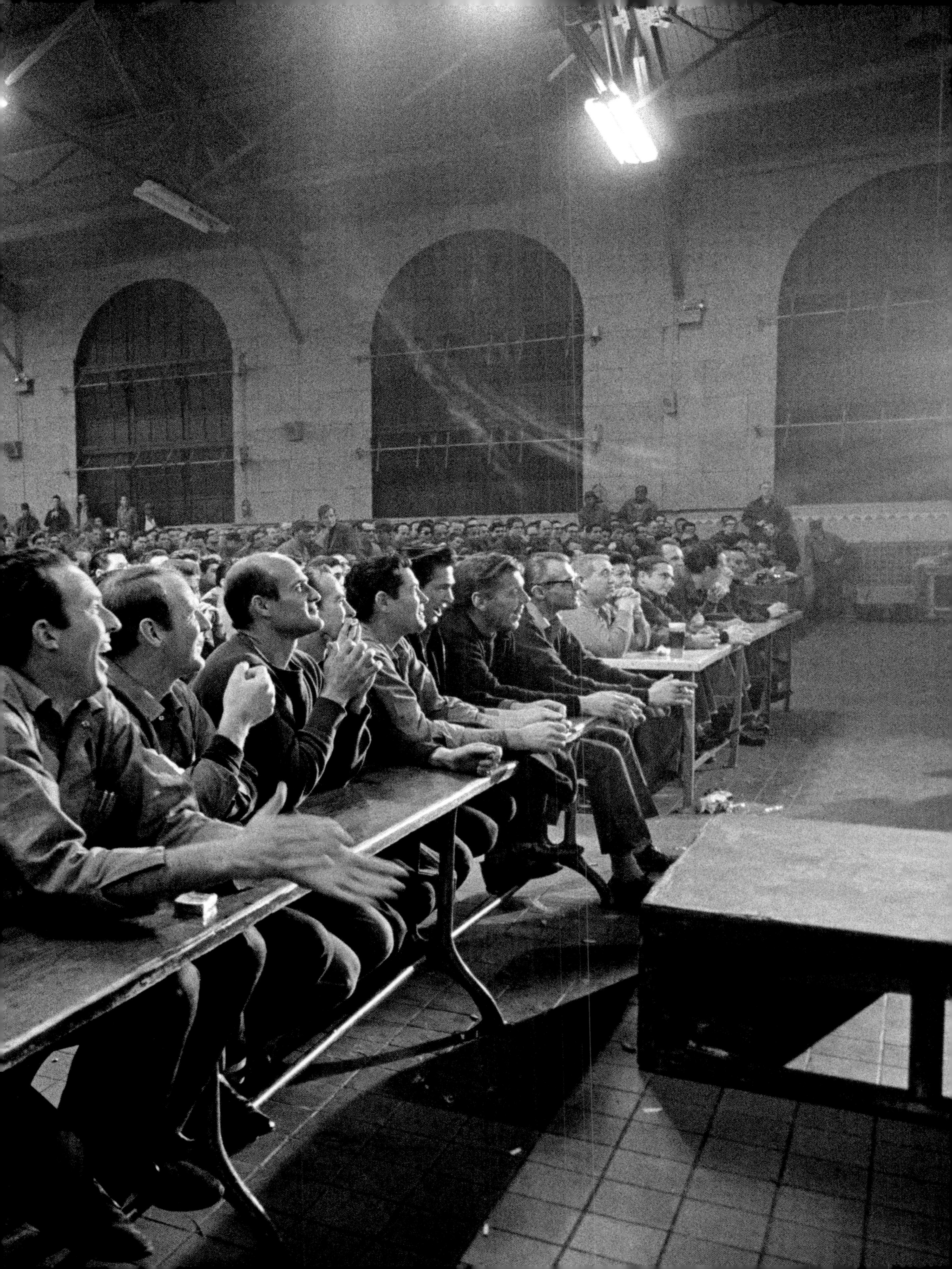

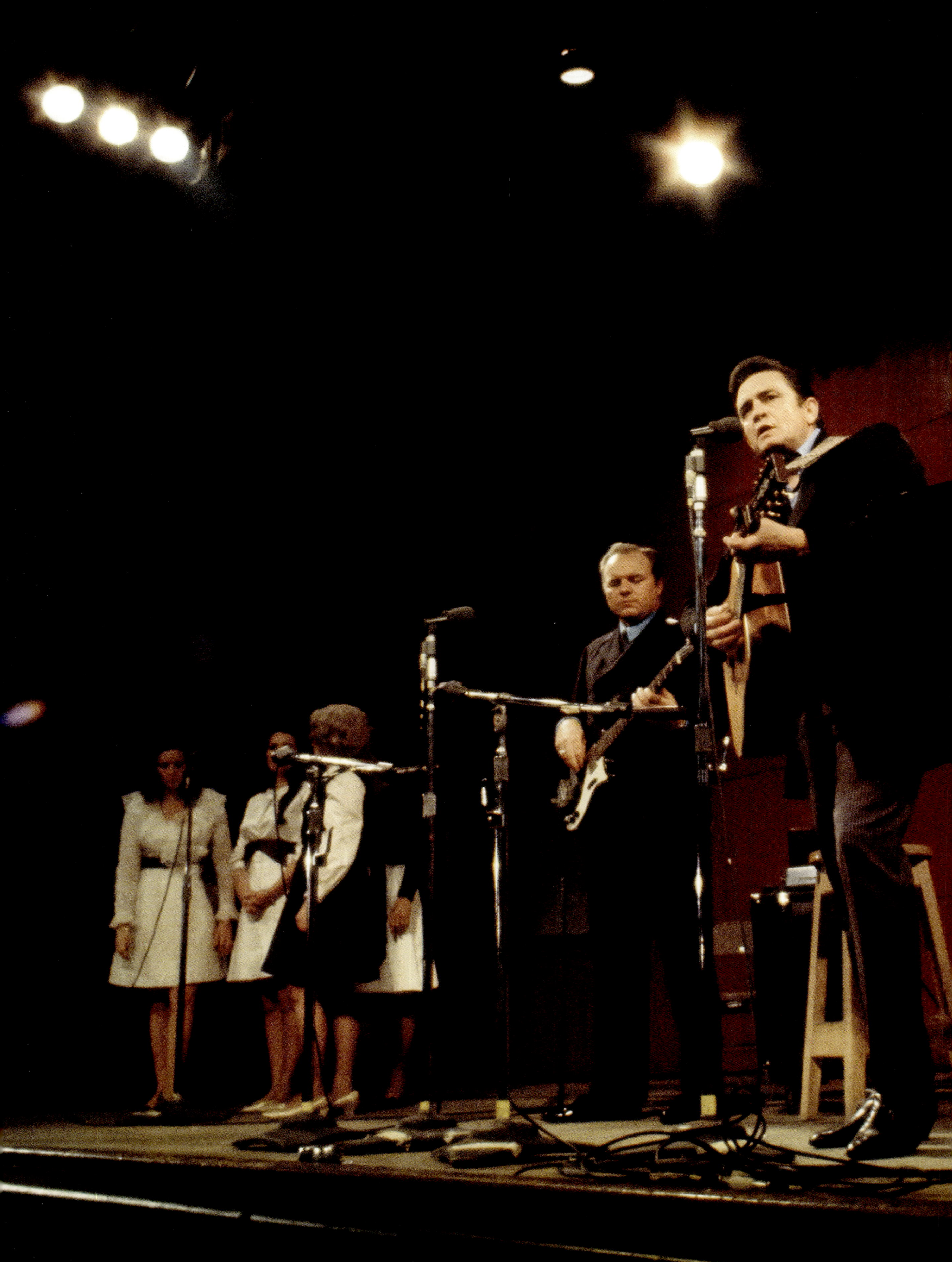

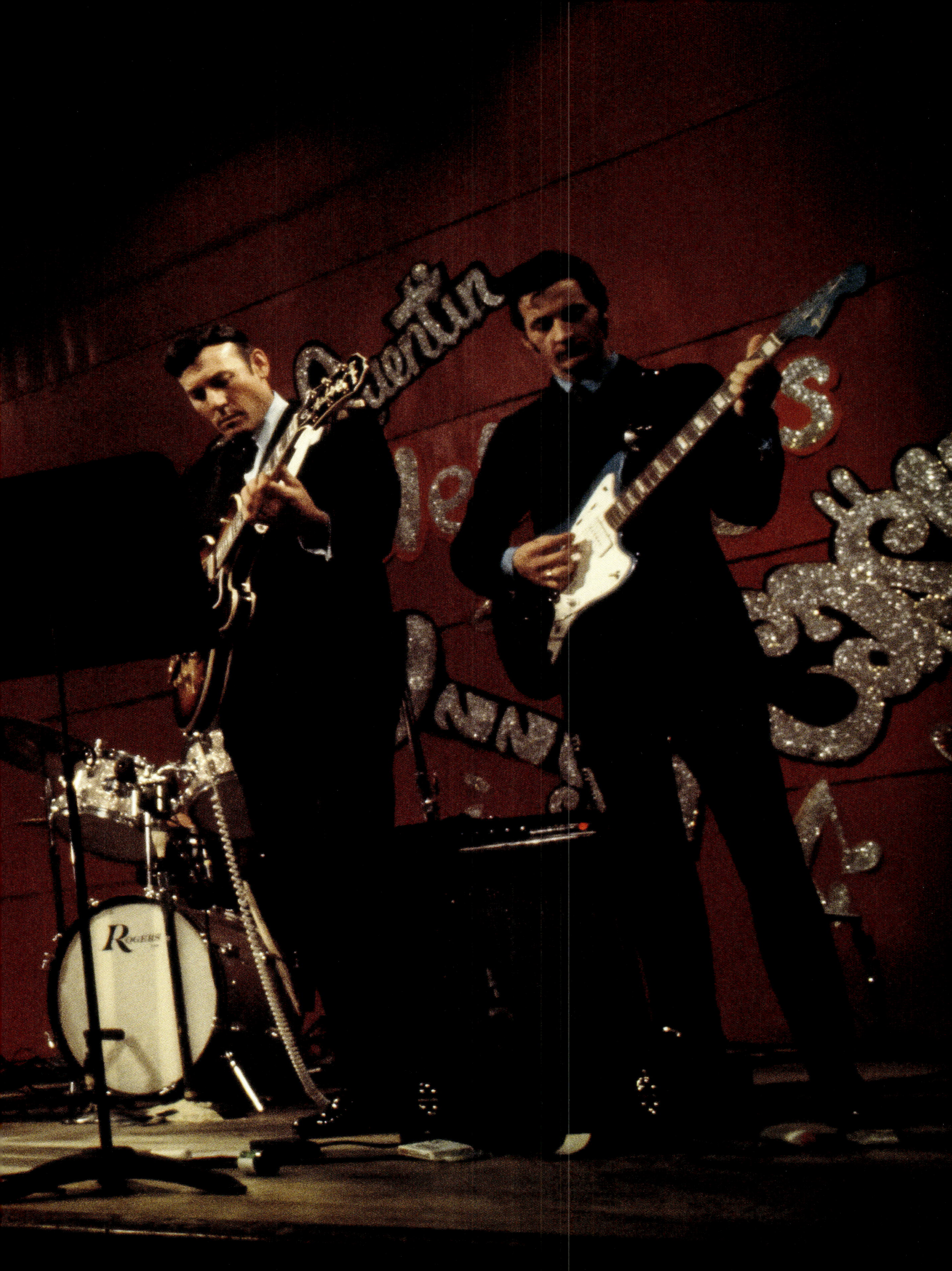

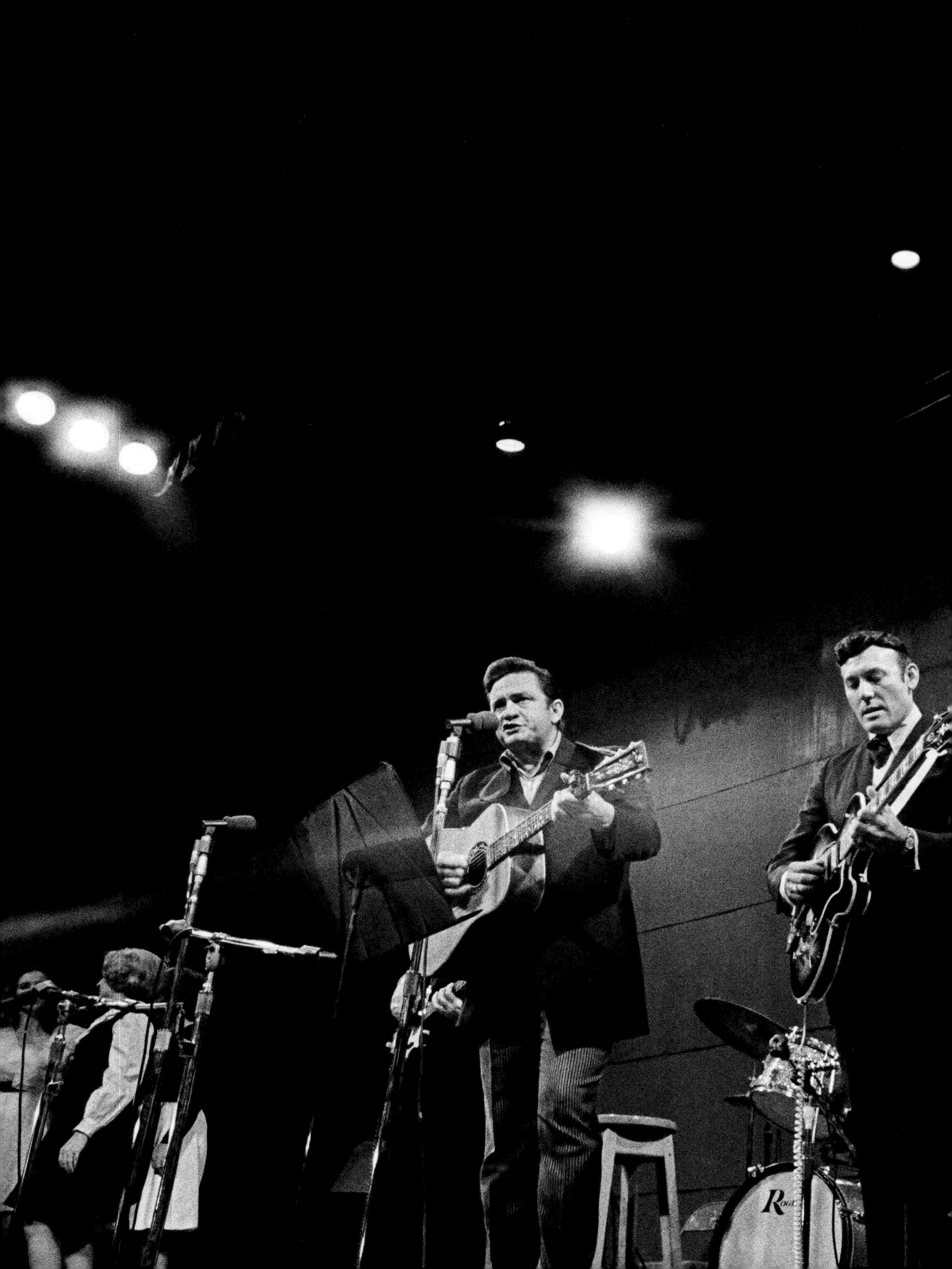

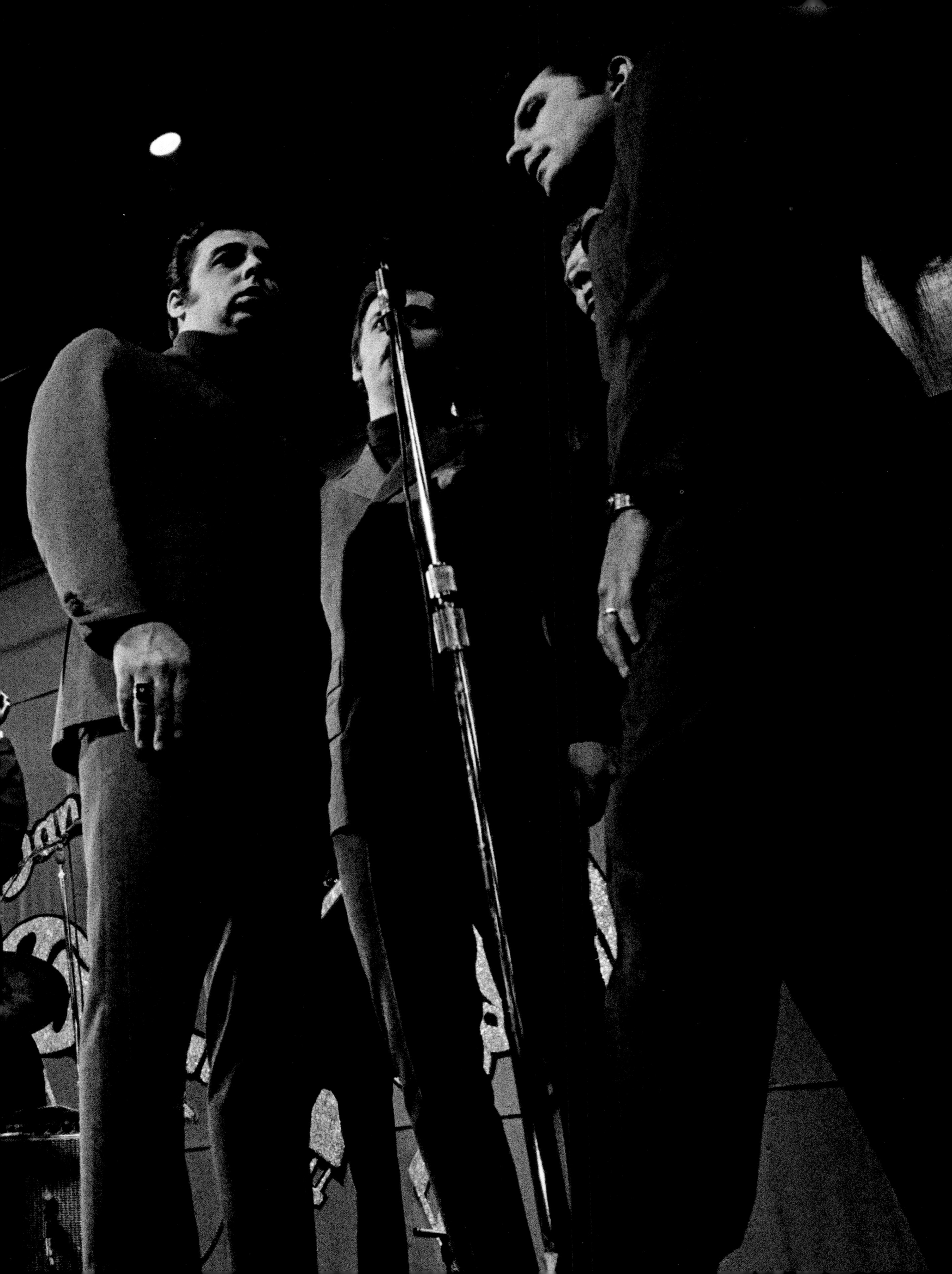

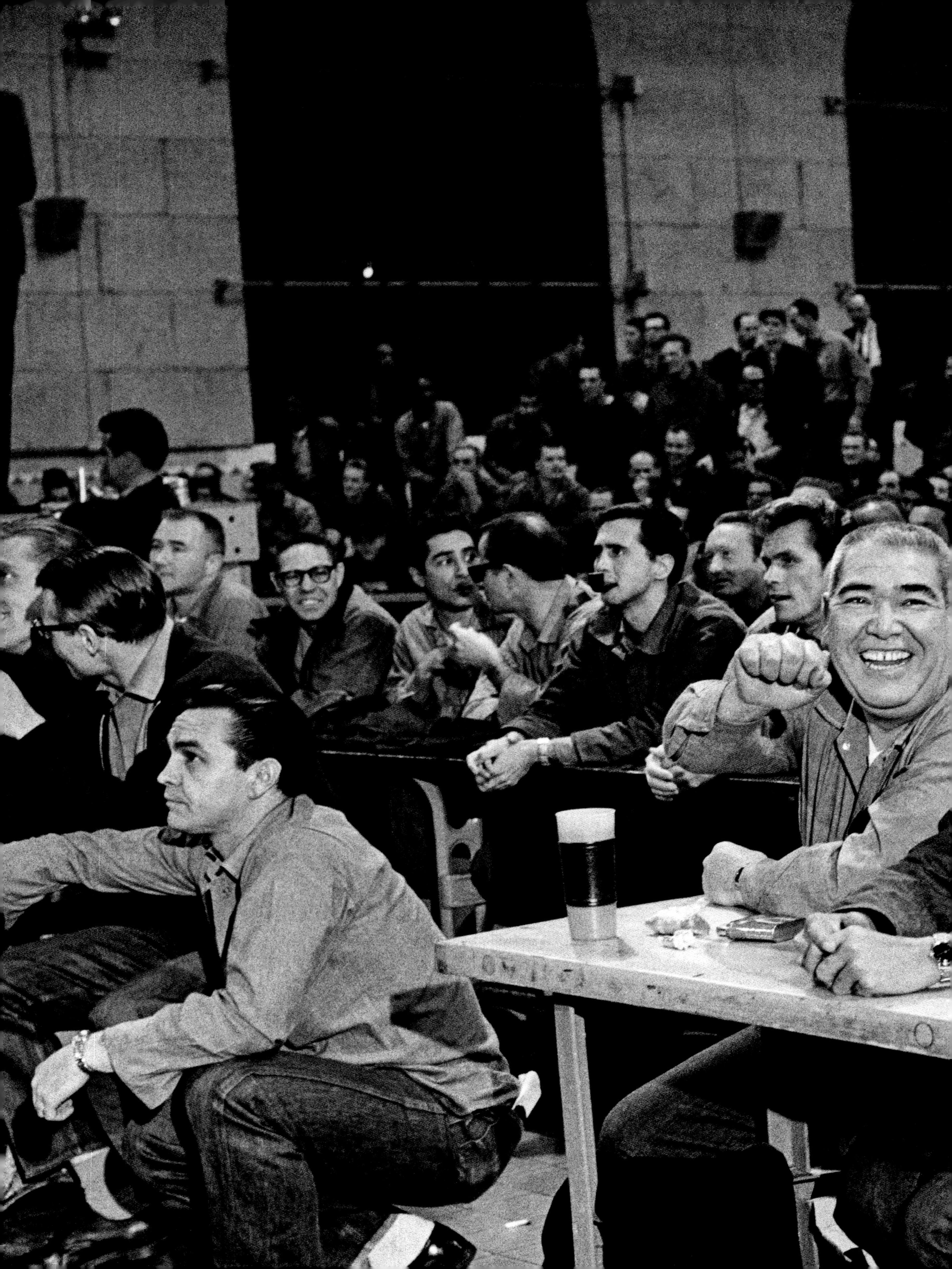

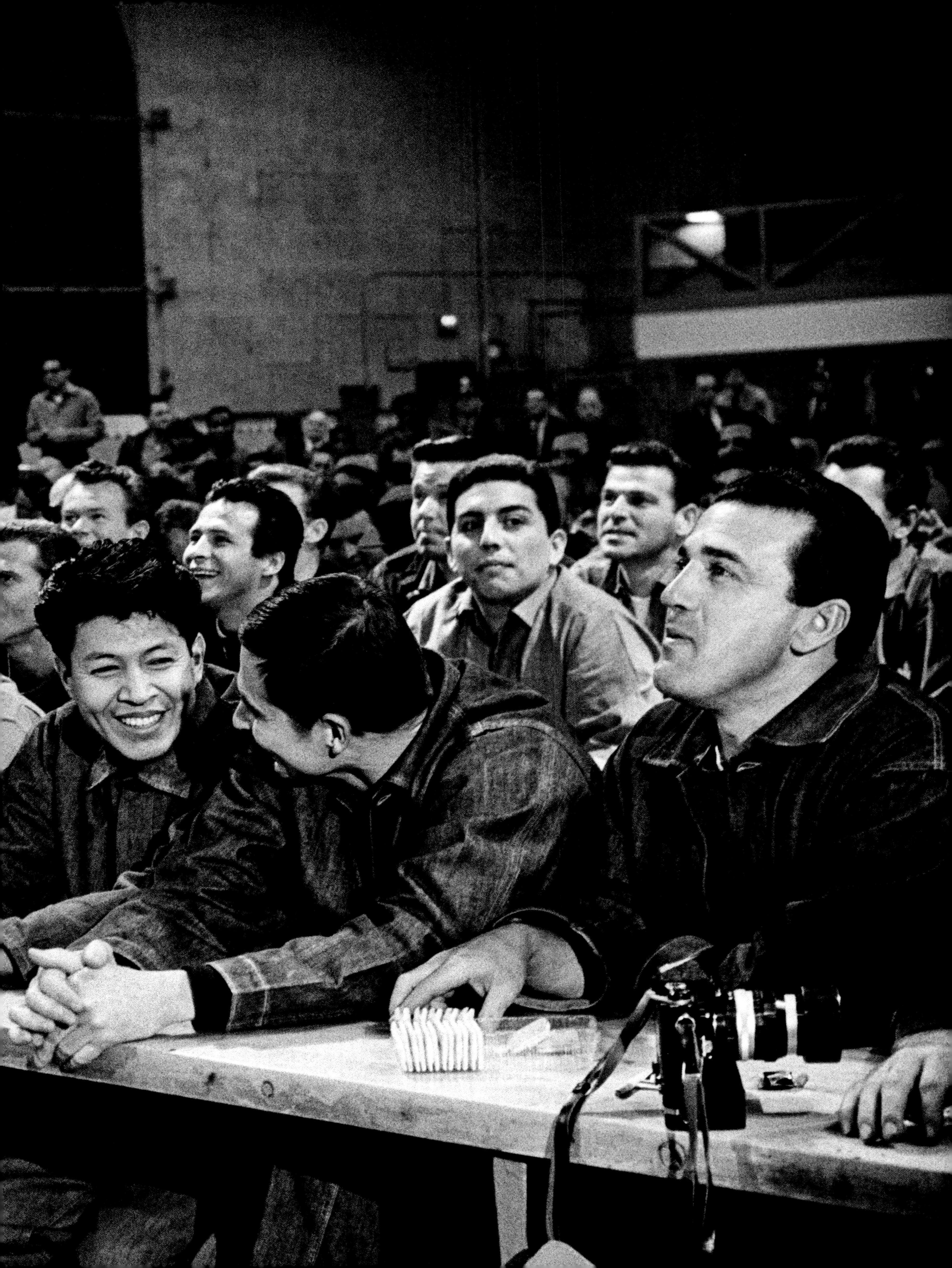

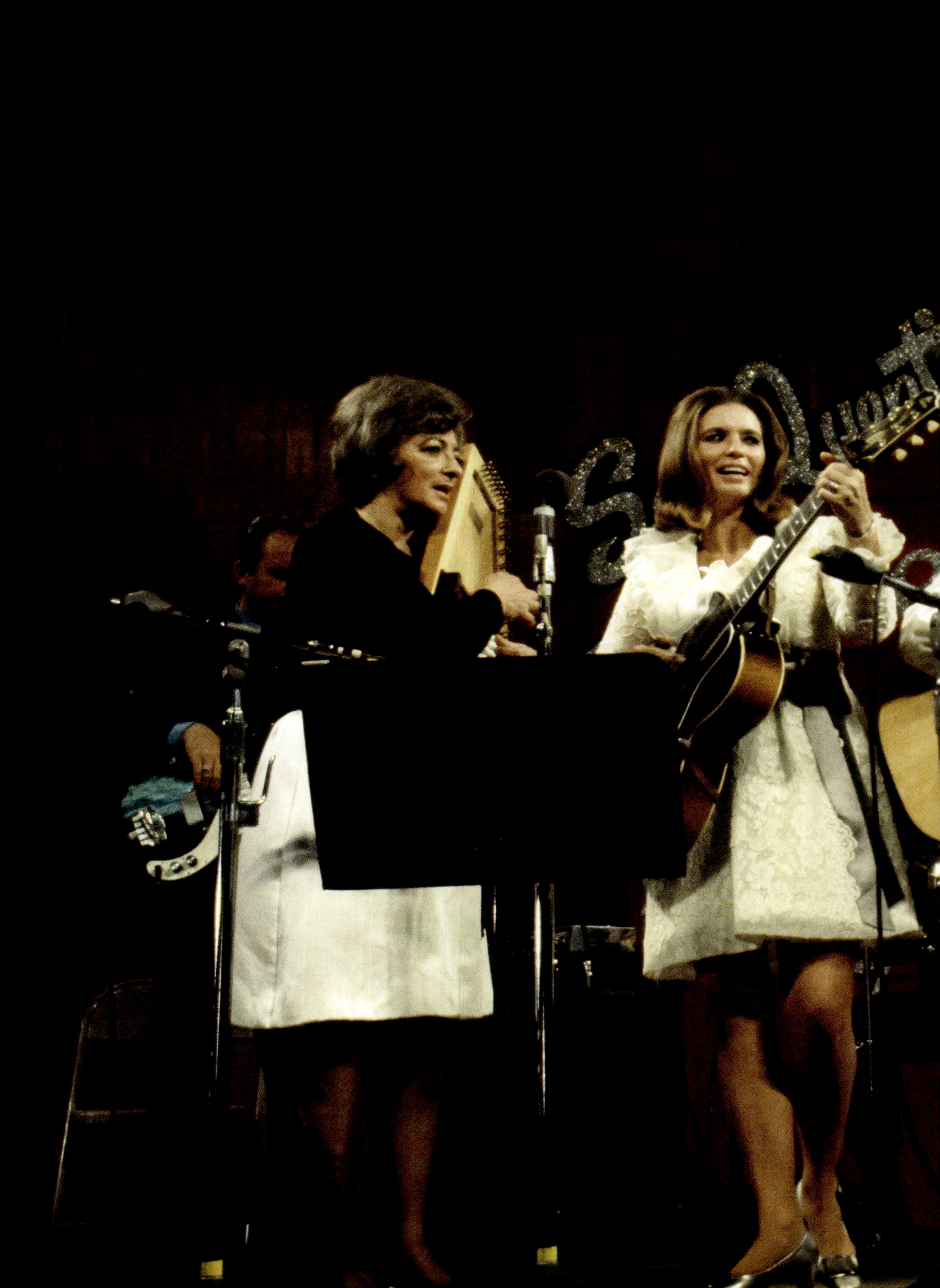

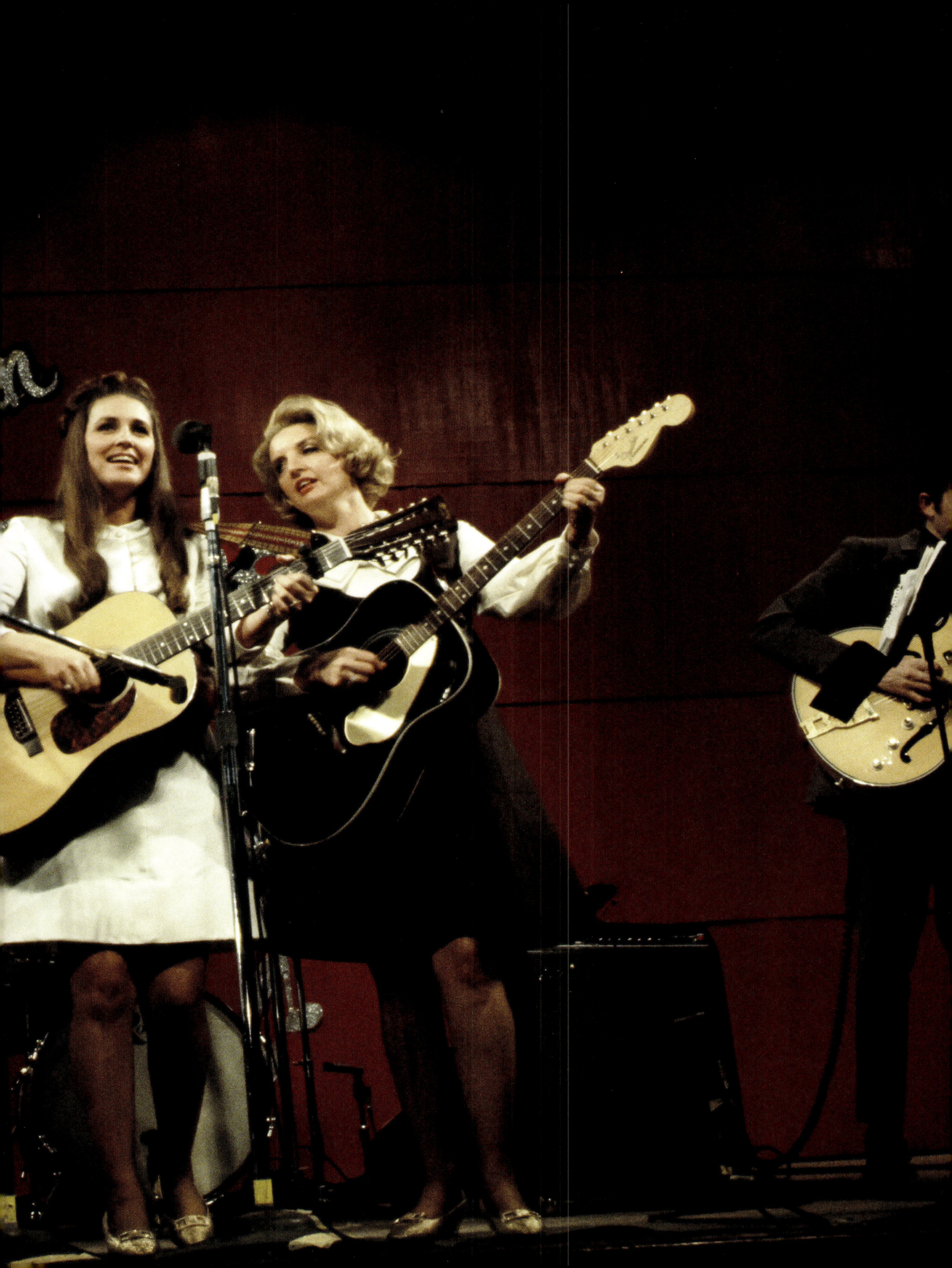

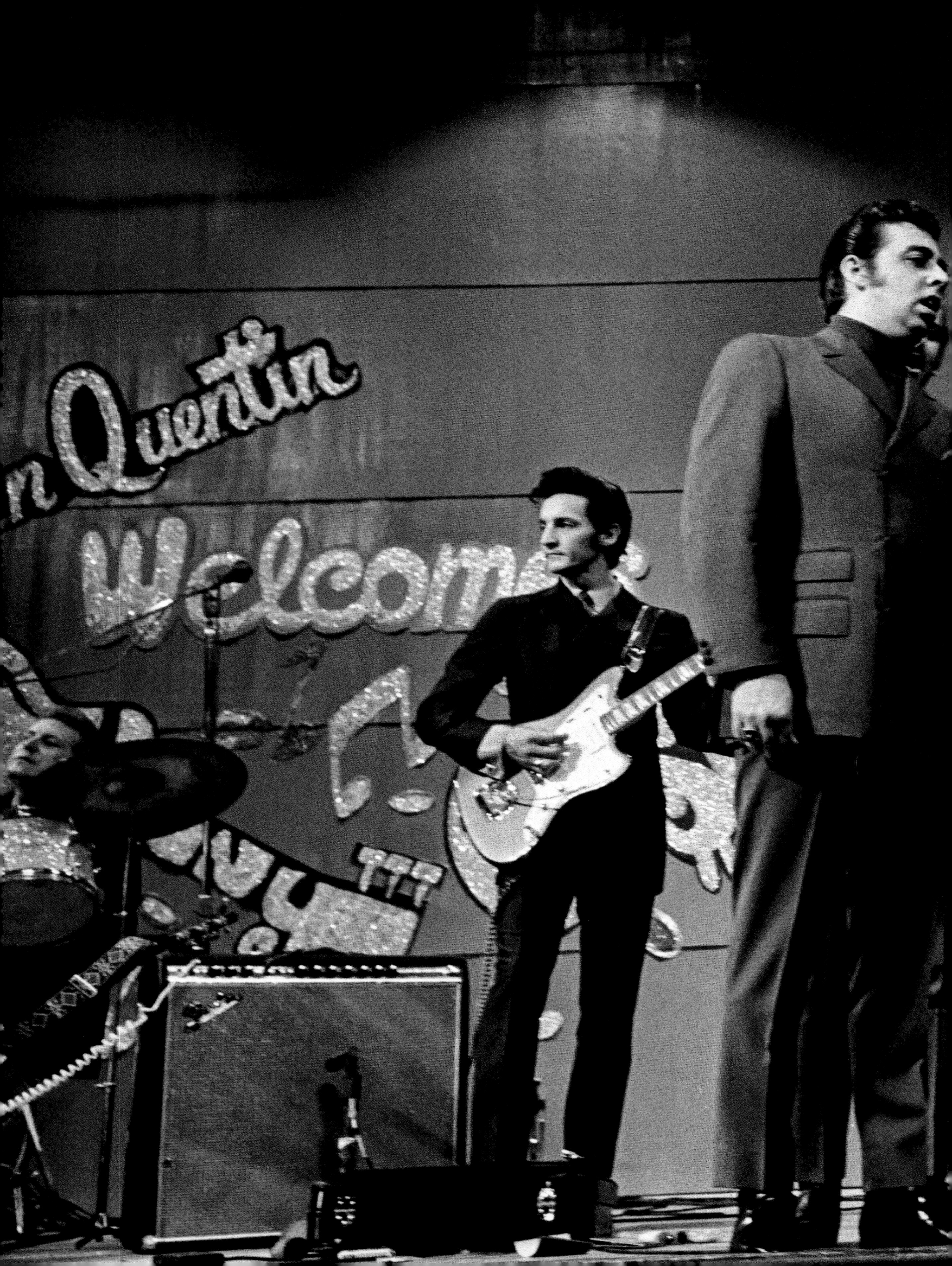

n Quentin
Welcome

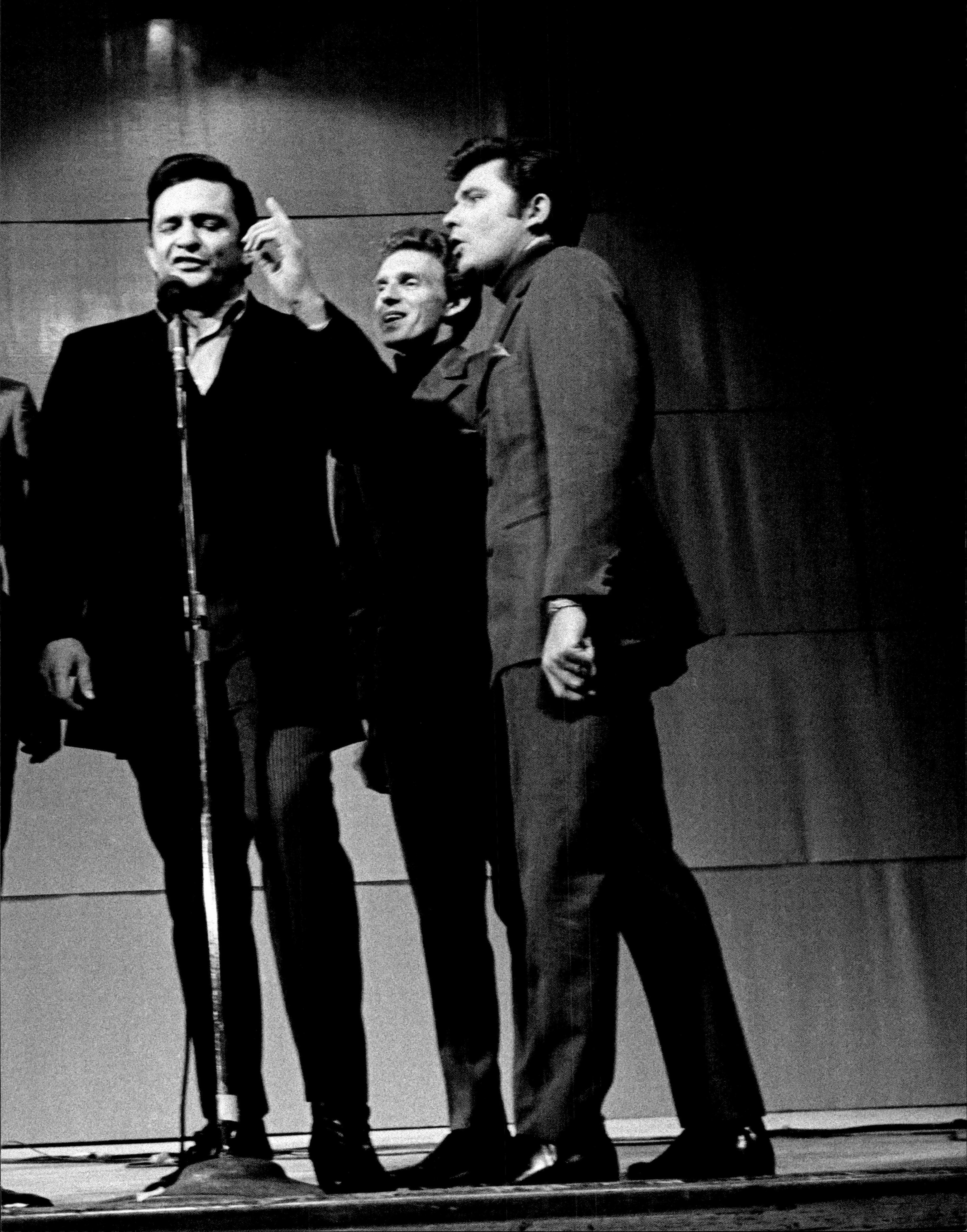

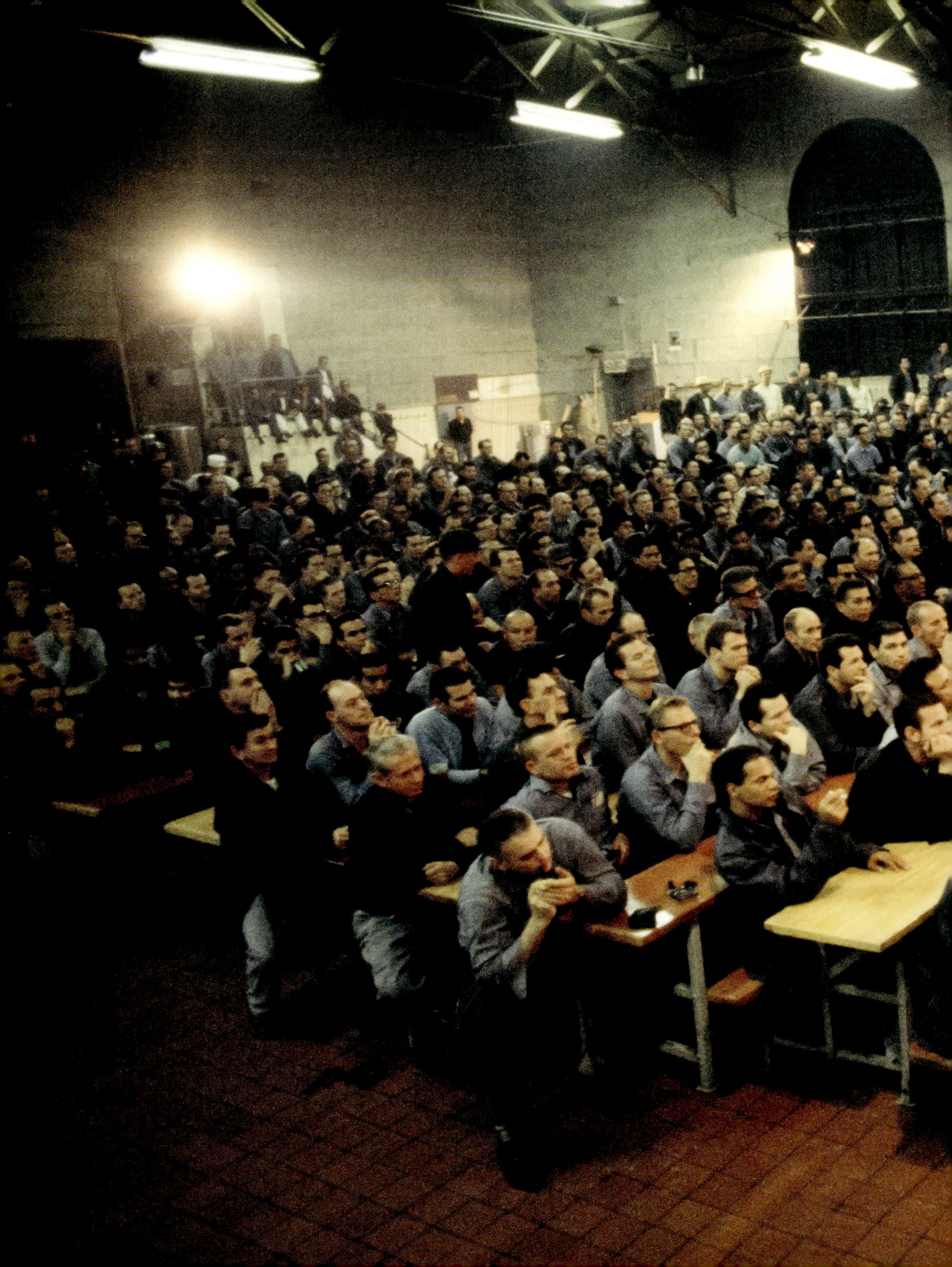

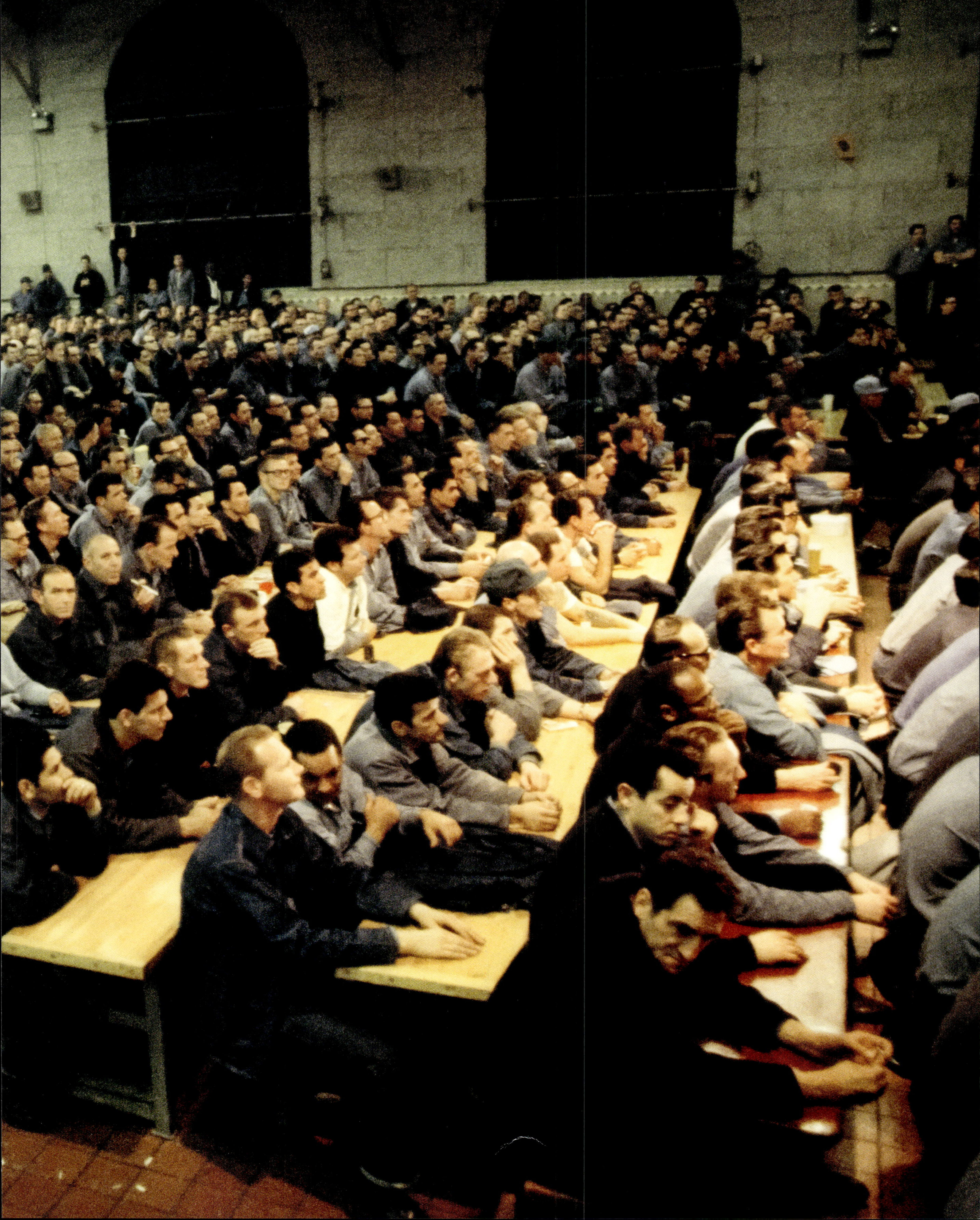

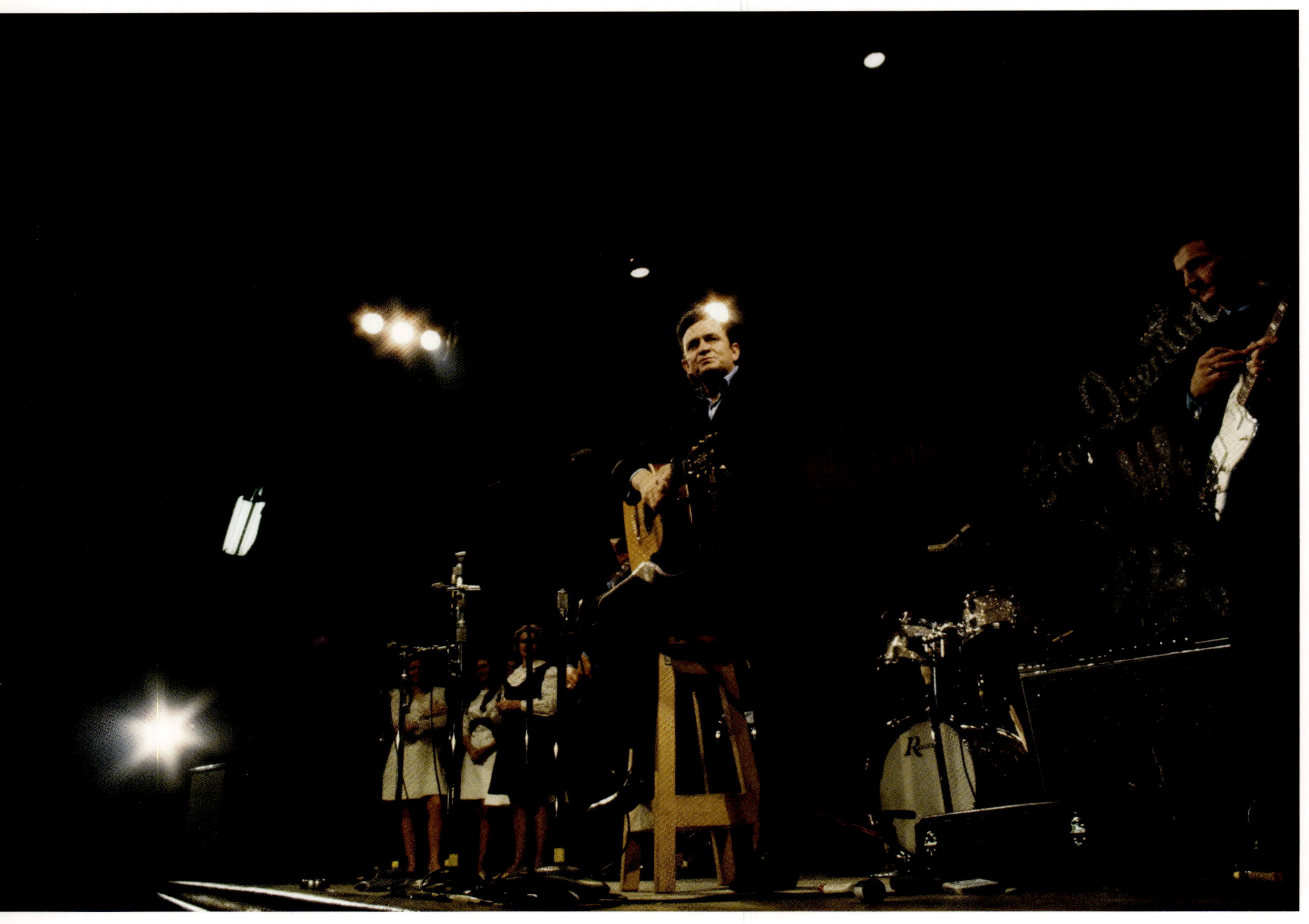

Johnny Cash's *At San Quentin* album was released on June 7, 1969 to coincide with the launch of *The Johnny Cash Show* on ABC. It was an enormous success, hitting #1 on the country album chart for an astounding twenty weeks, and holding the top spot on the pop album chart for an entire month. The single, "A Boy Named Sue," reached #1 on the country chart and #2 on the pop charts. Though improvised on stage, it would become the biggest selling single of Johnny Cash's career.

"I speak partially from experience," Cash had written in the liner notes for *At Folsom Prison* the previous year. "I have been behind bars a few times. Sometimes of my own volition—sometimes involuntarily. Each time, I felt the same feeling of kinship with my fellow prisoners." Though he'd spent a few nights in jail, Cash never served hard time. The extraordinary popularity of the *Folsom* and *San Quentin* albums, however, linked Cash and prison in the popular imagination, leading many to believe he had been an inmate. It was part of his romanticized mythology. Stripping away the myth, however, Jim Marshall's images stand as a testament to Cash's real-life magnetism. Jim's uncanny ability to capture the little moments that tell a deeply meaningful story is unparalleled in musical photography. He and Cash were the perfect match for one another.

In an interview for the *Johnny Cash at Folsom Prison* documentary Rosanne described her father in terms that could equally be applied to Marshall's approach to photography. "He was his best self on stage," she explained. "He took his problems to the stage and he worked a lot of them out onstage. He had this kind of showmanship and kind generosity of spirit and good natured-ness coupled with this absolute lack of need to please anyone, but to just do what he did to the best of his ability. It was such an odd combination."

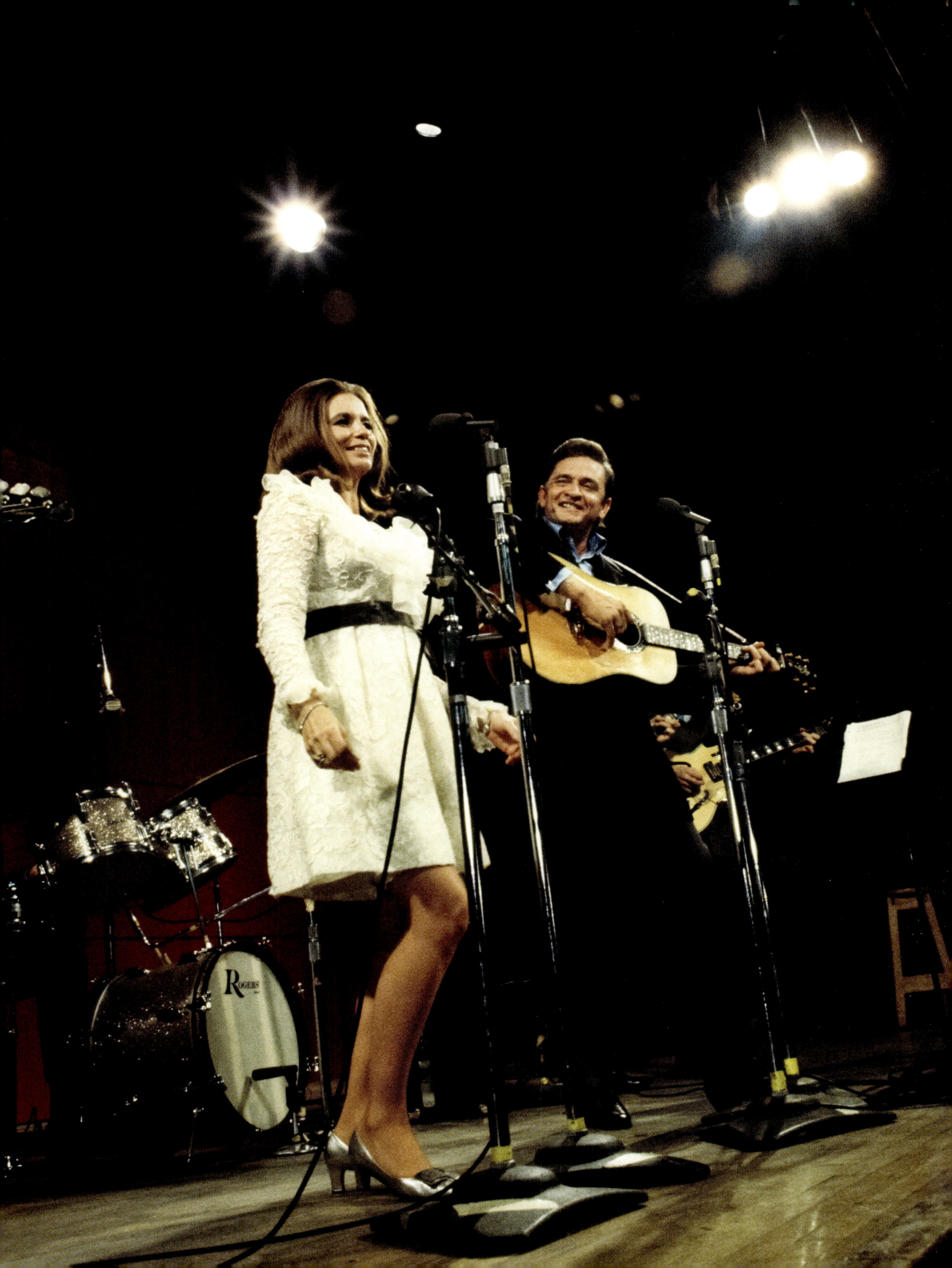

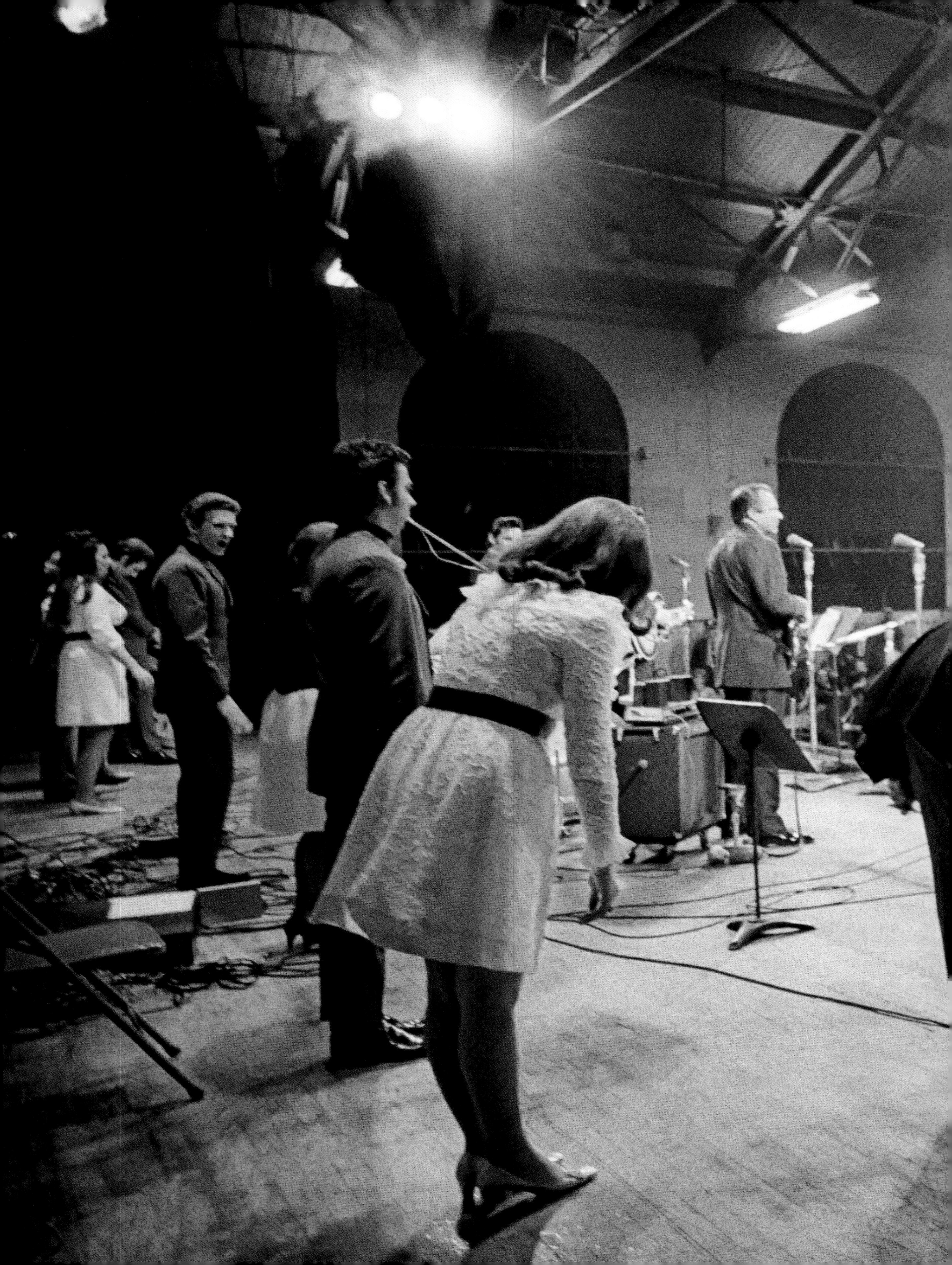

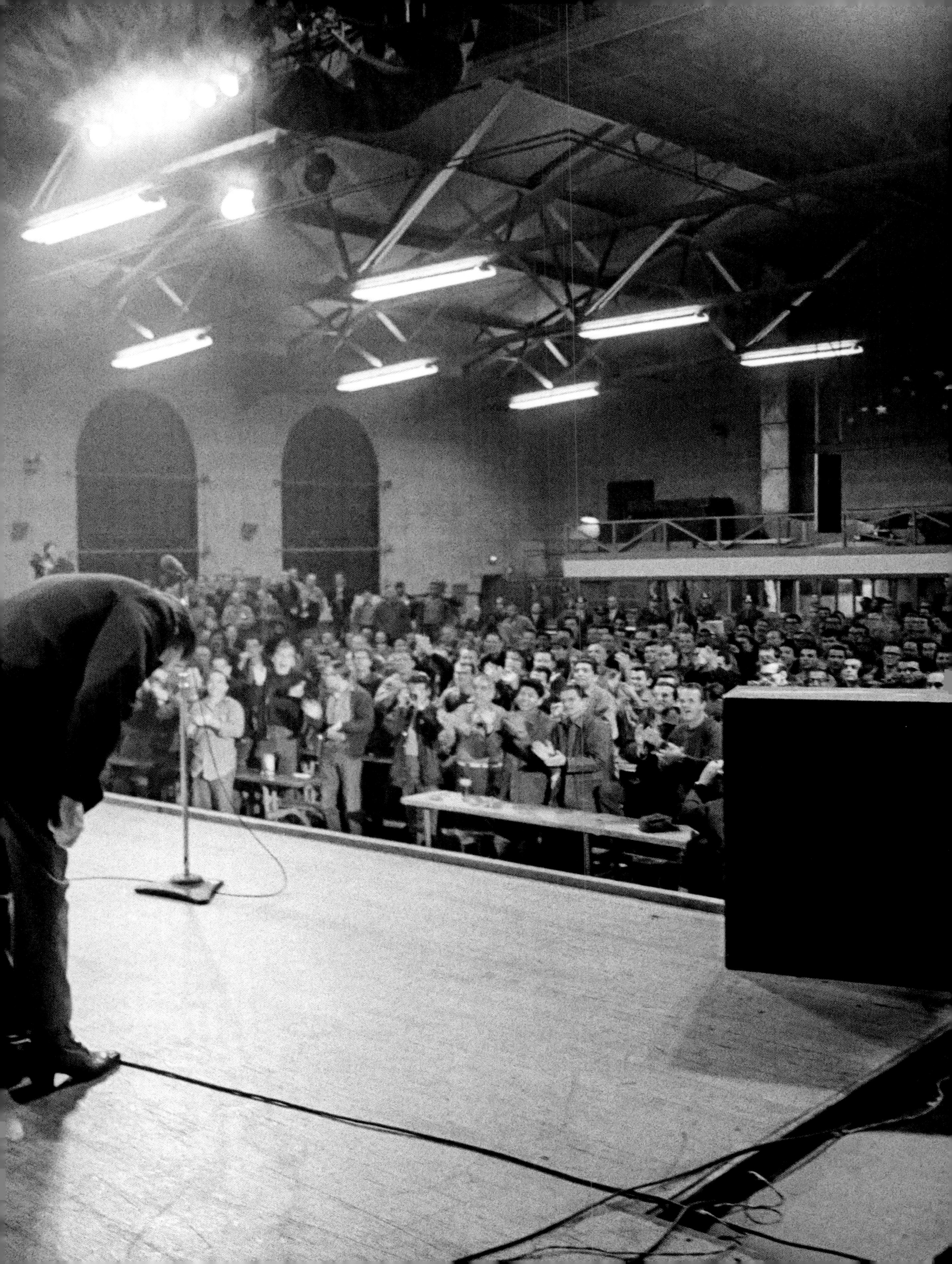

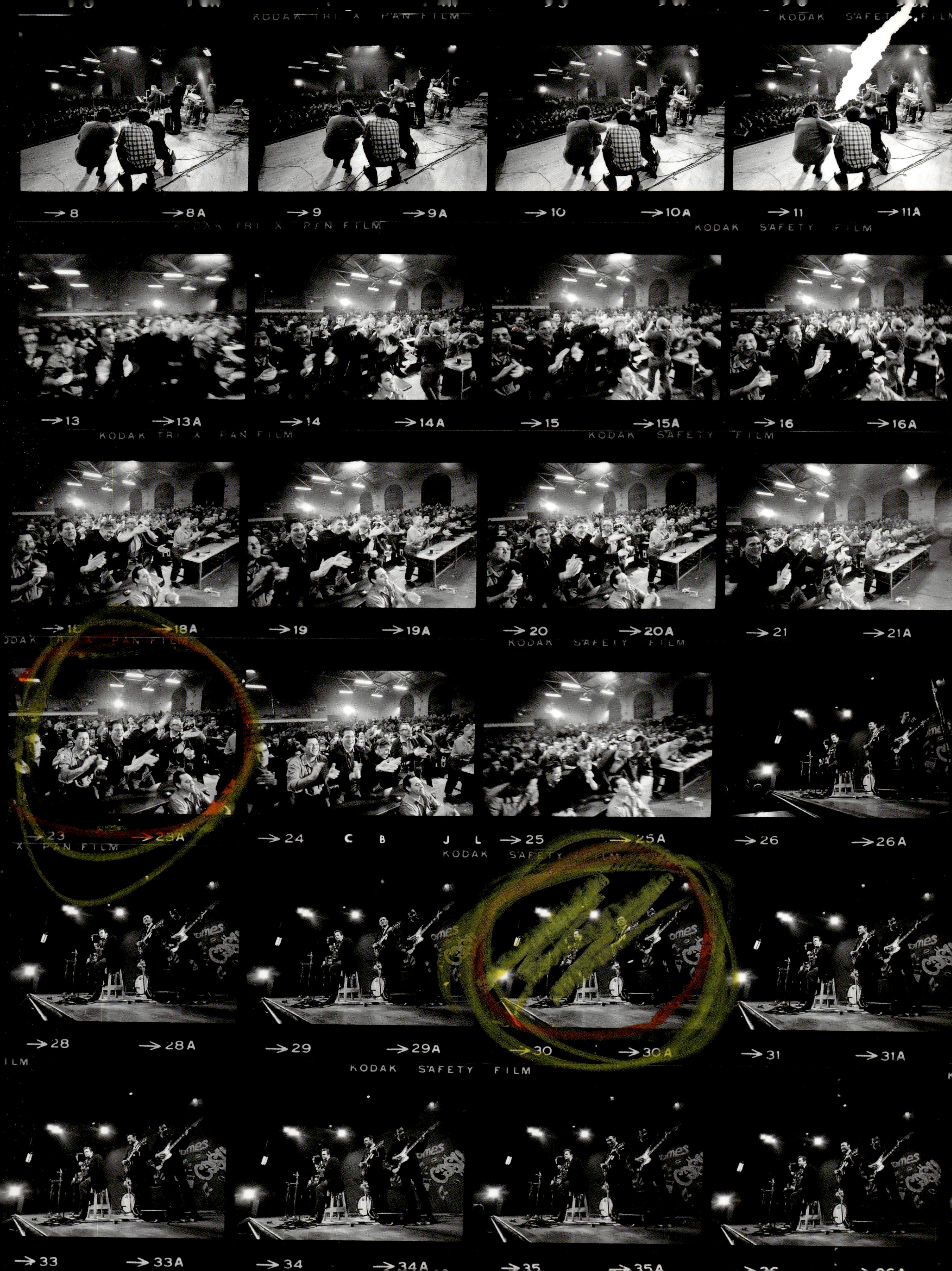

ACKNOWLEDGEMENTS

One of the only times I saw Jim cry was when he picked up the phone and was told Johnny Cash had passed away.

Jim first met Johnny Cash hanging out with Bob Dylan at a nightclub in Greenwich Village, New York in 1962. Jim and Johnny immediately hit it off. They stayed in touch and Jim then met up with and photographed Johnny Cash at the Newport Folk Festival in 1964. It was after that festival that they became lifelong friends.

Jim would then spend Thanksgivings at the Cash house in Hendersonville, Tennessee and got another one of his iconic shots of June Carter Cash resting her head on Johnny's chest. He also photographed Shel Silverstein singing "A boy named Sue" and Kris Kristofferson landed a helicopter there once to have Johnny listen to some of his songs. It is also where Jim photographed Waylon Jennings recording sessions in Cash's home recording studio.

I think this book is a testament to the trust and friendship Johnny Cash and Jim Marshall shared. They both felt like outsiders and fought to be accepted. Maybe that is why they both struggled with their inner demons. They both used their tools, one a guitar and one a camera, to shine a light on what they felt were important issues that needed to be talked about and changed.

They both lived their lives the way they wanted to and left us enduring, timeless legacies.

Thank you to Tony Nourmand and the Reel Art Press team. Thank you to Scott Bomar for his writing in this book and to BMG.

Big thank you to Marty Stuart for an insightful and warm introduction.

I continue to be thankful for John Carter Cash's respect, friendship and loyalty to his father's and Jim Marshall's unbreakable bond.

Thank you to Jay Blakesberg and Ben Kautt, as always, for the scanning that brings Jim Marshall's photographs to life and their continued support for Jim Marshall's legacy.

And finally, Bonita Passarelli. Thank you for being by my side with your guidance and love for every project we do. **AMELIA DAVIS**

Thanks to the John R. Cash Revocable Trust and the entire Johnny Cash team, including Josh Matas at Sandbox Management; Catherine Sullivan at Baker Sullivan Hoover; and Tiffany Dunn, Mary Lauren Teague, and Melissa Hazel at Loeb & Loeb.

Thanks to Marty Stuart and the Marty Stuart Congress of Country Music, Maria-Elena Orbea, and John Peets and Drew Bennett at Q Prime Artist Management.

Thanks to Michelle Bermudez, Lisa Del Greco, Walter Gross, Jennifer Kirell, Jaide Lewis, and Nicole Marroccoli at Sony Music.

Thanks to Caroline Gnagy for additional research and thanks to David Hirshland. **BMG**

First published 2018 by Reel Art Press/BMG

Reel Art Press is an imprint of Rare Art Press Ltd, London, UK

www.reelartpress.com
www.bmg.com

First Edition 10 9 8 7 6 5 4 3 2 1

ISBN: 978-1-909526-56-3

Pre-Press by HR Digital Solutions

This book is printed on paper Condat matt Périgord, ECF, acid free and age resistant. The Lecta Group uses only celluloses from certified or well managed forests and plantations.

Printed by Graphius, Gent

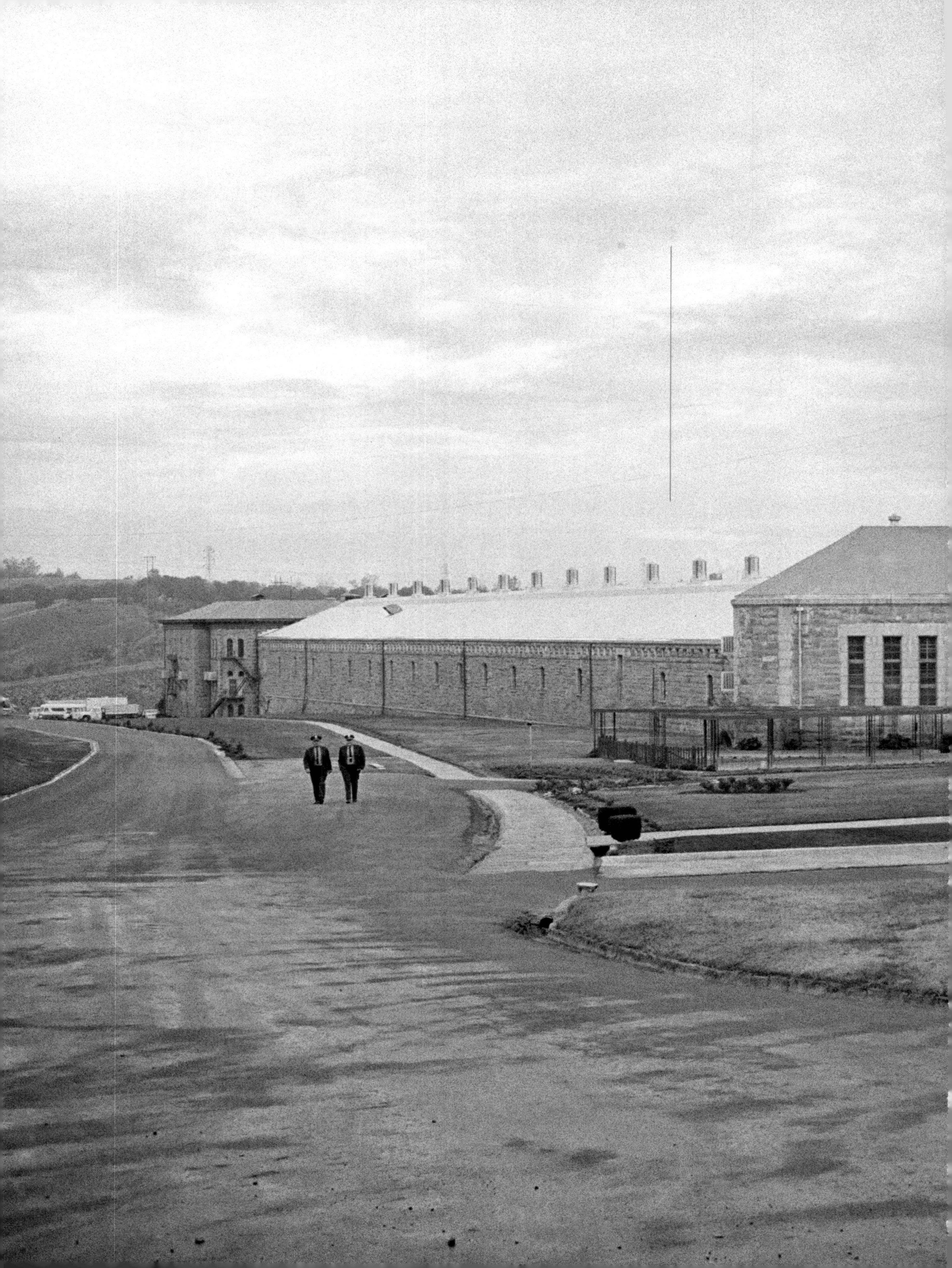